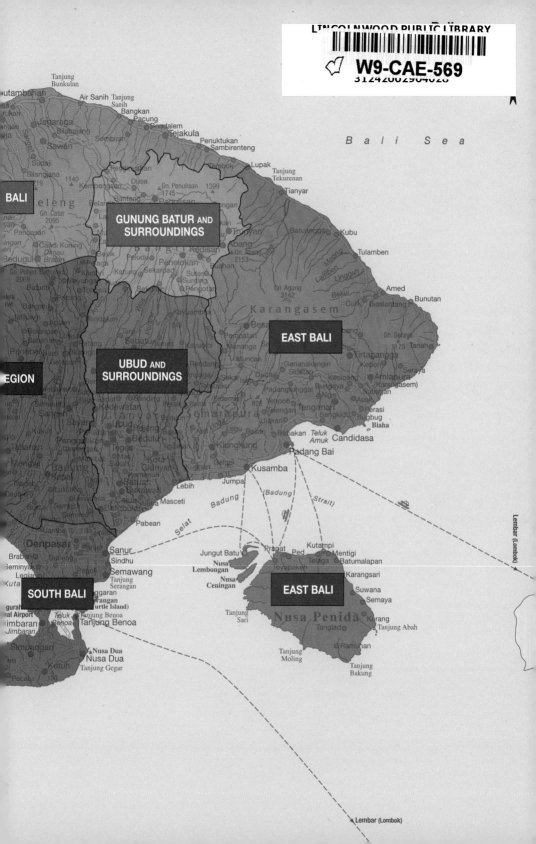

Bali Sea

BALI

GUNUNG BATUR AND
SURROUNDINGS

EAST BALI

UBUD AND
SURROUNDINGS

REGION

Karangasem

SOUTH BALI

EAST BALI

Nusa Penida

Tanjung Bunkulan
Air Sanih Tanjung
Sanih
Bangkan
Pacung
Bondalem
Tejakula
Penuktukan
Sambirenteng
Lupak
Tanjung
Tekurenan
Tianyar

Jagaraga
Bilabpiang
Sawan
Sudaji
Silangjana
1140
Kembangsari
Dusa
Gn. Penulisan 1399
1745
Penulisan
Batununggul
Kubu
Tulamben

Beleng
Gn. Catur
2095
Pancasari
Candi Kuning
Danau
Bedugul Bratan
Gn. Pohen Batukau
2069
Baturiti
Meyungan
Pacung
Trunyan
Abang
Gn. Abang
2153
Maong
Lamben
Linggah
Bekul
Amed
Bunutan
Biaslantang
Ciluk
Gn. Agung
3142

Penelokan
Katung Sekardadi
Selat
Pengotan

Kuyumba
Besi
Pempatan
Kintamani
Muncan
Sibetan
Gn. Seraya
175
Tanah
Tirtagangga
Kebon
Seraya
Amlapura
(Karangasem)
Subagan
Asak
Ngis
Perasi
Bugbug
Biaha

Sembung
Sangeh
Pelaga

Mengwi
Denpasar
Braban
Seminyak
Legian
Kuta
Kutuh
Pecatu

Sanur
Sindhu
Semawang
Tanjung
Serangan
(Turtle Island)
Pabean

Selat
Badung
(Badung)
Strait)
Kusamba
Jumpai
Lebih
Masceti

Padang Bai
Candidasa
Teluk
Amuk
Klungkung
Gelgel
Kamenuh
Bukawan

Jungut Batu
Nusa
Lembongan
Nusa
Ceningan
Toyapakeh
Prapat
Ped
Telaga
Kutampi
Mentigi
Batumalapan
Karangsari
Suwana
Semaya

Tanjung
Sari
Tanjung
Moling
Karang
Tanglad
Tanjung Abah
Ramuhan
Tanjung
Bakung

Nusa Dua
Tanjung Gegar
Teluk
Benoa
Tanjung Benoa

al Airport
imbaran
Jimbaran
Simpangan

Lembar (Lombok)

INSIGHT ⊙ GUIDES

BALI & LOMBOK

PLAN & BOOK
YOUR TAILOR-MADE TRIP

BRAZIL CHILE ECUADOR

TAILOR-MADE TRIPS & UNIQUE EXPERIENCES CREATED BY LOCAL TRAVEL EXPERTS AT INSIGHTGUIDES.COM/HOLIDAYS

Insight Guides has been inspiring travellers with high-quality travel content for over 45 years. As well as our popular guidebooks, we now offer the opportunity to book tailor-made private trips completely personalised to your needs and interests. By connecting with one of our local experts, you will directly benefit from their expertise and local know-how, helping you create memories that will last a lifetime.

HOW INSIGHTGUIDES.COM/HOLIDAYS WORKS

STEP 1

Pick your dream destination and submit an enquiry, or modify an existing itinerary if you prefer.

STEP 2

Fill in a short form, sharing details of your travel plans and preferences with a local expert.

STEP 3

Your local expert will create your personalised itinerary, which you can amend until you are completely satisfied.

STEP 4

Book securely online. Pack your bags and enjoy your holiday! Your local expert will be available to answer questions during your trip.

BENEFITS OF PLANNING & BOOKING AT INSIGHTGUIDES.COM/HOLIDAYS

PLANNED BY LOCAL EXPERTS

The Insight Guides local experts are hand-picked, based on their experience in the travel industry and their impeccable standards of customer service.

SAVE TIME & MONEY

When a local expert plans your trip, you save time and money when you book, even during high season. You won't be charged for using a credit card either.

TAILOR-MADE TRIPS

Book with Insight Guides, and you will be in complete control of the planning process, from the initial selections to amending your final itinerary.

BOOK & TRAVEL STRESS-FREE

Enjoy stress-free travel when you use the Insight Guides secure online booking platform. All bookings come with a money-back guarantee.

WHAT OTHER TRAVELLERS THINK ABOUT TRIPS BOOKED AT INSIGHTGUIDES.COM/HOLIDAYS

Trip to Portugal

Every step of the planning process and the trip itself was effortless and exceptional. Our special interests, preferences and requests were accommodated resulting in a trip that exceeded our expectations.

Corinne, USA ★★★★★

Trip to Vietnam

The organization was superb, the drivers professional, and accommodation quite comfortable. I was well taken care of! My thanks to your colleagues who helped make my trip to Vietnam such a great experience. My only regret is that I couldn't spend more time in the country.

Heather ★★★★★

DON'T MISS OUT
BOOK NOW AT
INSIGHTGUIDES.COM/HOLIDAYS

CONTENTS

Introduction

The best of Bali and Lombok 6
Bali 21
People 23
Geography 28

History & features

Decisive dates 34
An Island Where Cultures Meet 37
   🔍 Chinese influences on Bali 47
Religion and Rituals 51
   🔍 The cremation ceremony 57
📷 Festivals of Faith 58
Cuisine 61
   🔍 Melting pot cuisine 65
Performing Arts 67
   🔍 Gamelan music 73
Arts and Crafts 75
📷 Gifts to Deities and Demons 80
Outdoor Activities 83
Architecture 89

Places

BALI 101
■ SOUTH BALI 105
📷 Bali Beach Activities 122
■ UBUD AND SURROUNDINGS 125
   🔍 Ubud walks 138
■ GUNUNG BATUR AND
   SURROUNDINGS 148
■ EAST BALI 153
📷 Water Parks of East Bali 168
■ NORTH BALI 171
■ WEST BALI 181
■ TABANAN REGION 191
LOMBOK 201
■ WEST LOMBOK 203
■ THE GILI ISLANDS 213
■ NORTH AND EAST LOMBOK 217
■ CENTRAL AND SOUTH LOMBOK 223

Travel tips

TRANSPORT: BALI

Getting There 230
    By Air...230
    By Minivan or Car.................................230
    By Bus 230
    By Ferry 231
Getting Around 231
    From the Airport 231
    Orientation 231
    Public Transport 232
    Private Transport 233
    On Foot 233

TRANSPORT: LOMBOK

Getting There 234
    By Air...234
    By Sea 234
Getting Around 234
    From the Airport 234
    Orientation 234
    Transport...234

A – Z

Addresses 236
Admission Charges.............................236
Age Restrictions.................................236
Budgeting for your Trip.......................236
Business Travellers 236
Children..237
Climate...237
Clothing..237
Consulates 238
Crime & Security 238
Customs Regulations.........................238
Economy...238
Electricity 238
Emergency Numbers..........................238
Etiquette...238
Health & Medical Care.......................239
Internet 240
Left Luggage 241
LGBTQ Travellers 241
Lost Property 241
Maps...241
Media..241
Money...241
Opening Hours....................................242

Packing & Shipping.....................................242
Postal Services 242
Public Holidays 242
Public Toilets...243
Religious Services.......................................243
Smoking 243
Taxes & Tipping 243
Telephones 243
Time Zone 244
Tourist Offices..244
Travellers with Disabilities 244
Visas & Passports 244
Websites...244
Weights & Measures....................................244
Women Travellers...244

LANGUAGE

Bahasa Indonesia...245
Glossary 246

FURTHER READING

History & Culture 248
Fiction...248
Art/Music/Dance..248
General..248

Maps

Bali 102
South Bali...106
Denpasar...108
Sanur...112
Nusa Dua and Tanjung Benoa 114
Kuta Bay..118
Ubud and Surroundings...............................126
Central Ubud...132
Gunung Batur..149
East Bali..154
North Bali..172
West Bali 182
Tabanan Region..192
Lombok 204
Inside front cover Bali
Inside back cover Lombok

LEGEND

🔍 Insight on
📷 Photo story

THE BEST OF BALI AND LOMBOK: TOP ATTRACTIONS

△ **Surfing**. Bali and Lombok are iconic surfing playgrounds. In Bali, pros head to the outer reef breaks at Bukit Badung; in Lombok it's the southern shoreline. Newbies can hone skills in lagoons. See page 84.

▽ **Odalan (temple anniversary festival)**. These take place somewhere on Bali almost every day. They provide an ideal opportunity to see the island decked out in ceremonial splendour. See page 58.

△ **Gili Trawangan**. Just off the northwest coast of Lombok, this island escape has stunning beaches of powdery white sand in addition to the party reputation held by its bars and restaurants. See page 215.

△ **Jatiluwih, Bali**. A landscape of endless sculpted rice terraces against a mountain backdrop. See page 197.

△ **Dancing**. Kecak is one of Bali's most dramatic all-male dances. See page 70.

△ **Penelokan, Bali**. There are dramatic views to be had here of the active volcano, Gunung Batur, and its crater lake. See page 148.

△ **Gunung Kawi, Bali**. This ancient temple comprises an amazing complex of facades and monks' niches hewn from solid rock, all set on the banks of a river valley. See page 145.

▽ **Pottery**. Lombok pottery is best seen at Banyumelek and Penujak villages. See pages 207 and 224.

△ **Trekking**. In Lombok, don't miss the waterfalls and ancient forests in Rinjani National Park. See page 220.

▷ **Diving**. Aficionados head for Tulamben in the east or Pulau Menjangan in the northwest, Bali. Or try the Gili Islands in Lombok for their rich aquatic life – good for snorkelling too. See page 83.

THE BEST OF BALI AND LOMBOK: EDITOR'S CHOICE

Herons fly over the fields in Petulu.

BALI FOR FAMILIES

Bali Bird Park. See exotic birds from all over Indonesia, including the giant cassowary, hornbills, birds of paradise and more than 250 bird species in a lush garden setting. A special highlight is the enclosure containing the endangered Bali starling. See page 127.

Surfing schools. What better way to bond with your kids than by learning to surf together? Monkey Surf (https://monkeysurf.jimdo.com) in Kuta, Lombok takes beginners from age 4. One-on-one instruction in mellow waves is a great way to start. See page 84.

Waterbom Park. Located in Tuban, near Kuta, the artificial pools and rivers with slides, tubes and ramps make for wet and wild fun rides (under the watchful eye of life-guards). See page 117.

Bali Botanical Gardens. Located in Bali's cooler northern highlands, there are walking trails that meander through high-altitude pine forests. See page 177.

Reef Seen Aquatics. See baby turtles being reared until they are old enough to be released into the ocean. You can even sponsor the release of a hatchling. See page 182.

ONLY IN BALI

Petulu. At sunset, thousands of white herons return to roost daily in the trees at Petulu, Bali. Said to be a manifestation of human souls, the birds blanket the trees like snow. See page 143.

Nyepi. On the first day of the Balinese-Hindu New Year, no one is allowed outside (not even tourists) and all lights are turned off. See page 59.

Cremations. These are boisterous and colourful public ceremonies sometimes involving the entire Balinese village. See page 57.

Muncan. On the eve of the Bali-Hindu New Year, a pair of large male and female figures undergo the simulation of a public mating as part of a traditional fertility rite. See page 155.

Trunyan. The pre-Hindu Balinese people here do not cremate the dead (unlike Hindu Balinese) but instead leave them exposed to the elements. See page 150.

Makare. Using thorny leaves, macho males at Tenganan in east Bali draw each other's blood in this vicious ritual as offerings to demons. See page 164.

Taking offerings to an odalan (temple festival) at Pura Silayakti in Padang Bai, Bali.

See hornbills at Bali Bird Park.

BEST VIEWS

Antosari to Pupuan, Bali. North of Antosari, passing Belimbing and Sanda all the way to Pupuan takes you past incredible rice terraces. See page 193.

Pura Pasar Agung. Stunning setting for a remote temple on the slopes of Bali's Gunung Agung. See page 156.

Ujung to Amed. Breathtaking ocean views and black sand beaches on Bali filled with hundreds of outrigger canoes. See page 166.

Pura Luhur-Uluwatu. Spectacular ocean views from a cliff-top temple on Bali island. See page 115.

Lombok Strait. Magnificent sunsets across the Lombok Strait to Bali, viewed from along Lombok's west coast. See page 206.

Kuta, Lombok to Selong Belanak. Breathtaking views of the southern coast from its wind- and surf-lashed cliffs. See page 225.

Gunung Rinjani, Lombok. On one side you'll be treated to views of the crater lake; on the other, stunning vistas across to the coast. See page 220.

Dramatic coastline at Pura Luhur Uluwatu, Bali.

BEST BEACHES

Jimbaran. Greyish white sands and clean waters in a picturesque bay south of Kuta, Bali, but minus the persistent beach vendors. See page 116.

Nusa Dua, Bali. Gentle waves caressing white sands lined with luxury hotels, ideal for families with young children. See page 113.

Seminyak. Large expanse of grey sands with thundering waves, perfect for boogie boarding and surfing in Bali. See page 119.

Kuta Bay, Bali. Crowded with surfers, half-naked bodies basking in the sun and persistent vendors, Kuta draws people for its stunning sunsets. The firm grey sands are also great for walking. See page 117.

Pemuteran, Bali. Idyllic stretch of beach, sandy in parts, rocky in others, with a clutch of boutique hotels and nearby snorkelling and diving at Pulau Menjangan. See page 182.

Tanjung Aan, Lombok. Undisturbed sugary white beaches and calm waters. See page 226.

Selong Belanak, Lombok. Blessed with powdery white sands and aquamarine waters. See page 227.

Kuta, Lombok. Great beach on the south coast. See page 225.

Diver and a school of jackfish near where the Liberty wreck lies in Tulamben, Bali.

Legong dance performance in Ubud's municipal hall, Bali.

BEST TEMPLES AND ANCIENT SITES

Pura Puncak Penulisan. Atmospheric terraced temple perched on Bali's Gunung Batur's crater rim with swirling mists and ancient statues. See page 150.

Pura Luhur Batukaru, Bali. Ancient forests surround this remote temple at the foot of Gunung Batukaru. See page 197.

Yeh Pulu. Scenes of an unknown ancient Bali era are carved in stone amidst scenic rice fields. See page 142.

Pura Rambut Siwi. Serene temple built on a cliff overlooking Bali's quiet southwest coast. See page 187.

Pura Tanah Lot, Bali. Much-visited temple on an islet just off the coast. Sunsets here are glorious but it gets very crowded. See page 121.

Vihara Dharma Giri, Bali. Buddhist temple on the side of a hill with a 10 metre (33ft)-long reclining Buddha. See page 193.

Pura Beji, Bali. Pink sandstone towers with intricate carvings. See page 174.

Goa Gajah. Enter the gaping jaws of an ancient Balinese man-made cave. See page 139.

Pura Taman Ayun, Bali. Pretty temple with a series of soaring meru (pagoda), protected by a moat. See page 195.

Pura Ulun Danu Bratan, Bali. Supremely photogenic lakeside temple. See page 177.

Pura Tirtha Empul, Bali. Busy temple with a holy spring. See page 145.

Pura Lingsar, Lombok. Hindu, Muslim, Buddhist and Christian believers come to pray here. See page 208.

Pura Suranadi, Lombok. Among the holiest and oldest temples in Lombok. See page 209.

Pura Batu Bolong, Lombok. Dramatic temple perched on the edge of a cliff. See page 210.

Taman Narmada, Lombok. A complex of temples, pools, a lake and beautiful gardens. See page 208.

BEST FESTIVALS

Perang Pandan. June–July, Tenganan, Bali. Annual courtship ritual honouring the Hindu god Indra.

Bali Kite Festival. June–Aug, Sanur, Bali. Troupes compete with giant kites with wingspans up to 11 metres (36ft).

Bau Nyle. Feb–Mar, Mandalika, Lombok. Performances to welcome sea worms, symbolic of sacrifice for the greater good.

Karangasem Festival. June, Amlapura, Bali. Celebration of cultural arts held in conjunction with Amlapura's anniversary.

Ubud Food Festival. Apr, Ubud, Bali. A three-day culinary extravaganza with workshops, demonstrations and tours.

Tour de Lombok. Mar, Mandalika, Lombok. Cyclers from across the world race to the finish line.

Semarapura Festival. Apr–May, Semarapura, Bali. A commemoration of Semarapura's anniversary and the historic Klungkung puputan, showcasing local arts. See page 58 for more on festivals.

Holy spring at Pura Tirtha Empul, north of Ubud, Bali.

Gendang belek musician.

BEST CLUBS AND BARS

Ku De Ta. Chic dining and drinks spot that draws a beautiful crowd in Seminyak, Bali. **Pyramid**. Pharaoh-themed nightclub located between Kuta and Seminyak, Bali. **Sky Garden**. Kuta, Bali's hottest night spot, featuring international DJs on four stages and a buffet. **Sama-Sama Reggae Bar**. Great live music in a cool, laid-back atmosphere on Gili Trawangan, Lombok. **Engine Room Supper Club**. DJs in three different venues spin a variety of music in Kuta, Bali **The Bus Bar**. A '74 VW bus, great pizzas plus cocktails and beer make for a great apres-surf place in Kuta, Lombok.

BEST MUSEUMS AND GALLERIES

Neka Art Museum. One of the finest collections of Balinese and Indonesian paintings. See page 133. **Taman Werdhi Budaya Art Centre, Denpasar**. Good displays of the various Balinese visual arts. See page 110. **Symon's Art Zoo, North Bali**. An astonishing cacophony of colours and subjects displayed in the artist's home. See page 172. **Museum Puri Lukisan, Ubud, Bali**. A well-respected museum with a large collection of traditional and contemporary Balinese art. See page 132. **ARMA Museum & Resort, Ubud, Bali**. Run by a local art dealer, the museum has a fine collection of both Balinese and Indonesian art. See page 137.

ONLY IN LOMBOK

Gendang Belek. Traditional music featuring the big drums for which Lombok is famous (ask at your hotel for performance venues). **Bau Nyale Festival**. Takes place every year in February at Mandalika beach, near Kuta, Lombok. See page 225. **Ayam Pelecing**. Fried chicken doused with a fiery chilli sauce – a Lombok speciality!

Neka Art Museum at Ubud.

THE BEST OF BALI & LOMBOK: PLAN & BOOK YOUR TAILOR-MADE TRIP

The Indonesian islands of Bali and Lombok make the perfect pairing for a trip away, offering natural beauty, ancient culture, an abundance of charm and myriad things to do. From palm-fringed beaches and superlative surfing to tropical jungle treks, sea temples and traditional villages, this magical ten-day adventure delivers it all.

△ **Day 1, Uluwatu**. Nestled on Bali's Bukit peninsula in the south, Uluwatu is renowned for its stunning shoreline. Not all the beaches are suitable for swimming, but it's the perfect spot to sip a cold Bintang and watch the surfers at play. Do visit Pura Luhur Uluwatu, a sea temple perched high on the cliffs overlooking the Indian Ocean. See page 115.

△ **Days 3 & 4, Ubud**. Head northeast to Ubud, making a short detour via Celuk, a village famous for its locally-made gold and silver handicrafts. Ubud is Bali's cultural heart, home to scores of artists and craftspeople. The town's Neka Art Museum, which houses one of the finest collections of Balinese and Indonesian paintings, is well worth a visit. See page 130.

▽ **Day 5, Amed**. Amed consists of a cluster of picturesque beaches and villages along the east coast of Bali. The tranquil setting offers affordable homestays, restaurants and bars and is the ideal base from which to embark on mountain treks up nearby Gunung Agung. See page 166.

◁ **Day 2, Canggu**. This former fisherman's village on the west coast attracts a laid-back, creative crowd. The surfing is excellent - from beginner to pro - and surf shacks line the beach, alongside yoga studios, quirky shops and cafés serving the likes of turmeric lattes and goji berry shots. As dusk falls make the short trip to Pura Tana Lot, famous for its offshore setting and sunset backdrops. See page 120.

△ **Days 6 & 7, Lombok**. Catch the ferry from Padang Bai Port to the neighbouring – quieter and less-travelled – island of Lombok. Beach lovers will appreciate the pristine shoreline, fringed by coffee and coconut plantations. For an insight into the indigenous Sasak culture, visit one of the thatch-roofed villages that dot the island where colourful ceremonies, dance and music are an authentic part of local life. See page 201.

▽ **Day 8, Gili Islands**. A short boat trip off the northwest coast will bring you to the Gili Islands. Ringed by coral reefs with a rich tropical marine biodiversity, they're a snorkelling and diving paradise. Turquoise sea, soft white sands and coconut groves come as standard, though the islands are also the place to party with Gili Trawangan particularly popular for its beach parties and cocktails. See page 210.

△ ▽ **Days 9 & 10, Mt Rinjani**. Senaru is the gateway to Rinjani National Park and a magnet for trekkers looking to climb the majestic Gunung Rinjani, Indonesia's second-highest volcano. The Park itself is a haven of jungle-clad paths, waterfalls and rice fields. As you'd expect, the flora and fauna are captivating, with tropical birds, civets, monkeys and exotic butterflies to be spotted. See page 220.

You can plan and book this trip with Insight Guides, or we can help you create your own. Whether you're after adventure or a family-friendly holiday, we have a trip for you, with all the activities you enjoy doing and the sights you want to see. All our trips are devised by local experts who get the most out of the destination. Visit **www.insightguides.com/holidays** to chat with one of our local travel experts.

Entrance to a temple at Peliatan village, south of Ubud.

Buffalo racing in Makepung.

Jungutbatu beach,
Nusa Lembongan.

A notable bicycle relief at Pura Maduwe Karang.

BALI

Synonymous with paradise, if not blissful exile, Bali attracts visitors with its relative remoteness and unique culture. Tourism has had its impact, but it's still possible to get off the beaten track.

A powerful priest wanted to keep his misbehaving son in permanent exile and so prevented him from returning home to Java by drawing his cane across the narrowest point of land to create a watery divide. Thus Bali became separated from Java. This mythological tale has some truth to it as geologically the two islands were connected during the last Ice Age.

Detail from a carved wooden door, Ubud.

The source of all life for the Balinese lies in the mountains, for they are believed to be the abode of deities. Over the years, ash from repeated volcanic eruptions has created fertile soils watered by rivers flowing from crater lakes. The rugged range of mountains running from east to west has created distinct regions. To the north of this divide lies a coastal strip with fertile foothills while to the south are expansive beaches, the rice-growing centres and the nucleus of Bali's tourism infrastructure. The cooler central highlands are dotted with small farms hugging steep slopes, the west is largely dominated by a national park, and the eastern shore is lined with fishing and salt-producing villages, and some rice terraces.

The Austronesian Balinese are ethnically and linguistically related to Malays and Polynesians, with additional infusions of Indian, Chinese and Arab blood, from the merchants who either traded or settled on the island long ago. Centuries of aristocratic Balinese rule influenced by Javanese courts dating from the 10th century ended violently with the Dutch conquest of the island during the early 1900s.

Since then, Bali's natural beauty and dynamic culture have attracted huge numbers of people. Back in 1970, the first edition of this book was the very first in the *Insight Guides* series, conceptualised by the company's founder, Hans Höfer, as a highly-illustrated guidebook, focussing on the local culture. Fifty years on, while much

Balinese kecak fire dance at Taman Kaja temple.

more developed touristically, Bali remains a captivating destination and a cornerstone of the *Insight Guides* list.

Yet purists, residents and even a growing number of visitors fear for the island's future. Indeed, the first-time visitor expecting a tropical paradise in Bali will be saddened by the environmental degradation, extensive development and inadequate infrastructure. Thankfully, places of beauty and serenity still exist – but you must seek them away from the south and off the beaten path. The unswaying bonds of religion, family and community have also helped buffer the people from the more negative aspects of tourism.

PEOPLE

Community participation in time-honoured rituals that celebrate the cycles of life give the Balinese a strong sense of purpose. Village life survives, even though many young people are attracted to work in the richer tourist centres.

The Hindu god of creation Brahma and god of reincarnation Siwa (Shiva) fashioned human figures from dough. The first batch they baked was pale; the second was burnt and black. The last, however, golden brown and deemed perfect, were brought to life by the gods as the first Balinese.

During the 8th century, a legendary Javanese holy man led many of his followers to Bali, a wild and unpopulated place at the time. When a great number of them died there, he and the survivors went back home. After requesting divine blessings, the holy man returned with a smaller group and succeeded in establishing permanent settlements. These first people on the island are the ancestors of today's Bali Aga, aboriginal Balinese (see page 24).

ETHNICITY AND LANGUAGE

Myth and legend aside, the Balinese are one of the many diverse but related Austronesian ethno-linguistic groups inhabiting an immense area stretching from Indonesia to New Zealand, and from Easter Island to Madagascar. Most of these people live in Indonesia, Philippines, Malaysia and the Polynesian islands.

Although linguistically the Balinese language is closer to those spoken on the islands to its east, it has been heavily influenced by the Javanese language. This has led to a rich and complex language spoken by over 4 million Balinese people in a nation of an estimated 269 million. As an ethnic and religious minority in Indonesia, the Balinese are proud of their language and use it when communicating with family and friends.

Spoken Balinese has several levels, and the one used depends upon the caste, status, age and social relationship between speakers. Friends and equals speak what is known as Low

Locals in Seseh, Tabanan.

Balinese. A commoner will speak High Balinese to a superior or elder, who then replies in Low or Middle Balinese, depending on familiarity and degree of distance in status. Middle Balinese is polite and is used in most situations. An honorific vocabulary is used when speaking and referring to important persons such as a high priest.

An ancient language called Kawi or Old Javanese, introduced in the 10th century, is mainly used for poetry and drama. In theatre, people who play the roles of deities and royalty speak Kawi. As few people understand Kawi, it is translated into Balinese by servant-advisers.

Balinese is written in an alphabet derived from an ancient south Indian script, but very few young people are proficient in reading and writing it. It is mostly used in ancient texts and in the modern world for street signs and sign boards of schools and government offices.

When speaking with each other, younger people mix Balinese with Bahasa Indonesia, the national language, and some English. Complicated Balinese grammar is being replaced by the simpler Indonesian one. While purists worry the Balinese language is being lost, the more practical know that language and everything else changes according to the Balinese concept of *desa-kala-patra* (place-time-mode).

HIERACHICAL SOCIETY

The concept of caste was introduced by the Hindu Javanese Majapahit kingdom in the 14th century, but the Dutch colonials altered the system during the 20th century. The highest is the *brahmana* or priestly caste with males named Ida Bagus and females Ida Ayu. Next are *satria*, upper nobility with names like Cokorda, Dewa or Ngakan for males, and Cokorda Istri, Dewa Ayu or Desak for females. *Wesia* are lesser gentry, with males called Anak Agung or Gusti Ngurah, and females, Anak Agung Istri or Gusti Ayu.

On the school run.

⊘ BALI AGA

In Trunyan (see page 150) and Tenganan (see page 163) are villages of the Bali Aga, people who have retained old Balinese traditions from pre-Majapahit times, before Javanese and Hindu influences took root. The Bali Aga exist outside of the caste system. Their religion is ancestor focused, therefore exclusive of the Hindu Balinese and centred instead on the primacy of village origin and internal social hierarchy. It is their rituals which, more than anything else, give the Bali Aga their autonomy from the rest of Balinese society. One is the Mekare Kare or human blood sacrifice which involved combat between tribe members.

These *triwangsa* (three upper castes) comprise only 3 percent of the population.

Most Balinese are commoner *sudra* or *jaba* (outsiders). Commoner children are named by birth order with the prefix I for males and Ni for females. The oldest is always called Wayan, Putu or Gede; the second Made or Nengah; the third Nyoman or Komang; and the fourth Ketut, all of which invariably leaves foreigners confused. Birth order names are repeated for subsequent children, with Cenik or Alit (little), Balik (return) or Tagel (multiple) tagged on after their first names. The system is also used for children of higher castes with commoner mothers, such as Ida Bagus Made or Gusti Putu. A specific proper name always follows the birth order

What's in a name? Names for Balinese are very important because it is believed that naming a child can affect his or her life. Several factors have to be taken into consideration, therefore at least four names are given.

name and caste title. But nearly every Balinese has a nickname and prefers to be called by this. Even family relationship names, such as Nini

Villager with rooster for cock fighting, Seseh.

(grandmother) or Beli (older brother) are more commonly used than actual names.

Balinese identify more with their lineage groups than their caste. There are dozens of commoner clans, such as *pande* (metalsmiths) and *pasek* (ancestral groups). The upper castes have lineages descended from dynasties and priestly families. Many have rewritten their genealogies by finding and even creating connections with the 14th-century Javanese Majapahit kingdom in order to assert their status. Commoners, however, feel that a shopkeeper from the priestly caste need not be shown deference. Instead, such a person should show respect to a commoner medical doctor or lower caste community leader.

FAMILY AND SEXUALITY

Many Balinese households are crowded with up to four generations. Mothers and their daughters-in-law have private cooking spaces, which helps to maintain harmony. Infants are carried everywhere by their mother or older sibling. As the child grows up and begins to walk, he or she is free to wander about the village with other children, but an adult is usually nearby watching over them. Balinese children are rarely, if ever, spanked, which the Balinese believe would damage their tender souls. Children learn through

Mother and child from the market town Candikuning, north Bali.

guidance and example, and it is this raising of children with independence and respect that accounts for their maturity.

Young unmarried Balinese adults mix freely in public and frequently fall in and out of love. Amulets and love spells are sometimes used to enhance one's attractiveness to the opposite sex. Close physical contact between members of the same sex is common as a sign of friendship. This usually does not indicate homosexuality, which is tolerated as long as there are no open displays of affection, a rule that also applies to heterosexual relationships.

Sexual relations between Balinese teenagers are left to proceed in a natural way without interference from the parents, at least in the *sudra* caste that makes up the vast majority of the population. In the commonest form of marriage, the ceremony does not take place until several days after announcement of consummation or conception. And even in upper-caste 'arranged' marriages, the couple may sleep together for an agreed period before the wedding. To keep the population in check, the government encourages couples to have only two children. The Balinese have generally complied, and Bali's birth rate is among the lowest in Indonesia.

COMMUNITY RELATIONS

The Balinese are a very sociable people. During the day they are mostly outdoors, where children play in the streets. In the evening, they socialise at gathering spots or watch television together. Villagers even bathe naked together, males upstream from females but in view of each other. Oddly, most Balinese eat their daily meals alone. Even at receptions for ceremonies, they eat quickly and in silence.

The *desa* (village) is headed by an elected person called a *bendesa adap* who is responsible for

Preparing for a ceremony at Pura Samuan Tiga.

Abortion is not allowed by Indonesian law nor the Balinese religion as it interferes with the reincarnation of an ancestral soul. The legendary underworld punishment for this transgression is for the mother and the abortionist to walk a rickety bridge as the aborted foetus shakes them off into the hell fires below. However, this has not deterred some unwed young women.

Traditional beliefs dictate that children are reincarnated souls from the husband's side. In the case of divorce, the husband usually receives custody of the children, while the wife has to hope that her family accepts her return. Some divorced or widowed Balinese are known to remarry and have more children. A husband can take another wife if his first wife consents, but few do.

traditional affairs. There is also an appointed *kepala desa* (village head) responsible to the government. The village is divided into several *banjar*, a smaller unit of households, with an elected leader, the *klian banjar*. Members assist at communal festivals, each other's family ceremonies and during crises. *Banjar* membership is compulsory for married men.

Villagers are bound by the *awig-awig*, a set of oral and written rules of moral conduct and behaviour. Religion also guides every aspect of life, with some choosing to do additional devotional duties, like sweeping temple grounds. This brings them closer to the deities and increases their respect among villagers. The worst possible punishment for a Balinese is to be banished from the *banjar* for breaking moral codes. Help is not given, property can be confiscated, praying at temples is forbidden, exile from the village can occur and at death the person can be denied cremation.

TROUBLE IN PARADISE

Paedophilia in Bali is a growing concern, mostly perpetrated by foreigners who prey on children in impoverished areas. Bali also has a high HIV-AIDS rate due to exposure to tourism and intravenous drug use, which is another problem. The large number of unemployed young Balinese has caused a rise in crime along with drug and alcohol abuse, and while jobs are available in heavy labour and street-food vending, such work is viewed as undesirable and usually done by migrant workers from Java. There have also been a few incidents where unhappy villagers have blocked roads leading to hotels and created other disturbances when their demands at work were not met. Many people feel they are being grossly underpaid compared to the huge amounts of money tourists spend on accommodation and food.

As many young people work in the tourism centres and return home only for religious events, villages today are mostly occupied by children and older people. Few Balinese hold high positions in businesses because of the time off they need to attend ceremonies. This has caused them to resent migrant Indonesians and foreigners who have better jobs and salaries, and are not encumbered by religious commitments. A growing number of these outsiders are settling permanently on the overcrowded island, a situation made worse by migrants from other parts of Indonesia to what is perceived as a more prosperous Bali. All this has put additional strains on Bali's already limited resources. Today, Bali has a population of just over 4 million people, of whom about 90 percent are ethnic Balinese. The remaining are Javanese, Madurese, Sasak (Lombok), and other ethnicities. Lombok has a population of over 3 million with the indigenous Sasak making up 90 percent of the population. Small numbers of Balinese, Javanese and Buginese make up the rest.

Gambling at *tajen* (cockfights) has led to domestic problems since husbands and fathers spend a lot of time and money preparing their roosters, with fortunes made or lost during the fights. Traditional belief dictates that the spilling of blood for ceremonies is needed to appease demons. The fight is officially limited to three rounds but that does not stop cockfights from continuing for hours at a time, despite government attempts to ban them.

BALINESE WOMEN

Women are major players in the world of small business. Local women have long managed *warung* (road-side food stalls) or engaged in

Temple festival in Besakih village, East Bali.

home industries like weaving, all this on top of their household chores. These days women also run clothing boutiques, jewellery shops and restaurants. Women are also making their presence known in the arts, an area once dominated by men. Female painters are growing in number, and while women's gamelan music and dance groups have been around for years, today they are the norm. That they find time to practise while managing households is a tribute to their abilities and dedication. In another reversal of traditional gender roles, men are becoming experts at making certain offerings, especially the spectacular *sarad*, in which hundreds of colourful rice-dough sculptures are arranged against a framework of bamboo and cloth for temple ceremonies and weddings.

GEOGRAPHY

Volcanoes punctuate this enchanting island of rainforests, rice fields and monkeys. But the ingenuity and sheer determination of the Balinese has helped carve out a fruitful terrain from this wild and surf-lashed island.

Bali, one of 17,508 islands that make up the vast Indonesian archipelago, is located about 8 degrees south of the equator and 115 degrees east longitude. The island is separated from Java to its west by the Bali Strait, less than 3km (2 miles) wide and no more than 50 metres (160ft) deep. To the east, the Lombok Strait, an ocean trench that plunges down steeply to a depth of 1,300 metres (4,200ft) – the deepest waters of the archipelago – separates Bali from neighbouring Lombok island.

Lying east to west across the island are six volcanic peaks over 2,000 metres (6,500ft) high. The highest is Gunung Agung at 3,014 metres (9,796ft), considered the abode of the deities who cause eruptions to punish the Balinese for wrongdoings or for not showing respect.

By the same token, the rich, fertile mineral soil – a result of those eruptions – is regarded as a gift from the gods as it enables farmers to harvest up to three crops of rice a year in many areas.

Orchid at the Bali Botanical Gardens.

CLIMATE

Bali's tropical climate is tempered by cool ocean breezes. The northwest monsoon causes the greatest humidity during the rainy season from November to April. The dry season from May to October is far more pleasant. The average temperature at sea level is 26°C (79°F), with an average maximum of 32°C (90°F) in March and 29°C (84°F) in July. In the mountains, the temperature is always a few degrees cooler and the air less humid.

The mountains attract rain-laden clouds and ensure plentiful rainfall in many areas, averaging 2,150mm (85ins) yearly. Most of the island's rivers and streams run from mountain lakes, cutting deep ravines through soft volcanic rock.

PLANT LIFE

Originally, much of the island was covered by deciduous forests interspersed with grasslands. Vast areas of Bali have since been altered by agriculture, but it is still possible to see what the natural state of the island once was – even if today, original forests are only found in Taman Nasional Bali Barat (West Bali National Park). One such outpost is the vast Bali Botanical Gardens, near the shores of Danau Bratan, which plays home to more than 650 species of trees and more than 450 species of wild and propagated orchids.

The extreme west of Bali, Jembrana, is mountainous with patches of monsoon forest, but because of its arid nature, relatively few people live there. At the southern end of the island lies Bukit Badung, a jagged plateau joined to Bali by a narrow isthmus. This dry and barren limestone tableland stands out in sharp contrast to Bali's lush, alluvial plains.

The wide variety of vegetation ranges from many species of palm and bamboo through to flowering plants like frangipani, bougainvillea and orchids. Many Balinese villages have huge, centuries-old, sacred banyan trees. Pandanus and cacti grow in dry lowlands while tall pines and cypress trees thrive in the cool and moist starling, as well as 160 species of other birds and several kinds of mammals, including mouse deer, Muntjak (barking) and Javan rusa deer. Several species of monkeys and carnivores, such as leopard and civet cat, also live in this dense savannah forest. Unfortunately, the magnificent Bali tiger is extinct: the last sighting dates back to 1937 when one was shot dead by a Dutch hunter.

Of the domesticated animals, the most important are sway-back pigs and Bali cattle, but chickens and ducks are also commonly reared. Mangy street dogs can be found wandering all over the

Harvesting rice in Gianyar Regency, Bali, where verdant rice fields dot the landscape.

mountains. Lofty tree ferns, elephant grass and wild flowers often cling to cliffs.

ANIMAL LIFE

Many kinds of wildlife exist on the island: large insect-eating geckos are found everywhere and reptiles such as lizards and snakes are also common. Monkeys, especially macaques, are to be seen all over Bali. Of the native large mammal species, only the wild boar and deer remain.

Taman Nasional Bali Barat with its monsoon forests, coastal swamps and pristine seas, all once common throughout the island, provides glimpses of a unique environment. The park, originally set up by the Dutch and Bali's largest natural reserve, is home to the endangered white Bali

island. The long-haired Kintamani mountain dog, however, is prized as a pet and is believed to be descended from Chinese chows (see page 47).

RICE AND AGRICULTURE

The rice cycle relies as much on religious management as it does on nature and secular concerns. Rice determines the daily rhythm of life as well as many facets of social and religious organisation in most villages. Rice is personified by the goddess Dewi Sri, and offerings must be made to her in order for the harvest to be bountiful. When the grain appears on the stalks, she is said to be pregnant. Before harvesting traditional rice, a small and symbolic mock wedding ceremony is held. When farmers enter drained fields, they conceal the small knives that they carry to cut the grain so as not to frighten the soul of Dewi Sri dwelling in the rice.

Wet-rice cultivation is a complete ecosystem. Flooding the fields brings nutrients to the soil,

> In 2012, three areas exemplifying the Balinese cooperative irrigation system, called subak, were named as Unesco World Heritage Cultural Sites.

Fishermen at Legian Beach, south Bali.

which supports not only the growing rice, but also a complex food chain. One of Bali's most endearing sights is that of a small boy or old man herding a noisy flock of waddling ducks to feed on the insects, grubs and plants, while also naturally fertilising the fields.

The Balinese mostly grow baas putih (white rice) for daily consumption. They also cultivate padi bali (indigenous Balinese rice), gaga (non-irrigated rice), baas barak (red rice), ketan (glutinous white rice) and injin (glutinous black or purple rice). The last two are mainly used for desserts and offerings. During the 1970s, Indonesia participated in the infamous Green Revolution by introducing a new, high-yield variety of rice developed by the International Rice Research Institute in the Philippines. Although the intention was to make the country more self-sufficient in rice production, the grain had very little flavour and was unpopular with the Balinese.

The hybrid also rapidly depleted the soil so that large quantities of chemical fertilisers had to be used. The use of limited varieties of rice narrowed the genetic base, which ultimately led to crops becoming more vulnerable to pests. This was detrimental not only to human health, but also killed off much of the animal life in the fields and tainted the water supply. Given the extra expense that farmers had to bear in buying fertilisers and pesticides, it is hardly surprising that they are returning to the indigenous rice varieties and organic farming practices.

Although rice is the most important crop, farmers usually rotate it with corn, peanuts, chilli peppers, onions, soya beans and other vegetables during the dry season. Some crops are exported to other parts of Indonesia, but farmers have also found lucrative outlets in hotels and restaurants.

The temperate upland areas produce an astonishing array of fruits, vegetables and flowers. In north Bali where there is less water and therefore only one rice crop a year, farmers cultivate non-irrigated rice as well as fruits, vegetables, peanuts, cocoa, coffee, and spices such as cloves, cinnamon and vanilla.

IRRIGATION SYSTEMS

In order to grow rice, the Balinese have to divert water from the rivers to the paddy fields. Because the steep and narrow valleys preclude damming, the farmers have devised an elaborate irrigation system of tunnels, channels and bamboo aqueducts, known as subak, to carry the water. This is a centuries-old system, and an inscription on one tunnel dates the construction to AD 944.

Terraces that utilise the land to its maximum efficiency have been carved into the slopes, producing the verdant, classic Balinese landscape so beloved by artists and tourists. Water is brought up to the highest terraces by these channels and from there it uses gravity to flow downhill through the sawah (irrigated paddy fields). The system cannot work unless water is shared so all farmers belong to an irrigation society called subak. Members of these subak are responsible for repairing dykes and dams, and keeping tunnels and channels flowing freely.

Heading the island's irrigation system are lake temples dedicated to the goddess of the water, Dewi Danu. The Balinese believe that water is a divine gift. For example, Pura Ulun Danu Bratan and Pura Ulun Danu Batur, two important temples, are dedicated to the goddesses of these lakes. Temple priests set the schedule of planting and harvesting, and on a daily basis each farmer knows when he will receive water and when he must release it to the its bounty, regarding it as a place of demonic forces. Poorer Balinese who cannot afford to buy or lease irrigated land tend to make their living from the sea. Most of the catch is destined for restaurants catering to tourists rather than as a primary food source for the island's people. Prawn cultivation is also important. Most of it is exported to Japan with less than 1 percent sold to the local tourism sector. Another important resource is farmed seaweed, which is mainly used for thickening food and cosmetics.

Rice terraces at Belimbing, east Bali.

Seaweed farming at Toyopakeh harbour, Nusa Penida.

next *sawah*. Smaller temples and shrines where offerings are made are found along the system.

However, the divine nature attributed to water has not prevented rapid and unrestrained tourist development and its massive impact on the natural environment from causing a deterioration in water quality, the decline of water resources and the escalation of pollution. Hotels have been erected without regard to water supply and waste disposal capacity. With virtually no enforceable environmental protection laws, the island is under increasing stress.

THE SEA

Strangely, for an island people, the Balinese have mostly avoided the surrounding ocean and

⦿ LIFE ON THE LINE

Sir Alfred Russel Wallace (1822–1913), a British naturalist and contemporary of Charles Darwin, noted that there were marked differences in flora and fauna between Bali and Lombok. The large mammals of Bali and Java, elephants, tigers and rhinoceros, gave way in Lombok to marsupials and birds common to Australia. He concluded that Lombok Strait defined an ecological separation (later known as the Wallace Line) between the Asian and Australian continents. Although he wasn't wrong, modern scientists have since revised his findings. Lombok and the small islands to the east, including Timor, are now considered to be in a species transition zone called Wallacea.

Shadow puppets performance on Bali.

DECISIVE DATES

PREHISTORIC YEARS

2500–1500 BC
Migrants from southern China and mainland Southeast Asia reach the archipelago and mix with aboriginal peoples.

500 BC–AD 300
Bronze-age culture in Bali.

INDIANISED KINGDOMS

AD 78
Indian influences sweep the Indonesian archipelago.

AD 400
Hindu kingdoms emerge in west Java and east Kalimantan (Borneo).

AD 670
Chinese pilgrim records visit to Buddhist Bali island.

AD 882–914
Buddhist dynasty issues bronze inscriptions in Old Balinese.

AD 910
Political centre moves to central Java; rise of Buddhist kingdoms in Bali.

JAVANESE INFLUENCES

AD 989
Marriage of Buddhist Balinese king with Hindu Javanese princess leads to union.

1011
Airlangga succeeds to the throne in Java; his brother Anak Wungsu rules Bali.

1049
Civil war breaks out in Java; Bali becomes autonomous.

A young Balinese woman, c. 1940.

13th–15th centuries
Islamic sultanates in Sumatra and Malaysia control trade.

1284
Hindu-Buddhist Singasari kingdom retakes Bali.

1292
Singasari attacked by Kublai Khan; Bali becomes independent.

1293
Birth of Hindu Majapahit kingdom in Java.

1343
Majapahit invasion of Bali and Lombok.

1383
Gelgel kingdom founded in Bali.

Early 16th century
Islam spreads eastward in Java; Hindu-Javanese priests, aristocracy and artisans move to Gelgel, leading to Golden Age in Bali.

1515–28
Majapahit kingdom collapses; Bali becomes independent.

COLONIAL ERA

1596
Dutch ships arrive in Java.

1597
Dutch ships arrive in Bali.

1602
Dutch East Indies Company (VOC) founded.

1641
VOC takes over trade in the region.

1651
Civil war in Bali ends Gelgel rule.

1700
Bali breaks up into rival kingdoms that extend power to east Java and Lombok. Karangasem rules Lombok for the next 200 years.

1799
VOC bankrupted due to corruption; Dutch government rules archipelago as a colony until World War II.

1811–16
English rule the archipelago under Stamford Raffles. Colony returned to Holland after peace treaty signed.

1839
Danish trader Mads Lange opens trading port at Kuta, Bali.

1849
North Bali conquered through Dutch military force.

1894–96
Karangasem dynasty in Lombok and East Bali submits to the Dutch after the Sasak War.

1898
Dutch crush threats to Gianyar from other kingdoms and take control.

1906–8
Dutch defeat Badung, Tabanan and Klungkung royal families.

1917
Devastating earthquake hits Bali.

1920s–30s
New artistic developments as artists settle on Bali.

WORLD WAR II AND INDEPENDENCE

1942–5
Japanese Occupation during World War II; declaration of Republic of Indonesia on 17 August 1945.

1945–9
Dutch create State of Eastern Indonesia; after war of independence, the UN recognises Indonesia and Bali and Lombok become part of the new republic.

1963
Gunung Agung erupts, killing thousands.

1965
After failed alleged Communist coup against Sukarno, 500,000 people are massacred, over 100,000 on Bali.

1966
General Suharto formally replaces Sukarno as president. Modern period.

1970–1
Bali receives 15,000 visitors. Mass-tourism programme launched.

1997
Indonesia severely affected by Asian economic crisis.

1998
Riots in Jakarta leave over a thousand dead; President Suharto resigns.

2001
Megawati replaces President Abdurrahman Wahid, who resigns over falsified corruption charges.

2002
Terrorist bombs in Kuta kill more than 200 people.

2004
President Megawati loses re-election bid to Susilo Bambang Yudhoyono after heavily contested polls run

twice. A 6.5-magnitude earthquake and tsunami originating in Indonesia's Aceh province, on the northwest tip of Sumatra, reaches as far as the Maldives and kills 230,000 people in a dozen countries.

2005
On 1 October, three terrorist suicide bombs explode, one in Kuta Square and two on Jimbaran beach. Twenty die.

2014
Indonesia holds national elections. Jakarta Governor, Joko Widodo wins.

2015
Lombok hosts a record-breaking 1.9 million tourist arrivals.

2018
Earthquakes in north Lombok kill 600 people and injure thousands. Bali reports 15.8 million visitors.

2019
Joko Widodo declared president for a second term.

Joko Widodo on the campaign trail, March 2019.

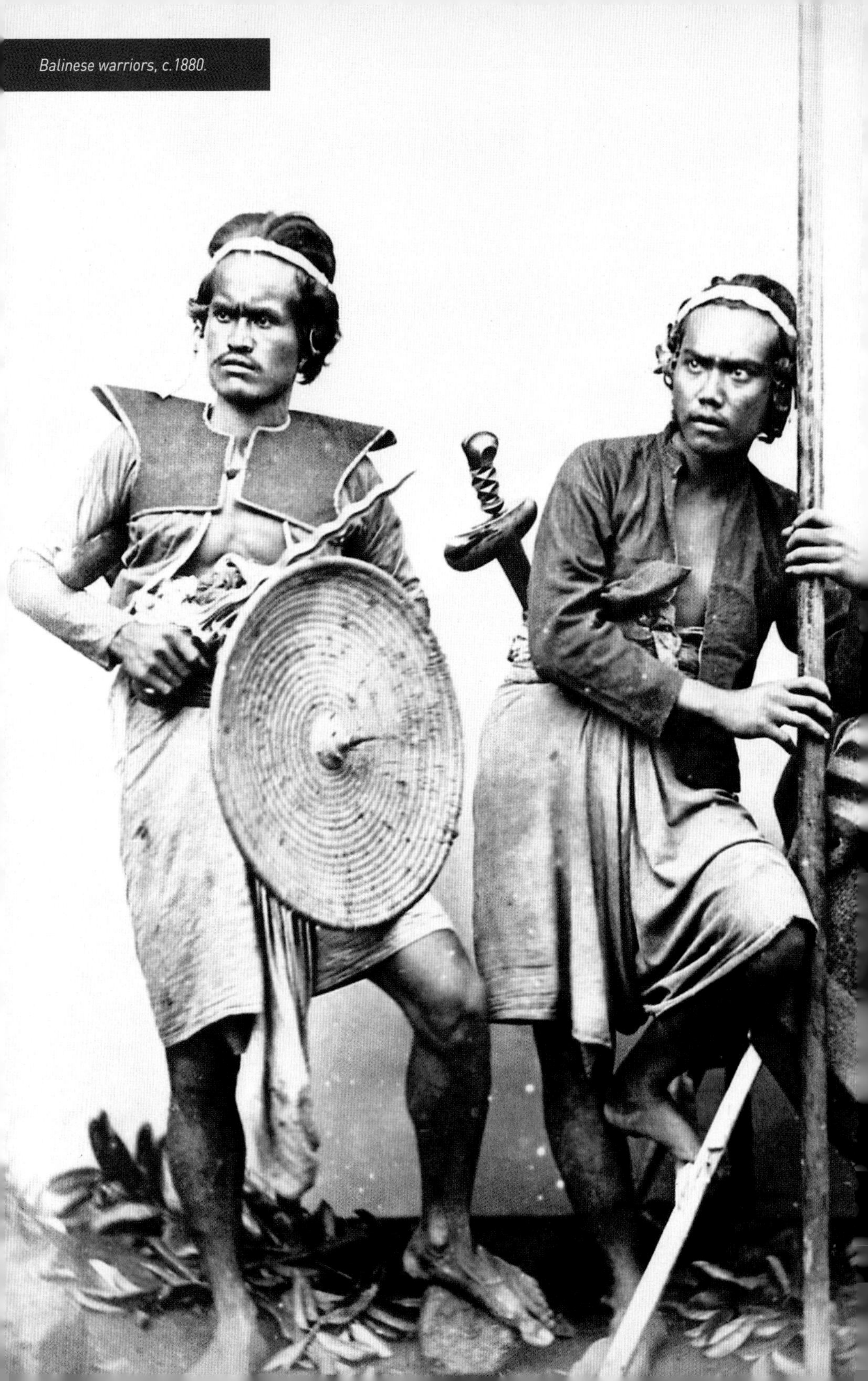

Balinese warriors, c.1880.

AN ISLAND WHERE CULTURES MEET

Despite years of influence from Indian traders and Javanese and colonial Dutch forces, Bali has emerged as an island with a strong sense of self-worth and individuality. Periods of calamity and war have shaped a unique land that brims with hope for the future.

Fossil remains indicate that the ancestors of the modern Balinese were Austronesian hunter-gatherers who migrated to the archipelago some 3,000 years ago from Northeast Asia. These people had contacts through trade with other islands in Southeast Asia, and by the 3rd century BC, the early Balinese had learned bronze casting and were making beautiful bronze kettle drums. Trade links were established 2,000 years ago with India and 1,500 years ago with China.

Unfortunately, a precise history of the social system of these prehistoric Balinese is not known. They practised various kinds of burial – in jars, without coffins and in sarcophagi – and this suggests some social stratification. Additionally, some of these sarcophagi, probably for those of the highest social status, are carved with masks and anthropomorphic figures.

Many of the burials of the prehistoric Balinese included grave goods – jewellery, tools and pottery – indicating a belief in providing for the afterlife.

The only other trace of these prehistoric people on the island are the megalithic structures that remain standing today: terraced structures, stone seats and *menhir* (monuments). Many of these structures are still used today for the veneration of deities as well as ancestors. The religious and social practices of the Bali Aga people, or aboriginal Balinese (see pages 23 and), who, until recently, were isolated communities, may represent vestiges of the prehistoric Balinese social system.

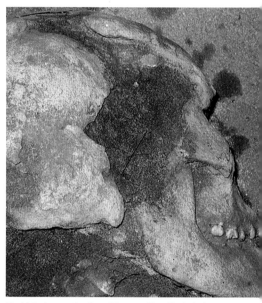

Prehistoric remains from Museum Situs Purbakala, Gilimanuk.

INDIAN INFLUENCES

Early Balinese rulers adopted certain imported religious and administrative practices originating in India that enhanced their status and power. An important belief was in the god-king, a divine incarnation on earth who exercised spiritual and political power through a hierarchy of priests. The realm and its people would prosper only as long as the king conducted himself in accordance with divine law. Although India provided social, theological and political models, the Balinese modified these to suit their own needs while retaining many indigenous practices. Indian deities, for instance, existed alongside the ancestral spirits.

Balinese contacts with India and with other Indian-influenced kingdoms in Southeast Asia were established by the 1st century, and a Buddhist dynasty was ruling Bali by the 7th century. Archaeological remains from this era include inscriptions in Old Balinese script on stone and copper, which reveal that shrines or temples were erected for various rulers. Statues may have been carved and bronzes cast to portray royalty or other important people. Ornamented caves, bathing places and rock-hewn temples were constructed near rivers, springs, ravines

Temple bas relief depicting hell.

☉ WIDOW WITCH

Bali's sacred Barong and Rangda dance (see page 68) is based on the semi-historical *Calonarang* tale. The story goes that the Javanese Hindu queen Mahendradatta used sorcery to kill her husband, the Balinese king Udayana, for breaking his promise not to take another wife. Their son Airlangga banished her and her unwed daughter to the forest. Transformed into the furious Rangda (demon witch), the queen used sorcery to cause more deaths in the kingdom. A Barong (mythical creature) sent his son to steal Rangda's book of sorcery, which the Barong then used to vanquish her. The Barong and Rangda dance represents the eternal struggle between good and evil.

and mountain tops, strongly indicating that these places were connected with ancient religious beliefs.

JAVANESE INFLUENCES

In AD 989, the Buddhist Balinese king Udayana married the Hindu Javanese princess Mahendradatta (see box) creating a geographic, political and religious union. A Hindu-Buddhist fusion that incorporated the ancient cult of ancestral worship was adopted as the state religion. During this time, Kawi (Old Javanese) replaced Old Balinese as the language of inscriptions and court edicts, indicating a Javanisation of Balinese royalty.

The couple's son, Airlangga, born in AD 991, married a princess from the Javanese Sanjaya kingdom. When his father-in-law was murdered, Airlangga waged years of warfare to defeat his rivals and enemies on Java. He finally gained control and ruled the island for the next three decades, while his younger brother, Anak Wungsu, was installed as regent of Bali. Airlangga divided his realm in Java among his two sons and retired to become an ascetic, but after his death in 1049, the brothers fought a long civil war against each other to gain supremacy on Java. As Bali was not involved in the struggle, it became an independent kingdom for the next 235 years until the short-lived east Javanese Singasari kingdom invaded in 1284 to retake the island. However, in 1292 Kublai Khan attacked Singasari for refusing to pay tribute to China and insulting his envoy; thus Bali became independent once again.

The recently founded east Javanese Majapahit kingdom sent its general Gajah Mada to Bali in 1343. The general was sent to quell the cruel king Bedulu, who was noted for his supernatural powers (he was said to be able to decapitate himself then restore his head, hence his name – meaning "different head"). According to legend, one day the god Siwa (the Balinese name for the Hindu god Shiva) was so offended by the king's audacity, that he caused the king's severed head to fall into a stream and be washed away. The king's minister replaced the king's head with that of a pig he killed. The tale follows that King Bedulu decreed that no one should ever look at his face again. When general Gajah Mada, who was staying at the royal court, looked up from his meal to gaze at the king's head, Bedulu became so angry that he was consumed by the fires of his own rage.

In reality, the Majapahit kingdom defeated the Balinese forces and proceeded to govern through a series of puppet rulers. A Javanese-style court along with its culture were introduced to Bali. Life changed when Majapahit broke up the old village structures. The Hindu caste system was introduced; at the apex were *brahmana* high priests, followed by royal *satria*, and *wesia* or merchants. Most of the population was commoner *sudra* or *jaba* (outsiders). Although the

The 16th century was Bali's Golden Age under Waturenggong, the king who welded the island into a strongly centralised kingdom based at Gelgel. He conquered Balmbangan in east Java and colonised neighbouring Lombok. Waturenggong also came to epitomise the concept of a just ruler. One of his biggest supporters, an arrival from Java, was a Brahmin high priest named Danghyang Nirartha or Pedanda Sakti Waurauh (Powerful Newcomer Priest), who is the ancestor of most Balinese high priests. He introduced rituals that were considered to be more powerful than those

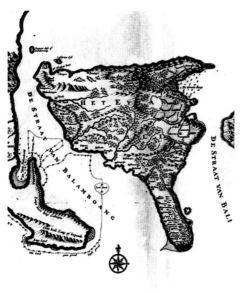

17th-century map of Bali.

17th-century European illustration of a Balinese raja.

royalty ruled, the high priests held the real power because of their knowledge of ancient texts. An evil or corrupt king could be replaced by a better one through the intercession of priests.

RISE AND FALL OF CLASSICAL BALI

The Hindu Majapahit kingdom began to crumble in 1515 with the rise of the Islamic sultanates in Java. Reluctant to succumb, the priests, nobles and artisans of the Majapahit empire chose instead to move to Bali, strengthening the Hindu culture that had taken root there. The Balinese in turn moulded the Majapahit influences to their own needs, reinventing the Balinese culture. Much of today's language, music, arts and literature are derived from this time.

previously performed, particularly the making of holy water, the key rite of the Brahmin priest.

Bali's first encounter with Europe occurred during this time. The contest by European powers to claim the fabled Spice Islands in the Maluku (Moluccas) area further east had begun. Although several European sea captains, including England's Sir Francis Drake, had sighted Bali, the first substantial body of information came from a Dutch expedition led by Cornelis de Houtman in 1597. He observed the height of the Balinese Golden Age, but soon after his visit the court of Gelgel began to decline rapidly. The Dutch failed to strike trade agreements with the Balinese in 1601, and for the next two centuries, encroaching Europeans largely ignored Bali.

INTERNAL PROBLEMS

A long period during which kingdoms rose and fell in succession began in Bali during the 17th century. The prime minister of Gelgel seized control in 1651 because the king's two sons were fighting for succession. The floodgates were opened when other lords saw their chance to become kings of their own domains. The concept of a single ruler was replaced by that of many, inspired by epic narratives such as the *Panji* or *Malat* romances that lent strength to the idea that a brave warrior could emerge from

nowhere and take a kingdom for himself. In the north emerged Buleleng, in the west Jembrana, and in the east, Karangasem took over Lombok. In the south a number of kingdoms appeared: Bangli, Tabanan, Badung, Gianyar and Mengwi; the latter expanded into east Java. In the same period, the tiny southeastern Klungkun kingdom, founded in 1665, took over the Gelgel throne. By the late 1700s, nine royal courts had emerged from the chaos, with Klungkung the strongest.

One of the more negative practices to emerge from Bali was slavery. It was a demand for slaves

Buleleng's court, c.1880.

⊙ A DANISH CONNECTION

Danish trader Mads Lange was trading rice from Lombok during the 1830s with China, Australia and Singapore. When the British established another trading post on the island in 1839, Lange left for Bali and landed at Kuta where he soon established a thriving trade. He cultivated relations with several Balinese kings and helped the Dutch develop commercial interests, all of which created conflicts of interest. By 1849, trade at Kuta was declining as ships went to the better, more accessible port in Singaraja. In 1856, Lange decided to return to Denmark but was poisoned while visiting a local lord, and died. He was buried in Kuta, where his tomb still stands today.

on the part of the Dutch and the ability of the Balinese to supply them that enabled petty kings to seize their moments of power with the common people as the victims. As wars were fought between rival kingdoms, villagers were forced to fight alongside their lords, and they had a vested interest in ensuring their lords won: defeat meant capture and being sold into slavery.

Opium was another commodity that the Balinese rulers exploited to enrich themselves. The Dutch held a monopoly in the region, but Balinese rulers who did not come under Dutch rule decided that they had a right to deal in the drug. The Balinese were also consuming 200 chests of opium a year, in addition to 20 to 30 chests being used by each of the courts.

During the 17th century in Dutch-controlled Batavia (Jakarta), out of 18,000 slaves, 9,000 were Balinese. Women were valued as wives and servants, men as labourers and colonial army soldiers.

By the beginning of the 19th century, in order to raise their status, the kings began rewriting genealogies that linked them to the ancient Javanese kingdoms. At the same time, many commoner families were increasing their power. Ultimately, it was the inability of the Balinese to present a united front against the Dutch that led to their downfall.

From 1811–16, Sir Thomas Stamford Raffles administered the Netherlands Indies for the Dutch government, which was exiled in London during the Napoleonic wars. He visited Bali and viewed the people as 'noble savages' preserving ancient Javanese civilisation, but failed to recognise their ability to adapt and transform these ideas to meet the future.

In 1815, Gunung Tambora volcano on Sumbawa island erupted violently. Bali was covered by volcanic ash that destroyed its rice harvests, and thousands starved to death. At least 25,000 people perished as a result of the eruption and its aftermath. A mudslide in Buleleng that same year killed 10,000 people. This was followed by outbreaks of cholera, dysentery, smallpox and rat plagues that devastated meagre food supplies, causing further famine and disease.

DUTCH INTRUSIONS

At the beginning of the 19th century, the Dutch were looking for ways to gain a foothold on Bali. Ash deposits from Tambora's eruption created a soil so fertile that the Balinese were able to export food to Singapore. But the Dutch were suspicious of Balinese dealings with the newly established British colony, Singapore. By the end of the 1830s, the Dutch were openly discussing trade, politics, plundering and slavery with the kings – veiled by deceitful treaties of friendship and commerce that would ultimately lead to Dutch sovereignty on the island.

The Dutch wanted to end the practice of plundering shipwrecks, which the Balinese regarded as gifts from the deity of the sea. The ship, cargo and everyone on board automatically became the property of the king who ruled the territory where the incident occurred. Thus, when a Dutch frigate went aground off Kuta in 1841, the Balinese naturally plundered it. The Dutch tried to get the Balinese to sign a treaty putting a stop to this but were rebuffed.

In 1846, the Dutch launched a punitive expedition against Buleleng in the north, but the Balinese put up a strong resistance. A second expedition was sent in 1848, and the

A Dutch East Indies Company vessel.

Balinese again fought off the Dutch attack. During the third expedition in 1849, backed by heavily armed soldiers, the Dutch attacked the fortifications at Jagaraja. Backed into a corner, the Balinese decided the only honourable course of action was to end it all in self-sacrifice. This was when the Dutch first witnessed a *puputan* (literally meaning "ending" or "finish"), a ritual suicide that traditionally signalled the end of a kingdom. Led by the Buleleng king, nobles marched into gunfire, and others committed suicide with daggers or poison. Thousands of Balinese men and women died.

Although the Dutch now regarded themselves as holding sovereignty, they did not interfere in the internal affairs of the southern and eastern Bali kingdoms. However, when Buleleng tried to rebel in 1853, the Dutch took more direct control.

END OF AN ERA

Between 1850 and 1888, Bali was hit by seven epidemics of smallpox and five of cholera, four rat plagues, and widespread dysentery outbreaks. In 1891, rival Balinese kings from Badung and Tabanan defeated neighbouring Mengwi and divided up the territory among themselves.

Dutch artillery firing on the Balinese.

⊘ DAGGERS OF DESTINY

Heirloom *keris*, daggers with straight or wavy blades, have been vital in the mythology connected to the rise of Balinese kingdoms. A *keris* unsheathed by a Majapahit invader conjured up demonic troops that made the Balinese flee. A king in north Bali pointed his dagger at ships to free stranded ones or cause them to become wrecked on reefs. A *keris* found in a piece of wood in a river helped found the Gianyar kingdom. In Klungkung, a *keris* kept away spirits of pestilence and epidemics. In north Bali, a lord stabbed his dagger into a mountain side, causing fresh water to gush out for irrigation and thus producing a bumper rice crop.

Meanwhile, the Balinese Mataram kingdom on Lombok enjoyed considerable influence and power, and had been overlords of Karangasem in east Bali since 1849. Most of the people living in Lombok were indigenous Muslim Sasak who rebelled when Mataram ordered them to fight in Bali. This gave the Dutch an excuse to invade Lombok and take over the British trade post.

In 1894, Dutch troops invaded Lombok and quickly conquered Mataram. At nearby Cakranegara, they were attacked by Balinese warriors. The Dutch sent reinforcements and the king eventually surrendered, along with his son and grandson. However, his nephew, Anak Agung Nengah, refused to surrender and chose the rite of *puputan*. Nengah led men, women and children who died either by the *keris* blades (see box) or rushed forward into the fire of the Dutch troops to be killed.

Worse was yet to come. In 1904, a Chinese-owned vessel registered by the Dutch colonial government struck a reef off Sanur in Bali and was plundered. Its owner greatly exaggerated the losses, and the Badung king, supported by the Tabana king, refused to pay compensation. In retaliation, the Dutch blockaded the Badung and Tabanan coasts and assembled a large military expedition.

In September 1906, the Dutch launched perhaps one of the most shameful episodes in colonial history. Dutch troops marched into Denpasar, and as they approached the palace its gates opened and the royal court dressed in white and ornamented with their finest jewellery filed out and stopped before them. A priest plunged a golden *keris* into the king's chest, while others turned their weapons upon themselves. Some, armed only with spears or bows and arrows, charged at the Dutch. The Dutch fired at them, then looted jewellery from the corpses and sacked the palace ruins.

That afternoon a similar scene was repeated at the smaller Pemecutan court in Denpasar. News of the *puputan* in Badung turned Dutch public opinion against their government's policy in the East Indies. Karangasem, Bangli and Gianyar reluctantly accepted Dutch authority.

If the Dutch had hoped that events would end there, they were mistaken. The final act of Bali's tragedy took place in 1908 when the Klungkung monarch objected to the Dutch imposition of an opium monopoly in his kingdom. In opposition, Balinese burned down a Dutch opium shop in Klungkung and killed a dealer. The Dutch retaliated by attacking Klungkung in April 1908. In response to the attack, the king, carrying his ancestral dagger, slowly emerged from the palace. His court and more than 200 people accompanied him to face the Dutch. The king knelt down and thrust the blade into the ground because a prophecy had foretold that this magical weapon would open up a chasm in the earth and swallow the enemy. Unfor-

maintain local traditions. Ironically, the Dutch thought that if Balinese culture was to be saved, then the Balinese had to be taught how to become more 'authentically' Balinese. The reform policy did go some way towards protecting the Balinese culture.

Foreigners were excluded from owning land. The opening up of tea, rubber, sugar and tobacco plantations were opposed in order to protect the Balinese from exploitation rampant elsewhere in the colony. Christian missionaries were prohibited from converting the Balinese.

Body of Badung's king after the 1906 puputan.

tunately, the prophecy proved to be false, and a Dutch bullet killed the king. His wives knelt around his corpse and drove *keris* blades into their hearts while the others began the *puputan* ritual. Klungkung palace was razed.

After nearly 600 years, the Balinese courts that had descended from the Majapahit empire of Java were gone. Bali was now completely under the control of the Dutch colonialists.

PARADISE: COLONIAL STYLE

International protests condemned the Dutch, forcing guilty officials to make amends by introducing reforms. This coincided with what has come to be known as "Balinisation", controlling by indirect rule while attempting to

Bali came to be regarded as a 'living museum' of ancient Hindu-Javanese culture, partly as a way of establishing the island's identity. Sadly, it was an unrealistic view that ignored independent developments on the island. During this time, many Dutch scholars came to study Balinese history, art, culture and religion, but they focused on the esoteric Brahmin high priests, and ignored the ordinary lives of the people. With the aid of Brahmin priests, the Dutch restructured the caste system, understanding little of the system's inherent mobility and flexibility. This rationalisation by the Dutch – not only of the caste system, but also of the political units, labour and rice farming – threw the traditional Balinese system into chaos. The restructuring was only advantageous to the upper-caste members who became strong supporters of the Dutch.

From the 1920s onwards, increasing numbers of visitors, including artists, sociologists, economists, dancers and musicians, were captivated by Bali's exotic charm. Their tales of travel to the island only served to promote Bali's image as an island paradise. A few influential foreign artists and anthropologists were keen to promote the island, but their works were skewed interpretations of the real Bali. Most of their

price of pig and copra (dried coconut flesh) exports and halving the value of the local currency. Poor peasants sold their lands to members of higher castes, while others became tenant farmers to pay off debts to the aristocrats who took their land as collateral.

The alliance between upper castes and the colonial government was increasingly challenged by educated commoners, especially in 1938 when the Dutch reinstated descendants of the royal families as figurative heads of power in their former kingdoms.

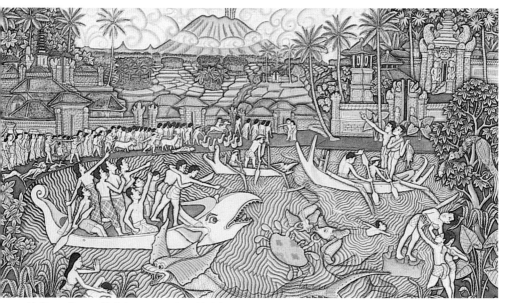

Ida Bagus Nyoman Rai's impression of the 1963 Gunung Agung eruption.

writings implicitly supported colonialism and implied that the Balinese had little to do with the development and direction of their own culture and history.

CRISES AND CONFLICT

While resident foreigners created an image of paradise, the Balinese lived with reality. In 1917, a devastating earthquake struck the island, flattening villages and destroying some of the most important temples. More than 1,000 people were killed. This was followed by a rat plague that destroyed crops, then by the worldwide Spanish-flu epidemic that claimed thousands of Balinese lives. The Great Depression in the 1930s hit Bali hard, quartering the

In February 1942, with the spread of World War II, Japanese forces landed at Sanur, marched unopposed into Denpasar and took control of Bali. The military secret police arrested Balinese who associated with the Dutch. As elsewhere in Asia, the Japanese occupiers were brutal, proclaiming themselves anti-colonial, when they were harsher than the Dutch. They ostensibly promoted Balinese culture and fostered nationalism, hoping to garner support from the locals against the Dutch.

When the Japanese surrendered in August 1945, Indonesian leaders Sukarno and Mohammad Hatta declared Indonesia as independent republic. Bali had no strong centre of power, so an interim administration struggled to keep

In the Margarana Incident of November 1946, Balinese nationalist I Gusti Ngurah Rai and his forces were surrounded by the Dutch at Marga, Tabanan. Rather than surrender, they resorted to puputan (suicide).

order and gain recognition, while the old kingdoms tried to reassert themselves. Some were pro-Dutch, like the Klunkung king, while others, like I Gusti Ngurah Rai (see box) were nationalists who supported an independent Indonesia.

The Dutch returned in December to reclaim their former colony and established the State of Eastern Indonesia. They imprisoned members of the anti-colonial administration, and the struggle for independence went underground. Four years of bitter fighting left more than 2,000 Balinese dead. When the United Nations officially recognised Indonesia as a republic in 1949, the Dutch had to withdraw. Bali became a province of the new nation. Today the island is divided into eight *kabupaten* (counties or regencies), each name for one of the former kingdoms who ceded their powers to the new republic, and the municipality of Denpasar. There is further division into *kecamatan* (sub-districts) and *desa dinas* (administrative villages). More numerous and important to the Balinese are *desa adat* (traditional villages), which are subdivided into *banjar* (hamlets or wards), a system unique to Bali.

PROBLEMS IN PARADISE

From 1946 to 1949, the split between the pro-Dutch and nationalist factions was pronounced, with many nationalists jailed, tortured or killed by other Balinese. These divisions were compounded by the split between feudal and modern forces, and tensions continued even after the Dutch departure in 1949. Members of the aristocratic castes moved increasingly into business. Political affiliation was similarly divided between the nationalists and socialists, a situation that was to change dramatically in the late 1950s.

Sukarno, then president of Indonesia, claimed empathy with the Balinese because of his background (his mother was Balinese) but did little to enhance the spiritual and material welfare

of the people; rampant inflation and corruption under his administration did not help. Nationwide attempts at land reform went some way in loosening the grip that the aristocratic landowners held over their tenants.

When Sukarno banned the Socialist Party, many of its members joined the Communist Party, which was especially strong in Bali. The island was a place of tension and continual political rallies during the early 1960s. Many Balinese feared that supernatural powers were being provoked. In 1963, the Gunung Agung

A young Sukarno.

eruption during the Eka Dasa Rudra ceremony, staged once a century, reinforced this belief. Villages were destroyed and thousands died in the disaster and ensuing famine.

During the early 1960s, many Balinese supported the PKI (Indonesian Communist Party). They urged people to claim back farmland that was owned by a minority. Support came from thousands of Balinese who were badly affected by the 1964 famine after Gunung Agung's eruption. A split developed between supporters of PÑI (Nationalist Party of Indonesia) and PKI, largely seen as a challenge to the old feudal and caste systems. Rallies advocated the overthrow of the caste system. The arts were entwined with propaganda as the Communist organisation

LEKRA (Institute for People's Culture) encouraged and sponsored musicians, dancers, puppeteers, writers and artists to spread their proletarian message.

When an abortive coup took place in Jakarta on 30 September 1965, the floodgates were opened. The Communists supposedly murdered some high-ranking military officers, but within a few hours the military, led by General Suharto, put a quick end to the attempt to take over the government. The speed of the countermeasures strongly indicated prior knowledge of the inci-

Artist at work in Ubud.

dent, which was played out in order to remove President Sukarno because he was gravitating towards the Soviet Union and its allies.

The Cold War became feverish in Bali, where PNI and other anti-Communists obliterated PKI in a bloodbath that claimed more than 100,000 lives. Old scores were settled between villagers, castes and family members, the massacre ultimately having little to do with politics. The surprise is that from this tragedy, Bali has emerged as a tourist paradise.

FOCUS ON TOURISM

Suharto's government, which came to power in 1966, identified Bali as the best site for mass tourism. This was supported by the World Bank, which drew up a tourism development plan that proposed a huge tourist resort at Nusa Dua that would make profitable use of the dry and infertile land. Because most hotels in Nusa Dua tended to be owned by foreign and Jakarta-based companies, the overall benefits for the Balinese were initially questionable. But local entrepreneurs began to further develop other tourism centres in the southern beaches and Ubud, where Balinese involvement and employment were greater.

Despite the negative aspects of tourism – like kitschy mass-produced souvenirs and blatant sales of land to developers – there is no doubt it has helped to revitalise the island's arts and crafts industry, and performing arts, as well as fund extensive temple renovations. Today, Balinese music and dance schools are packed with students. In fact many villages have their own performing arts groups and stage full-length performances for religious ceremonies, although most visitors only see condensed renditions of dances and shadow plays.

A VULNERABLE INDUSTRY

In the late 1990s, Bali remained an outpost of stability while most of Indonesia was torn by conflicts sparked by the Asian economic crisis and a succession of presidents. However crises in the early 20th century exposed the weakness of an economy so dependent on tourism.

Visitor numbers fell after the 9/11 terrorist attacks in the US, but more devastating was the Kuta nightclub bombings by Javanese Muslim radicals on 12 October 2002 that killed 202 people and injured 240 more. The terrorists were caught and brought to trial a year later, but just when visitor arrivals were showing signs of improvement bombs exploded again in Jimbaran and Kuta on 1 October 2005. This time 20 people were killed. The threats posed by Muslim extremists in the nation with the world's largest Islamic population (even though Bali is predominantly Hindu) combined with the unpredictability of natural disasters like volcanic eruptions and earthquakes, all negatively affected tourism. Yet, despite this, Bali's tourism industry has continued to grow, with annual foreign visitor arrivals breaking all previous records. 2018 was another record-breaking year, with over 6.07 million foreign tourists visiting Bali.

CHINESE INFLUENCES ON BALI

A 6th-century Chinese trade journal refers to an island called P'o-li (or Poleng), a description which seems to have been of a larger place possibly including east Java.

Although Chinese impact on Bali is not well documented in historical annals and is not obvious to the first-time visitor, Bali has had a distinct Chinese connection from as far back as AD 670, when a Chinese pilgrim-scholar on his way to India wrote about visiting a Buddhist country called Bali.

During the 11th century, a Balinese king married a Chinese princess of the Kang clan and converted her to Buddhism. The couple named their kingdom Bali Kang or Balingkang. The Hindu gods supposedly made her childless, so she died of sorrow and became Batari Mandul, the Barren Goddess, whose stone image is enshrined at the Pura Puncak Penulisan (see page 150) temple. The long-haired Kintamani mountain dogs from here are said to be descended from her pet Chinese chows. Princess Kang is worshipped by Balinese and Chinese as Ida Ratu Ayu Subandar, the Divine Harbour Queen, deity of trade and patron goddess of merchants. Pura Besakih and Pura Ulun Danu Batur temples both have large shrines in her honour.

DANCE AND DESIGN

Barong, of which there are various kinds, is a Balinese dance form usually performed by two men. The female figure in the pair of barong landung (tall protective spirits) wears a white mask with Chinese-like facial features – an image identified by many as Princess Kang. These masked mythological creatures animated by two dancers are also found in China and many other parts of Asia. In Bali, moreover, the Chinese-style lion called barong sae is just like the traditional Chinese lion dancers in that it dances to the sounds of gongs, drums and cymbals during certain auspicious times of the year in front of houses, businesses and temples.

Balinese architecture in the south also points to distinct Chinese styles. Both Balinese and Chinese homes and temples are surrounded by walls, which are sometimes inlaid with Chinese porcelain plates or ceramic lattice tiles. Just inside the gate, an aling-aling (privacy wall) is constructed to prevent demons and malign influ-

Chinese temple architecture is evident on Bali.

ences, which can only move straight, from entering. In both China and Bali, separate buildings with upward curving roof corners are arranged around an open central courtyard. A few Balinese textile patterns and woodcarving motifs are shared with the Chinese, such as karang cina (Chinese foliage).

Beyond the Chinese Buddhist temples in every major town, one need not look far to find other vestiges of Chinese influence. Chinese copper-alloy coins with centre holes are used in offerings and strung together to create ritual objects. They are also used as sacred images of the Hindu deities of prosperity and fertility as well as for shrine hangings and effigies.

Kecak fire show takes place in Gianyar Regency on Bali, during the full moon.

Temple festival offerings at Pura
Gunung Lebah, Ubud.

RELIGION AND RITUALS

The combination of Hindu traditions from Java and Bali's own animist beliefs has imbued the island with a spiritual richness and depth. Everyday life revolves around these beliefs, and temple ceremonies govern the calendar.

Religion to the Balinese-Hindus is inseparable from everyday life. Instead of taking their holidays away from home, they will use their holiday entitlement to attend ceremonies. Every time a small *canang* offering, filled with flower petals and incense, is laid upon the ground; every time an artisan carves out the features of a mythological creature; every time a young baby touches the ground for the first time, or ashes are cast into the sea, substantiation of their living culture is being manifested, acting as a constant reminder of the Balinese-Hindu passion for an authentic existence. While there are a small number of Christian, Buddhist and Muslim Balinese, Hinduism is the religion of the vast majority. The important thing for visitors to understand is that cremations and other ceremonies are not tourist attractions but genuine religious events. The fact that the Balinese allow outsiders to take part in them does not detract from their religious significance.

The Balinese religion is called Agama Hindu Dharma or Agama Tirtha, the religion of holy water, because of its important use in worship and ritual. Bali is the only island in Indonesia – which has the world's largest Islamic population – where Hinduism is the predominant religion.

The Balinese have long regarded the universe as a structured entity in which everything has its place. They also recognise the duality of nature: male and female, good and evil, day and night, life and death. Order and harmony are personified by deities who live on mountain tops and bestow their blessings on humans. Demons symbolise disorder and dwell beneath the sea, seeking chaos and destruction. Offerings must be made regularly to acknowledge the life-sustaining forces and prevent disasters such as earthquakes and epidemics.

Sanghyang Widi Wasa, the Supreme Being.

FUSION OF FAITHS

Buddhism was the state religion of Bali's early kingdoms since the 7th century. In the 10th century, Bali's King Udayana married a Hindu Javanese princess and the two religions fused. During the 16th century, high priests moved from Java to escape the encroachment of Islam. They introduced the caste system to Bali and placed themselves at the top of the hierarchy.

Bali's higher gods are Hindu and Buddhist, all manifestations of Sanghyang Widi Wasa, the Supreme Singular Deity of Universal Order. Siwa (Shiva), the destroyer and reincarnator, is the main focus of Hindu-Balinese worship. Two other gods, Brahma the creator and Wisnu (Vishnu) the preserver, are also worshipped.

> For Balinese, filing the six upper teeth into an even line diminishes the six negative aspects of human behaviour. These are passion, greed, anger, intoxication, ignorance and jealousy.

In some temples there is a three-seat shrine for these gods. During ceremonies, the shrine is decked out with coloured banners: red for Brahma, white for Siwa, and black for Wisnu.

ancestors, *buta yadnya* for demons, *dewa yadnya* for deities and *resi yadnya* for priests.

For instance, an expectant mother will undergo a ceremony between her fifth to seventh month to make sure that the baby develops safely. During the pregnancy, neither parents may cut their hair or help to bathe corpses for funerals. At birth the amniotic fluid, blood, fat covering the skin, and placenta are regarded as *catur sanak* or the 'four siblings', guardian spirits of the baby. The placenta is buried at home outside the north pavilion staircase; right side for a boy, left side for a girl.

Lace worker in Seminyak.

Participant in a purification ceremony.

The Balinese also worship a number of deified ancestors and spirits of mountains, lakes, rivers and trees. Other Indian aspects are the belief in the soul and the idea that every action has a reaction. Reincarnation is due to suffering caused by inappropriate behaviour. The goal is to escape from the cycle of rebirth and become one with the divine Supreme Being.

RITUALS OF BIRTH AND CHILDHOOD

Every event from birth to death must be divinely acknowledged to make it legitimate. A series of rites of passage marks these changes from one stage in the life cycle to another. There are five categories of *yadnya* (rituals): *manusa yadnya* for the living, *pitra yadnya* for the dead and

When the baby is 12 days old, a spirit medium, in a trance, will reveal which ancestor has been reincarnated. In the first major ceremony at the age of 42 days, the baby receives its name and demonic forces are sent away. The ritual obligation for the parents ends, and they can pray at temples again. The child, however, cannot touch the earth until it is 105 days old when the *telung bulan* or *tigang sasih* (three Balinese months of 35 days each) ceremony is held. From a bowl of water, the baby chooses an object that symbolises its future: a coin means business while an inscribed palm-leaf signifies scholarship. After this ceremony the baby can be taken to temple.

During the baby's first *otonan* (210-day birthday), it is welcomed into the community and its head is shaved clean. By the third birthday, the child is counted as a member of society.

ADVANCING TO ADULTHOOD

Puberty is marked for an adolescent girl by her first menstruation and for a boy by the deepening of his voice. Celebrating these changes today is rare except in some high-caste families. A *mapandes* or *potong gigi* (tooth-filing) ceremony marks the passage into adulthood (see box). Uneven teeth and pointed canines are too much like those of demons and animals. Because of the expense of a tooth-filing ceremony, however, it is common to hold it with a wedding. In addition, a corpse or its drawn effigy often has its teeth filed before being cremated, as it is feared that the soul cannot enter heaven if it looks like a fanged demon or animal.

Every Balinese is expected to *nganten* (get married). The most common way is by *mapedik* (request), in which the family and friends of the boy visit the family of the girl, presenting them with offerings and gifts. *Ngorod*, or elopement, is more economical (some say romantic) and just as common, with the boy abducting his girlfriend by car. Her family may feign outrage when they find her gone, even though they may have known of the plan.

In either case, the couple goes through a ceremony that seals the marriage. A formal wedding is held later at the groom's home when a priest sanctifies the union, and prayers are made to the ancestral deities. The aim of marriage is ultimately to have children, and the wedding ceremony is full of symbolism suggesting this. Bride and groom take turns sitting on a coconut to represent fertility. The groom uses a *keris* (dagger) to stab three times through a small mat held by the bride – the sexual symbolism is obvious.

Death and cremation ceremonies (see page 57) are even more elaborate and can go on for days.

TEMPLE FESTIVALS

Balinese usually visit a temple on holy days and during its *odalan* (anniversary celebration) held every 210 days of the Wuku calendar or 355 days by the lunar-solar Saka year (see page 58). The event may last a single night, for three days, or for 11 days or more during large festivals.

When preparations for an anniversary celebration begin, the temple comes to life. Villagers clean courtyards, unfurl banners and flags, and dress shrines and statues with cloth and ornaments. Men erect altars and structures from wood, bamboo and thatching, while the women prepare offerings (see page 80) from flowers and leaves. The men do most of the temple cooking (a task they rarely attend to at home) to feed those who *ngayah* (participate in preparations). *Tajen* (cockfights) are staged to appease the demons that require blood sacrifice, but the associated gambling activities are strictly entertainment for mortals.

Prayers at a temple.

⊙ APPROPRIATE TEMPLE ATTIRE

Dressing properly for temples is required. Even when nothing special is happening, everyone is modestly dressed with a sash tied around the waist, symbolising control of earthly desires. During temple ceremonies, visitors with exposed legs must wear a sarong. Bare shoulders or exposed midriffs for women are not allowed. Full formal dress may be required at important festivals, with a man wearing a tied headcloth and a shorter cloth over his sarong. Bathing before going is mandatory, and clothes worn at a cremation should be washed before being used at a temple. Women who are menstruating or anyone who has a bleeding wound cannot enter a temple.

Sacred images are taken out of storage and adorned by priests with flowers, ornaments and textiles. These images and statues are presented with offerings, worshipped, and are even entertained with music, sacred songs, poetry, puppetry and dances. Everyone takes pains to dress in their best clothes for a temple's anniversary celebration. At the closing of the festivities, priests politely request the spirits of visiting deities to depart. Images are undressed and stored away, cloths removed from shrines and parasols closed.

PRIESTS AND HEALERS

Through ritual knowledge, the *pedanda* (*brahmana* high priest) and *empu* (clan high priest) transmit divine power to preside over important ceremonies and create extremely potent holy water. The *pemangku* (local temple priests), who mostly come from the lower castes, create less powerful kinds of holy water, in addition to taking on very active roles in temple rituals and in presenting offerings. The Balinese require various types of *tirta* (holy water) in their spiritual life, each with a specific use. These cover all

A Balinese man is treated for his ailment using traditional medicine.

⊘ TRADITIONAL HEALING

Herbal recipes for curing physical ailments are recorded in traditional manuscripts. Although prescription drugs are available, many Balinese still go to healers for these remedies. To counteract attacks of witchcraft, a *balian* (spiritual healer) recites incantations and burns incense while subjecting the victim to a painful massage in order to force out the offending spell. Mystical syllables are invisibly written over the body for protection, and sometimes magical charms are given to be worn or even imbibed by the sufferer. Making vows to the deities can also cure mysterious illnesses, as does the drinking of *tirta* (holy water) from certain temples.

situations including removing spiritual impurities, eliminating crop pests, cleansing the dead, restoring fertility, bestowing knowledge, receiving divine blessings or curing illnesses.

Even with today's modern medicine, when a Balinese is struck by a mysterious illness the cause is often ascribed to the work of demons, black magic or the violation of a religious law or custom. They are likely to visit a *balian* (spiritual healer), who uses traditional remedies, massage, amulets or talismans to cure them. Some healers even use esoteric knowledge to help locate a lost object or determine auspicious days.

A *balian* is said to have the power to contact the spirit world in order to help or harm people. A healer always has a spirit guide; the relationship is potentially dangerous and has to be treated with great care and respect, and nourished with constant prayers and offerings. It is believed that certain kinds of sickness are caused by spirits and that the only cure is to learn to communicate with a particular spirit, who will not only neutralise the illness but will also work with that person on future occasions to help others. There are various ways in which Balinese become healers. Many are people who once suffered from serious illness and went to a *balian* for help. They either acquired healing powers through contact

with spirits during their treatment or by studying with the *balian* they consulted.

Different healers are known for different sets of skills, some of which fall more into the sphere of traditional, rather than spiritual, medicine. A *balian tulang* specialises in setting broken bones, while a *balian manak* is a midwife. Others such as the *balian tenung* specialise in divining and prophesying. A *balian usada* heals people with the help of *lontar* (palm-leaf manuscripts) that contain magical knowledge about medicine and healing. Although many *balian usada* are highly

A priest sprinkling holy water at a ceremony.

⊘ TRANCE AND SPIRIT POSSESSION

A boy prances barefooted on hot coals while riding a hobby horse. A old woman with tears streaming down her face screams in an ancient language she never learned. A man rushes at a masked witch figure to stab her with his dagger, but instead turns the blade into his bare chest and bends it without piercing his skin. A young dancer stands on the shoulders of a man and does backbends with her eyes shut. These and many other incidents are quite common in Balinese rituals.

Known generally as *kerauhan* (arrival) or *kesurupan* (descent), trance and possession are how supernatural powers are considered to make their

presence and power felt, enabling holy people, prepubescent children, and other selected individuals to perform unusual feats.

Deities and spirits show their pleasure or displeasure in these physical acts. Anything said by someone in a state of possession is carefully listened to and heeded, as a message from the numinous. A missing offering, an improper action, an unholy presence, or any number of things is enough for this to happen. Eventually, people are brought back to consciousness with splashes and gulps of holy water.

And it's all quite normal for the Balinese.

> *Night-time contests between practitioners of black magic happen in 'hotspots', especially coastal areas facing the Nusa Penida island, home of the lord of black magic, Ratu Gede Mas Mecaling.*

literate scholars who are consulted because of their ability to interpret these manuscripts, it is the *lontar* itself that is believed to contain the magical energy.

manifestations are known as *leyak*, living humans who can change their spirits into another form, such as a strange animal or a headless body. These *leyak* practice *desti*, literally "left-handed" or black magic. The human form of *leyak* will often remain asleep in bed while the spirit roams outdoors, so it is difficult to know who the *leyak* really are.

It is rare for a Balinese to speak openly about *leyak* for fear that such a practitioner will overhear and harm the speaker. Victims are more than likely to be members of a sorcerer's immediate family, the motives being revenge for simple affronts, jeal-

Pura Luhur Batakau, one of Bali's holiest temples.

The most common type of healer is the *balian taksu* who is consulted on matters relating to illness due to a curse – perhaps caused by a deceased person who is not happy for some reason and haunts the living. The *balian taksu* will begin the session by making offerings and falling into trance. The guiding spirit will be summoned and will speak through the healer, questioning the client to find out what the problem is before revealing the cause and cure.

THE DARK SIDE

Many Balinese will tell you stories of strange creatures they have encountered at night: monkeys with golden teeth, bald-headed giants, or even a strange ball of light hovering in the sky. These strange

ousy or greed. Babies are most susceptible before their first 210-day birthday ceremony, often crying or suffering mishaps for no apparent reason.

Not all *leyak* are harmful, however, as some practitioners just enjoy the thrill of supernatural transformation. Moreover, Balinese believe that both constructive and destructive forces are necessarily present in the world. They believe the important thing is that neither good nor evil gets the upper hand. Learning to become a *leyak* involves many years of study in secret and considerable self-sacrifice. The Balinese accept the fact that there are individuals who seek to study the black arts for evil purposes, but they are also deeply aware that a person who uses supernatural forces to harm others exposes himself to danger.

THE CREMATION CEREMONY

A soul merely borrows a physical human body, which upon death is returned to the five elements – wind, earth, fire, water and ether.

Balinese-Hindus believe that upon death, the physical body is returned to the five elements so as to release the soul and enable it to reincarnate on earth or unite with the divine Supreme Being. Friends, family and neighbours gather to share memories and provide comfort when someone dies. No weeping or grief is openly displayed, for this makes the soul unwilling to leave. The corpse should be cremated upon death, but this is so costly that a family often waits years to share expenses in a joint ceremony. In the meantime, the body is purified and buried in the village cemetery. A priest, however, cannot be buried and will be cremated as soon as possible.

Once a *ngaben* or *pelebon* (cremation) date is set, ritual specialists, priests, knowledgeable people, friends and neighbours help mobilise the communal spirit. If a body has been buried, the soul is brought home first in an effigy. The corpse is washed, but if there is no body, the action is simulated on a drawing of a human figure. A priest will give advice to the soul for its upcoming journey, guided by a lamp hanging outside the gate.

When the sun is overhead, village men bring down the effigy or corpse and place it inside a colourful *wadah* or *bade* (cremation tower) of wood and bamboo sparkling with gold paper, mirrors and other ornaments. Odd numbers of tiered roofs crown the tower depending on the caste of the deceased: Brahmins have 11, a noble has nine, and commoners have up to seven. A priest's tower has no roofs, but rather is an open throne decorated in white, yellow and gold, the colours of purity. Dozens of men carry the tower in a noisy procession, spinning it at crossroads to confuse the soul so that it cannot find its way home to disturb the living.

At the cemetery, the body or effigy is taken down and a pair of young chickens set free, symbolising the soul's release. The body and effigy are placed in a *patulangan* (sarcophagus) of wood, bamboo, cloth and paper. A priest or noble uses a bull, but others have fanciful animals like a winged lion or elephant-fish.

Inside the sarcophagus, the shroud is opened and holy water is poured over the remains. Letters of

A bull-shaped cremation sarcophagus.

introduction to the deities are placed inside along with money to pay the underworld demons. The sarcophagus is then closed and set ablaze.

DEIFIED SOUL

After the corpse is reduced to ashes, the soul is deified in a *nyekah* or *mukur* ceremony. At least 12 days later, the family gathers and pulverises the charred bone fragments and puts them with sandalwood, bamboo, flowers, leaves and spices into a yellow coconut. Following prayers and other rituals designed to speed the soul of the deceased onto the next level, the effigy is cast into the sea. The deified ancestor is then received in the family temple.

📷 FESTIVALS OF FAITH

Incense, offerings, food, music, dance –
festivals are feasts for deities and
demons as well as a wonderful spectacle.

Temple festivals are great opportunities to see Bali in all its ceremonial splendour – replete with women balancing offerings of food, flowers and fruit on their heads, music, sacred dances and temple rituals, even an illegal cockfight or two, amid much noise and activity.

The Balinese follow two calendar systems. The Saka solar-lunar calendar year begins in AD 78 and has 354 days with a 13th month added once every three years. The Pawukon (or Wuku) calendar is set by a cycle of 210 days with concurrently running 1- to 10-day periods, the conjunctions of which determine the *odalan* (temple festivals). Together these two calendar systems determine the incredibly complex schedule of holy days and anniversaries celebrated throughout Bali.

The most important Pawukon festival is **Galun-gan**, an island-wide five-day festival when ancestral souls visit their descendants. Pigs are slaughtered for offerings, temples are festooned with decorations and ritual feasting takes place. Ten days later, during **Kuningan**, the spirits take their leave.

Women carrying sacred offerings. At the start of a temple ceremony, the invisible spirits are invited by priests to occupy physical objects that worshippers then focus upon.

Village girls dressed in traditional costume to celebrate their local odalan, or temple festival, in Seseh, Tabanan.

The drummer sets the tempo and dynamics for the gamelan music that accompanies ceremonies, processions and dance performances during festivals.

Men performing the Melasti ritual before Nyepi.

Nyepi: day of silence

Nyepi marks the Balinese Saka New Year and occurs in March or April on the day that follows the dark moon of the spring equinox. This is when all of the island retreats into silence for 24 hours. On this day, dedicated to meditation and prayer, there are no flights into or out of Bali, nobody works, cooks or travels, shops remain closed, all streets are deserted and no lights are switched on, even after sunset. The general explanation is that the quietude will trick the *bhutas* and *kalas* (demons) into believing that the island has been abandoned so that they, too, will leave.

Nyepi is perhaps the most important of the Island's religious days and the prohibitions are taken seriously. Hotels are exempt from Nyepi's rigorous practices but the streets are closed to both pedestrians and vehicles (except for emergency vehicles). *Pecalang* (village wardens) are posted to keep people off the streets and the beach.

The night before Nyepi, however, is filled with activity. Exciting street processions take place as the evil spirits are driven away with gongs, drums, cymbals, exploding firecrackers, bamboo cannons and huge, scary, highly creative papier-mâché monster effigies known as *ogoh-ogoh*, some of which are later burnt amid much revelry.

Sacred verses are chanted by the pedanda (Brahmana high priest) while ringing a bronze bell, burning a sacred fire and sprinkling tirta (holy water).

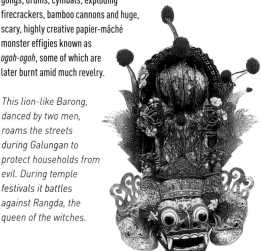

This lion-like Barong, danced by two men, roams the streets during Galungan to protect households from evil. During temple festivals it battles against Rangda, the queen of the witches.

Bowls of traditional Indonesian food at a cookery school in Ubud.

CUISINE

Bali's fertile volcanic soils and surrounding seas provide an abundance of tempting fish, fruit, meat and vegetables. International cuisine is so widely available that it can be hard to find authentic local flavours.

As odd as it may seem, it's surprisingly difficult for visitors to find genuine Balinese cuisine in Bali. This is because the local restaurants, street vendors and *warung* (road-side food stalls) generally offer Indonesian or Indonesian-Chinese food. The numerous restaurants in the main tourism areas, on the other hand, serve an astonishing array of international cuisines, from Italian, French and East-West fusion to Indian and Japanese. But if you search hard enough, you can track down genuine Balinese dishes at some market stalls (especially on the main market days), at some *warung* and at an increasing number of restaurants that have begun to realise that visitors actually want to try authentic Balinese cuisine.

A favourite delicacy is pepes ikan, made with minced, spiced fish. The juices are enclosed within a banana leaf parcel and the experience is an explosion of moist, fragrant, smoky flavour.

The balmy tropical climate and volcanic soil have blessed Bali with a superb range of fruits and vegetables, not to mention several varieties of rice. And it's not just tropical produce. Up in the cool hills, temperate-climate vegetables such as carrots, cabbages and broccoli are grown. In fact, everything from coffee to cloves, cardamom to corn, and grapes to guavas can be found in this fertile island, while fiery hot chillies and fragrant herbs are frequently planted between the paddy fields.

As with the rest of Indonesia, Balinese food has been influenced by centuries of foreign trade and by Dutch colonialism. Many spices and seasonings used to flavour Balinese cuisine

Nasi tumpeng is served on important occasions.

were introduced, including the ever-present chilli, which was brought to Asia by the Portuguese and Spanish in the 16th century. The Chinese, who traded and eventually settled in Bali, as elsewhere in Indonesia, have also influenced the food, with noodles, soy sauce, bean sprouts and bean curd being the main contributions.

SPICE AND SEASONINGS

Spices, herbs and a range of other seasonings lend excitingly different flavours to Balinese meat, poultry, fish and vegetable dishes. A heady citrus fragrance is provided by fresh lime juice from the distinctive *limo Bali*, kaffir lime leaf and lemongrass. Ginger and its relatives – the bright yellow turmeric, *galangal* root and the camphor-scented *kencur* – go hand in hand with shallots and garlic, pounded to a paste with chillies that range from the plump little fiery *tabia* to long, slender ones. A distinctive salty tang is provided by *sera* (fermented shrimp paste), while the sweetness of palm sugar is often offset by the sour *asem* (tamarind).

Herbs include basil, *pandan wangi* (fragrant screwpine) and *daun salam*, which looks like bay leaf but has a different taste. When it comes to dried spices, the Balinese have a limited range compared to the West Sumatrans, who are famous for their fiery Padang dishes. Along with black peppercorns, the Balinese cook makes use of coriander, cinnamon stick or grated nutmeg. *Kemiri* (candlenuts) are often ground to give a rich flavour and texture to the main spice paste called *basa gede*, the basis of many Balinese dishes.

Although almost all these seasonings are found elsewhere in Indonesia, the way the Balinese combine them makes a distinctive difference. Like other Indonesian cooks, the Balinese use coconut milk squeezed from the grated flesh of a ripe coconut to provide the liquid in many dishes. However, by first roasting the coconut chunks directly on hot coals before grating it, the Balinese add a wonderful, faintly smoky tang to their food.

A TYPICAL BALINESE MEAL

Balinese meals are always centred on rice, except for breakfast, which is generally a very simple affair. The housewife may come back from the market with sticky sweet cakes, which will probably be eaten with fresh fruit and washed down with coffee or tea. Before the midday meal is enjoyed, offerings of a few grains of cooked rice, incense and flowers must be made to all the resident gods and spirits in the family compound. Once they have been fed, it's time for mortals to tuck in.

The rice will be accompanied by a range of vegetable dishes, with protein in the form of meat (pork is more popular than beef, as consuming beef is forbidden for Hindus), fish or poultry. *Tempe*, a nutty slab made from fermented soy beans, is a delicious and inexpensive source of protein. As the poultry – especially ducks, which are marched off to the paddy fields each day to fertilise the growing rice and perform insect patrol – is not usually tender, it is often finely chopped with a cleaver before cooking, as are fish and prawns. One very popular way of cooking is to wrap minced and highly seasoned meat, fish or poultry in banana leaf parcels and steam them, or set the parcels directly onto hot coals to roast. Known as *tum*, these banana leaf packets are served in most Balinese homes. Although these dishes will be seasoned, additional spicing is available with an accompanying chilli-based *sambal*.

There may also be slices of crunchy cucumber to provide a refreshing contrast, as well as something crisp, like deep-fried *krupuk* (wafers made from tapioca flour flavoured with fish,

A market vendor and her wares in Denpasar.

⊘ BABI GULING

The best-known Balinese dish is spit-roasted pig, known as *guling celeng*, or by its Indonesian name, *babi guling*. The inside is stuffed with a mixture of chopped herbs and spices, and the skin is basted with turmeric juice before the pig is spit-roasted over glowing charcoal. A full meal will include tender flesh and portions of crisp skin; a few slices of spicy sausage made from the intestines stuffed with blood and seasoned meat; and *lawar*, an intricate mixture of pounded pork, a touch of pig's blood, steamed vegetables and seasonings. All this is eaten with steamed rice and a vegetable dish of young *nangka* (jackfruit).

prawns or *melinjo* nuts) or *peyek* (deep-fried rice flour fritters seasoned with tiny anchovies or peanuts). One dish will probably be flavoured with the thick, sweet soy sauce found everywhere in Indonesia, so that taken overall, the meal will have a wide range of flavours (sweet, sour, hot, spicy, fragrant) and textures.

Evening meals usually comprise whatever was left over from midday, served with rice and another dish or two – perhaps an omelette or fried noodles. Dishes that Westerners regard as dessert, such as black rice pudding and

The Balinese version, *saté lilit*, is infinitely more delicious, consisting of finely minced fish mixed with pounded herbs, spices and grated coconut. In some tourist restaurants, this pounded mixture is wrapped around sticks of fresh lemongrass rather than wooden skewers; the result is positively ambrosial.

The Balinese, like the Chinese, will eat anything, including eels, snails and frogs from the paddy fields, along with dragonflies and other exotica. Too sensible to waste anything that nature provides, the Balinese use the tender heart of the

Nasi campur (rice with vegetables and meat) for sale at a food market.

rice flour dumplings filled with palm sugar, are eaten as a between-meal snack by the Balinese.

BALINESE STAPLES

Probably the best-known Balinese dish is *babi guling*, or spit-roasted pig (see box). Also very popular with visitors but generally prepared for special festivals is *bebek* (duck) or *ayam* (chicken) *betutu* marinated with fragrant herbs, spices and chillies then wrapped in banana leaf and steamed. Once the duck is tender, the package is cooked over charcoal to impart a faint smoked flavour.

Saté (satay) elsewhere in Indonesia consists of morsels of meat or poultry threaded on skewers and cooked over charcoal, served with a sweet peanut gravy, enlivened with sliced chilli.

banana stem as a vegetable, generally cooking it in a spicy chicken stock to make *ares*. Unripe papaya is also used to make a spicy soup, although in Bali soup is not drunk as a separate course but enjoyed with rice and other dishes.

One of the most common fish found in Balinese waters is tuna, which is often transformed into a spicy salad. Steaks of tuna are slathered with a paste of chilli, garlic, shallots, turmeric and ginger and then fried. The fish is then flaked and mixed with a fresh *sambal*, fragrant with lemon-grass and kaffir lime leaves. The result, *sambal be tongkol*, will put you off tinned tuna for good. Even simple grilled fish takes on a new flavour, with whole fish being seasoned with lime juice, salt and a fiery *sambal* before being roasted over charcoal and served with fresh tomato sauce.

The most interesting vegetable dishes include *pakis* (young fern tips) with a dressing of garlic and *kencur (aromatic ginger)*; young jackfruit simmered in spicy coconut milk, palm heart curries or salads, and the tender leaves of the star fruit tree blanched and mixed with spiced coconut milk. All types of leaves, from star fruit to tapioca to spinach, can be used for *jukut urab*. The leaves are blanched and mixed with bean sprouts before being combined with

A selection of Balinese sticky cakes.

grated coconut, chilli, garlic and a touch of dried shrimp paste.

One of Bali's most refreshing dishes is eaten as a snack, and favoured by pregnant women. Simple *warung* indicate that *rujak* is on the menu by a stone mortar and pestle, and a basket of green mangoes, papaya, pineapple and cucumber (you'll also find it served out of boxes balanced on bicycles and prepared at the road side). Place an order and the vendor will start slicing the basic ingredients: bird's-eye chillies, a chunk of palm sugar and some roasted shrimp paste are thrown into the mortar and ground to a paste, with a little sour tamarind and salt added. If you don't want it too hot, ask to go easy on the chilli *(tidak pedas)*. The result is

mouth-puckeringly sour and sweet at the same time, as well as salty and spicy.

SWEET AND STICKY DESSERTS

The Balinese have a sweet tooth and love to snack on little cakes and dumplings. Many visitors have discovered the delights of the seemingly bizzare *bubur injin*, black rice pudding in which purplish-black glutinous rice is simmered with fragrant screw pine leaves until it reaches the consistency of a porridge. It is then sweetened with palm sugar and served with thick coconut milk to make what is arguably the archipelago's most delicious breakfast or snack or dessert.

Since bananas are so abundant, it's not surprising to find them either dipped in batter and deep fried, boiled and rolled in grated coconut or simmered in coconut cream sweetened with palm sugar. Little dumplings of glutinous rice flour combined with tapioca flour are cooked in coconut milk to make *jaja batun bedil*. Yet another variation on the glutinous rice theme is *wajik*, made by cooking glutinous rice with water and fragrant screw pine before steaming it with palm sugar and coconut milk. The resulting sticky mixture is spread on a tray and cooled before being cut into chunks.

DRINKS HOT AND COLD

Skip the usual fizzy drinks in favour of local favourites like *kopyor* (young coconut water), served with slivers of the tender coconut flesh. Another excellent option is *air jeruk*, which is juice squeezed from the local green-skinned oranges – completely different in flavour to navel oranges. If you see a blender outside a stall, you'll know they're serving fresh fruit drinks, spiked with sugar syrup, ice and evaporated milk; try *sirsak* (soursop), *apokat* (avocado), *mangga* (mango), *nanas* (pineapple) and *pisang* (banana).

Tap water is not safe to drink so opt for sealed bottles. Tea and coffee are normally served without milk but laden with sugar unless you specify that you want it *pahit*. Drinking the local coffee or *kopi tubruk*, made by stirring the grounds, sugar and boiling water in a tall glass, is an acquired taste but worth it for the richly roasted flavour.

Should you want to relax over an alcoholic drink at the end of the day, check out the Indonesian Bintang beer, best served icy cold.

MELTING POT CUISINE

Since the mid-1990s hundreds of restaurants have opened in Bali, serving a variety of cuisines from all corners of the globe.

Bali's dining options are quite incredible, and at prices that constantly amaze tourists when they convert the cost back to their own currency (sans alcoholic beverages, which are quite pricey). Most of the best international restaurants are located around Seminyak, Petitenget and Kerobokan, site of the trailblazing eatery La Lucciola, with Seminyak's Jalan Laksmana/Kayu Aya earning itself the name Eat Street. Since then the trend has spread throughout the island's southern tourist areas, with Ubud also offering some of Bali's most exciting dining options. Even more remote areas, such as Lovina (north coast) and the Amed district (east coast) can lay claim to some great-value (albeit more simple) international dining.

VARIETY IS THE SPICE

Eateries in Bali cover the gamut from simple roadside *warung* to chic fine-dining restaurants. Some are beach side, others river side and some even high up in magnificent mountain locations.

Once the food was solely local or Indonesian, but now more than a dozen world cuisines are represented. Pure Balinese restaurants are difficult to come by and Bumbu Bali (in Nusa Dua), Merah Putih (in Kerobokan) and Sate Bali (in Seminyak) are rare finds, but superb. The contrasts are many; a small bustling Greek tavern (Mykonos, Seminyak), the flavours of Moroccan tagines (Khaima, Seminyak), fresh home-made pasta (Massimo, Sanur), or the elegance of fine dining (Mozaic and CasCades, Ubud). The settings are just as varied: majestic views from above the Ayung River (Kudus House, Ubud), beach side with stunning sunset views (La Lucciola and Ku De Ta, Seminyak; Ma Joly, Tuban) and romantic garden settings (Sarong, Petitenget, and Slippery Stone, Seminyak). Watch the dolphins while you breakfast (Villa Agung and Kubu Lalang, Lovina) or eat among the fishing boats (Café Indah, Amed).

FUSION FARE

International chefs who have made Bali their new home have also created some brilliant fusion fare. Whether you call it Pacific Rim, Modern Australian or Modern French, Californian or New Asian – or whatever fancy name bandied by the international cooking gurus – the hallmark of this trend is the

Sushi and oysters – grazing food at Ku De Ta.

clever combination of Asian flavours with Western methods of preparation (or is it the other way round?). In expert hands the right balance can produce sensational results.

At Blue Fin (in Tuban), one of its best dishes combines baked scallops, octopus, squid and shrimps with a chilli mayonnaise and fish roe sauce. Mama San (in Kerobokan) serves pungent Asian comfort food in fine-dining style with dishes such as roast Peking duck with hoisin sauce, Thai fish cakes with sweet chilli sauce, and black sticky rice with mango and coconut cream.

People used to come to Bali only to surf and shop. Now many come just to eat.

A Balinese dancer in full regalia.

PERFORMING ARTS

Balinese dance and drama are staged purely for entertainment, or more soberly for temple ceremonies. Performed for deities, demons and mere mortals, frenzied spirit possession and trance are key features of some sacred dances.

Dance, drama, puppetry and music often take place during religious ceremonies to entertain both divine and human audiences. Performers are often possessed by spirits and go into a state of trance in order to dispel evil forces. In the last century, many newer forms of dance and drama have emerged. Many of these are derived from sacred forms but have been adapted for secular situations, like performances staged for tourists.

> *Serving as an exorcism of black magic, the Balinese hold the Barong and Rangda dance sacred to their religion; powerful forces are at work and elaborate preparations are made to ensure a balance between good and evil.*

The dances are often typified by subtle, controlled gestures and a fixed mask-like face with unfocused eyes and closed lips. The dancer's limbs form precise angles and the head sinks down so far that the neck disappears. At other times, gestures replicate nature, hands flutter like a bird in flight, and limbs follow sudden changes of direction as the performers move in slow horizontal zigzagging circles. The eyes become expressive and beguiling as they flicker and dance, movements become jerky, sometimes provocative and occasionally erotic.

SANGHYANG

Perhaps the most riveting of the dances is *sanghyang* (divine), which refers to a particular spirit that possesses a dancer. *Sanghyang dedari* is performed by two prepubescent girls to ward off an epidemic or some disaster. Through special songs

Dance practice in progress.

and incense, *dedari* (celestial maidens) are invited to enter their bodies. The girls then perform simple dances and versions of the *legong* (see page 69).

In *sanghyang deling*, two girls hold sticks connected with a string from which hang two dolls. To the sound of sacred songs, divine spirits make the dolls vibrate and twirl. The spirits then enter the girls, who dance with their eyes shut. But don't expect the soaring steps of Western dance; the dancers stand on the shoulders of two men who hold only their ankles, and from this perch they gracefully sway and bend their bodies while warding off evil spirits. Back on the ground they stomp on glowing embers and are eventually brought out of the trance by a temple priest with holy water and prayers. In *sanghyang jaran*, the spirits of horses possess men dancing on hobbyhorses. They run through the temple grounds and prance barefooted on burning coals.

WOMEN'S DEVOTIONAL DANCES

Sacred dances like *gabor* and *pendet* are usually performed by women to present offerings to the visiting deities of a temple during a temple ceremony. They carry ritual objects and offerings while improvising dances before the shrines. *Panyembrama* is a secularised version in which the dancers toss flower petals.

Rangda the widow-witch is one scary character.

Rejang and *sutri* are slow dances regarded as offerings to the deities. Young girls, unwed maidens, and/or post-menopausal women move slowly in long lines towards shrines or in a circle around them, holding their waist sashes and gracefully fluttering fans.

BARIS: MEN'S CEREMONIAL DANCE

Baris gede (rows of great warriors) are named after the weapons that are carried by four to 16 dancers. *Baris tumbak* uses long lances, *baris panah* has bows and arrows, while *baris bedil* bears wooden rifles. In *baris tamiang* they hold small round shields, and in *baris dadap* they carry narrow wooden shields. The lines of dancers often divide into two groups

to engage in a mock battle that may lead to trance.

BARONG AND RANGDA

One of Bali's most popular dances, *barong* is a protective spirit in mask and costume danced by two men, especially around a village between the Galungan and Kuningan holidays. There are many types of *barong* costumes, the most common being *barong keket* or *barong ket*, a mythological red-faced creature with bulging eyes, huge teeth, deer antlers and a golden headdress full of mirrors.

The mask of Rangda, the widow-witch who rules the demons of illness and haunts graveyards, represents negative cosmic forces. She is both feared and respected because she can protect people from harm. Rangda is the Hindu goddess Durga in her malevolent manifestation as the consort of Siwa (Shiva).

The Barong and Rangda confrontation is more than just a struggle between good and evil. The Balinese believe that one cannot exist without the other, that they are essentially two sides of the same coin. So ultimately the battle ends in a state of balance with neither side really winning or losing. When the Barong appears, he snaps his toothy jaws, shakes his shaggy body made of hair or feathers, and swishes his mirrored tail. He protects everyone from harm. Rangda is even more frightening to behold. With pendulous breasts, tresses of goat hair, terrible fangs protruding from her mouth, long finger nails, wide eyes, a lolling tongue and fake human entrails wrapped around her neck, she embodies every imaginable destructive force. She growls and speaks in ancient Kawi (Old Javanese) during the performance.

Men, and sometimes women and children, sit nearby with drawn *keris* (daggers). In a state of trance, they get up to attack Rangda who uses her magical white cloth to cast a spell so that instead of stabbing her they turn their blades on themselves. However, the power of the Barong prevents them from harm (an injury is said to be a sign of divine displeasure). A temple priest will revive those who are possessed by sprinkling them with holy water.

TOPENG AND WAYANG WONG

Topeng (mask dance) is performed at temple ceremonies, tooth-filings, weddings and cremations.

A solo dancer changes wooden masks to assume the roles in the entire story. Some performances have up to five dancers known as *topeng panca* (five masks), which allow for more drama and humour since several figures appear at once to interact with each other. Episodes are drawn from the *Babad*, histories of the Balinese kingdoms based on legendary events and characters.

Wayang wong uses fantastic, sacred wooden masks of humans, monkeys and ogres. Most dramatic dance performances show an episode from the *Ramayana*. Adviser-servants provide

replace them in many roles. All-male *arja muani* or *arja cowok* groups are making a comeback today and are popular because of their risqué humour and hilarious routines.

PREMBON AND SENDRATARI

Prembon (merger) blends together elements of *topeng* (mask dance) and *arja*. After some introductory mask dances, a story from the Javanese-Balinese romances begins, but the story is of minimal importance; the Balinese dialogue features lots of humour.

Baris is a ceremonial dance for men.

An example of a type of Barong mask.

humour and translate poetic Kawi (Old Javanese) dialogues into common Balinese for the audience. The play finishes in a great battle with the monkeys defeating the ogres.

ARJA

Arja is a folk opera that developed during the 19th century. The dancers must be trained in singing *tembang* (Balinese poetry). In order to hear the voices, musical accompaniment is light, using small drums and gongs, flutes, cymbals, and a bamboo instrument called *guntang*.

Themes are mostly from Javanese-Balinese romances. Packed with sentimentality and melodrama, *arja* was originally performed only by men, but during the 1920s women began to

Sendratari, from the words *seni* (art), *drama* and *tari* (dance), was specially created for a festival in the 1960s by teachers at the government performing arts high school in Denpasar. Dancers mime the words spoken by a narrator from stories drawn from Indian epics and Javanese-Balinese semi-historical legends.

LEGONG

The graceful *legong* dance developed during the 18th century following a king's divine vision. The original temple version, *sanghyang legong* or *topeng dedari*, is a non-narrative sacred dance with several *topeng* (masks) worn by two performers portraying celestial maidens. Today, it is a dance by three prepubescent girls who tell a story through mime. The costumes are stunning, with the dancers dressed in gold brocade and wearing flower-bedecked headdresses. The stories are mostly drawn from Indian epic literature and Javanese-Balinese romances.

GAMBUH

Gambuh first was performed in the 18th-century Balinese courts, but today it is mostly done for temple ceremonies. Males formerly danced all the parts, but now women play the female roles and the refined princes. Stories are from Javanese-Balinese romances, but the elegance and proper presentation of the dance and music are more important. Wearing colourful costumes and elaborate make-up, dancers are accompanied by very long bamboo flutes, bowed lute and drums. Stylised dialogues in courtly Kawi are translated into Balinese by attendants for the audience.

KECAK

The popular *kecak* dance was developed during the early 1930s in Bona village in Gianyar. Derived from the *sanghyang dedari* dance, it

Kecak is performed by an all-male ensemble.

⊙ HINDU EPICS: THE BASIS FOR BALINESE PERFORMING ARTS

A basic understanding of the epic Hindu *Ramayana* and *Mahabarata* tales are key to a greater appreciation of Balinese dance and drama.

Ramayana: Prince Rama, his wife Sita, and his younger brother Laksmana are exiled into the forest due to the plottings of his stepmother, who wants the throne for her own son. One day Laksmana cuts off the nose of an ogress that tries to seduce him. Her husband, King Rawana seeks revenge, and sends an ogre disguised as a golden deer to tempt Sita. Rama pursues and kills the golden deer, but with its dying cries, it imitates Rama calling for help. Sita then orders Laksmana to go and help his brother. Disguised as a holy man, Rawana deceives and abducts Sita, causing Rama to enlist the aid of a monkey army to fight the ogres. The monkey king sends his general Hanoman to find Sita, and after many battles, resulting in the deaths of most of the ogres, Rama finally kills Rawana. In a trial by fire, Sita proves that Rawana never violated her during captivity.

Mahabharata: The five noble Pandawa brothers are tricked out of the right to their own kingdom by their 100 devious Korawa cousins. Forced into exile, the Pandawas begin preparations for battle. During the great Bharatayuddha war, most of the Korawas and their allies are killed. The Pandawas reign for a long time before going to heaven.

has been added to and adapted, incorporating scenes mostly from the *Ramayana* epic or other Hindu legends.

Kecak is an amazing cacophony of interlocking sounds and movements. Dozens of bare-chested men, wearing lengths of black and white *poleng* cloth around their waists and a single red hibiscus flower behind the ear, sit in concentric circles and chant in various rhythms without any musical accompaniment, their arms reaching up and fingers outstretched. The "chak-'chak-chak-a-chak' sounds and vigorous hand gestures are aesthetic elements for narrating the story, such as a dense forest or battling enemies. The players move in unison, hands stretched out, pulled in, or resting on the shoulder of the next person, waists rotating left and right, while creating at least four different rhythmic patterns. Other dancers then enter the arena to present a core episode of the Hindu epic, the *Ramayana*. The *kecak* is probably the best known of the many Balinese dances and is sometimes called the monkey dance because at the end of the story, the players of the voice orchestra gyrate like monkeys as Prince Sita is finally rescued by the monkey army.

KEBYAR AND JANGER

Kebyar (flash of lightning) began during the early 20th century in north Bali performed by two young women dressed as men. It was further developed in south Bali by the dancer I Ketut Marya, better known as Mario. This genre is also called *bebancihan* (cross-dressing); however, either sex can dance it. The genius lies in the arm and finger gestures, torso movements and facial expressions. In *kebyar duduk* and *kebyar trompong*, the dancer actually sits most of the time and even plays the *trompong* (gong chimes).

Janger was also choreographed in the early 20th century. Twelve girls in traditional costumes with fan-shaped headdresses sing folk songs while fluttering fans and performing repetitious dance movements. Twelve boys, their youthful faces painted with moustaches and sporting gilded head-cloths and beaded bibs, do frenzied movements partly based on martial arts, accompanied by rhythmic shouts.

THE ART OF WAYANG KULIT

Wayang kulit (shadow play) probably originated in ritual performances to bring ancestors into contact with mortals. The shadows on the screen are the spirits, the screen represents the world, the lamp symbolises the sun, and the *dalang* (puppeteer) embodies the supreme deity, the greatest puppeteer.

Most of the storylines of Balinese *wayang kulit* are taken from the great Indian epics *Ramayana* and *Mahabharata* (see box) which relate the exploits of heroes and maidens. These stories have been performed to enraptured audiences for centuries. While Balinese *wayang kulit* is probably derived from 10th

Wayang kulit dalang (puppetmaster).

century Javanese sources, it has been adapted and modified over time into a very different modern form.

Wayang ramayana for instance uses episodes from the *Ramayana* and *wayang parwa* from the *Mahabharata*. *Wayang gambuh* and *wayang arja* take stories from the Javanese-Balinese romances. *Wayang babad* tells the legendary histories of Balinese kingdoms. *Wayang cupak* concerns the adventures of the glutton Cupak and his heroic brother Grantang. *Wayang Calonarang* is potentially dangerous because it tells the story of an 11th-century Javanese queen who was banished from the palace for practising black magic. A powerful puppeteer can summon and challenge *leyak* (people with dark supernatural powers), but if a performance is not properly done it can bring disaster.

The puppets used in all types of *wayang* are made from cattle parchment pierced with filigree designs, painted and gold-leafed. They are manipulated by rods attached to the body and arms, which are joined at the shoulders and elbows. A comic character will have a moveable lower jaw.

While *wayang kulit* is entertainment, the Balinese are also very much aware that within the stories are important moral lessons. Most

A wayang kulit shadow puppet.

performances are regarded as sacred because they occur only during religious occasions like temple festivals. A *dalang* can be hired to perform as a fulfilment of a religious vow.

The shadow puppets in the episode being performed are introduced to the audience one by one. Good and noble characters such as gods, kings, princes and their attendants are on the right, while evil characters like ogres, demons and witches are on the left.

Puppet shadows are traditionally cast by a coconut oil lamp that is suspended above the centre of a vertical screen of tightly stretched white cotton cloth. Warm, flickering flames create a muted and ethereal effect upon the screen, which brings the shadows to life. The

dalang sits on the side of the lamp to manipulate the puppets. On each side of the puppeteer sits an assistant who keeps the puppets in order, and behind him are the musicians. The audience mostly prefers to watch the magical shadows, but a small group of men and boys usually sit on the *dalang*'s side to watch him at work.

The accompanying music, using two or four metallophones or a small gamelan (see page 73) orchestra supports the drama. Musical signals from the *dalang* are conveyed by means of large wooden knobs that he holds in his left hand and between the big and second toes of his right foot to rap the side of the *gedog* (puppet box). Verbal cues are concealed in the narrative.

MASTER STORYTELLER

The *dalang* is a remarkable person with extraordinary stamina to remain seated during a performance that can last up to four hours without a break. His skills and knowledge are equally impressive, for he has mastered the characters, dialogues and plots for dozens of stories, which he tells without using any script. The puppeteer's knowledge includes details of Balinese religious practice and philosophy, familiarity with folk tales and proverbial knowledge, plus being in tune with current events and local gossip, and adept at comedy.

Because of the wide variety of characters, the *dalang* must have knowledge of Kawi (Old Javanese) and of High, Middle and Low Balinese languages to bring the puppets to life. Royalty is addressed in High Balinese, while common characters are addressed in Low Balinese. The comic *panasar* (servant-advisers) are there to provide humour, pungent critique, slapstick comedy and translate Kawi and High Balinese into everyday language for the audience. Each character has a particular way of speaking, and the puppeteer in one fell swoop must switch from the low pitch of a hero to the sweet high tones of a princess and then to the rough and gruff growls of a giant.

It takes years to master all of this knowledge and skill; a young boy will often follow his puppeteer father to performances and act as his assistant. Others may follow a calling and study from a proficient *dalang*, while some take up the art after a profound mystical experience.

🔍 GAMELAN MUSIC

Gamelan accompanies every theatrical, religious and social event, its music serving as entertainment for both deities and humans.

Any given *banjar* (neighbourhood) usually owns a gamelan (*gambelan* or *gong* in Balinese) set, and anyone may join a *sekaha gong* (music club) – there are children's gamelan clubs where boys and girls as young as nine years old play. Almost two dozen kinds of traditional ensembles exist, ranging from a small *gender wayang* duet or quartet of bronze metallophones to accompany *wayang kulit* (shadow puppet) plays, to a huge *gong gede* temple ensemble with up to 40 players. Ancient *gamelan selonding* have few instruments with iron keys, while *gamelan saron-gambang* uses only a handful of instruments with wooden or bronze keys. *Gong balaganjur* and *gong batel* are ceremonial processional groups using a full set.

Some ensembles are named after the dance form that they accompany, such as *gamelan joged*, which uses *grantang*, *rindik* or *tingklik* (small bamboo xylophones) and some bronze instruments for *joged* (social dancing). *Gamelan jegog* only has bamboo instruments, and the deep tones produced by striking the bigger xylophones with padded large mallets resonate through the body so that the listener can feel the vibrations. *Gamelan tektekan* uses single-tuned bamboo tubes and wooden cowbells rhythmically played by dozens of dancing men.

GONGS AND KEYS

A gamelan primarily consists of different sizes of *gangsa* (metallophones with bronze keys suspended over bamboo resonators) and *reyong* or *trompong* (racks of small knobbed gongs). They are set in carved and gilded wooden frames. *Gangsa* of various size have different functions; high-pitched *kantilan* plays rapid interlocking elaborations, while the very low *jublag* plays the basic melody. All *gangsa* are paired and tuned slightly out of pitch with each other to create

pulses of sound that make Balinese music shimmer and vibrate. At the heart of the ensemble are two *kendang* (drums). These control the tempo, with the drummers using their hands and knobbed sticks. Small *ceng-ceng* or *rincik* (cymbals) accent the music, while a small, single *kempli* gong keeps the beat. Large hanging gongs and

A gamelan orchestra.

small *kempur* are struck at important points. The singers are a recent addition to the gamelan.

Gongs and keys are forged by hand in the same methods used for centuries. Tuning to the five- or seven-note scale is done by painstakingly filing and hammering away at each piece. The small *gamelan angklung* in south Bali uses a four-note scale, but in north Bali they use a five-note scale. A standard scale does not exist, so each ensemble has its own unique sound.

For the Balinese, gamelan instruments have spiritual power. No one steps over an instrument, as this would offend the ensemble's spirits. Respect is shown by presenting them with offerings on particular holy days and before performances.

Making intricate carvings on coconut shells.

ARTS AND CRAFTS

Originally, art on Bali was an obligation to the deities. It still is today, but tourism has changed much of Bali's aesthetic purpose. The beauty of the handiwork is still apparent in stone and wood carvings, textiles, metalwork and painting.

Balinese art has its primary expression in religion, not as a conscious production for its own sake. Bronzes and stone carvings of deities survive from the early centuries AD but the tropical climate is unkind to all but the hardiest of materials: soft volcanic stone quickly erodes, cloth paintings decay in the humidity, and woodcarvings are eaten by termites. Over the years, earthquakes and volcanoes have destroyed numerous works of art. Replacements thus had to be made every few generations.

Art is expressed through music, dance, carving, painting, and especially in offerings for religious ceremonies (see page 80). Not all Balinese have the sense of originality that distinguishes artists, but many of them are great craftspeople. Crafts range from woodcarving to weaving, from metalwork to painting. Particular villages are famous for their families of skilled craftsmen.

A paras stone carving at Batubulan.

> *Balinese silverwork is enhanced by a technique called granulation, where small pellets and tiny coiled silver wires are heated until soft enough to adhere to the piece, in order to form a pattern or decorative feature.*

WOOD AND STONE CARVING

Carving goes back many centuries to when temples and courts needed symbolic decorations and embellishments. Hard tropical woods and soft *paras* (sandstone) are used for gates, beams and pillars in many buildings. Sacred wooden images, architectural carvings, and cases for gamelan musical instruments are often painted and gold-leafed. During the 1930s, carvers began moving away from stylised religious figures and created new forms from mythology and everyday life. Some highly imaginative and beautiful sculptures became elongated and distorted. The natural shapes of branches and roots also suggested the finished woodcarved forms to many artists. Most carvings in these new styles were unpainted to show the natural beauty of the grain.

Today, most carvings are made in Gianyar Regency. Wood is used in Mas, Peliatan, Selakarang and Kemenuh; stone is favoured in Batubulan and Singapadu, while coconut shells and cattle bones are used in Tampaksiring.

MASKS

When someone from the West puts on a mask, they're usually pretending to be someone else;

> *Cheap factory printed batik pieces look good on one side only, while expensive handmade ones feature distinct and intricate patterns and vivid colours on both sides.*

but in Bali when someone dons a mask, especially a sacred mask, they become someone else. Sacred masks, most famously used in the *topeng* and the Barong dances, have a power called *tenget*, which enters the body of the performer who wears one. These very powerful masks are brought to life through a ceremony conducted by a *pedanda*, a Brahman high priest. They are kept in special shrines and receive offerings every full and new moon, and whenever they are used. They also get special offerings on the day known as Tumpek Wayang.

Masks may represent gods, animals, demons, or humans. They can be half masks, three-quarter face (extending to the upper lip), or full face; some even have a movable jaw.

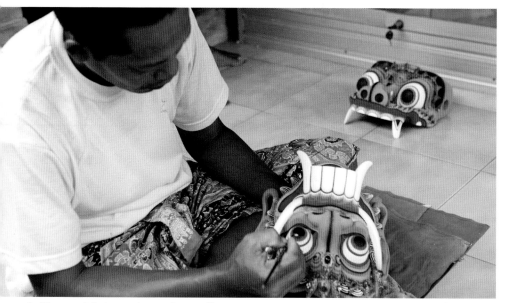

Crafting a mask for topeng dancers, Batuan village.

⊘ ILLUSTRATED TEXTS

Lontar (palm-leaf manuscripts) are made from dried leaves of the fan palm *(Borassus flabellifer)*. These long, thin books are held together by cords strung through centre holes in the leaves. They are inscribed with historical accounts, calendars, poetry, medical texts, stories and prayers. Some may be illustrated with stylised diagrams or very detailed figures.

Leaves are first boiled in spices, dried, trimmed, and then inscribed with a sharp metal stylus. The surface is rubbed with soot mixed with a little oil or burned candlenuts and wiped clean with a cloth, leaving residues in the fine etched lines. The oil also keeps the dry leaves flexible.

More than 30 different tools are used in mask carving. After endless sanding at least 40 coats of paint are applied to achieve a strikingly glossy surface. The mask carver, known as the *Undagi Tapel*, is likely to come from a family of carvers, and most come from Mas or Singapadu villages. Those who make masks for the temple must be members of the Brahman caste since only they know the required rituals involved in making a sacred mask.

With the birth of tourism, visitors started to show an interest in masks as wall decorations, thus initiating a new line of business for the carvers. Today, thousands of people worldwide collect these colourful and compelling objects.

BALINESE TEXTILES

Bali's claim to fabric fame is a weft ikat cloth called *endek*. Plastic raffia is firmly tied around the weft or horizontal threads of a cloth before it is woven and then dyed so that the wrapped areas resist the colour. This is repeated in other parts with different dyes, while previously tied areas are untied to receive new colours. Finally, all the threads are untied and woven, and the intricate patterns emerge. Some *endek* is made from silk, but cheaper cotton and rayon are more widely used. Semi-mechanised looms produce great quantities in Denpasar and Gianyar but some of the finest *endek* comes from Sidemen in Karangasem and Gelgel in Klungkung.

A masterpiece of Balinese craftsmanship, double-ikat cloths called *geringsing* are woven only in Tenganan in Karangasem (east Bali); Japan and India are the only other places where double ikat is made. Both the handspun cotton warp and weft threads are tied and dyed with the same patterns before the cloth is woven, which requires special skills and a great attention to detail. Cloths are handwoven in a back-tension loom, and the dyed threads must be properly aligned so that the unique patterns emerge.

The rich colours of these cloths, with groups of geometrical or floral patterns, are produced by dyeing them with indigo and morinda, a shrub whose roots produce a reddish-brown colour. *Geringsing* is considered sacred, and its name can mean "illness free". It can also mean "speckled", a fitting description of the shimmering colourful patterns. Since it is widely believed that the cloths protect the wearer from earthly and supernatural enemies, they are used in religious ceremonies.

Songket is a brocade cloth with gold, silver or coloured weft threads forming intricate designs on the surface of the cloth. They tend to be heavy and dense, due to the weaving technique that is done from the back of the cloth. In the old days, *songket* could only be worn by aristocrats, but today these expensive fabrics are available to anyone who can afford them. The main centres of *songket* weaving are Gelgel in Klungkung, Sidemen in Karangasem, Singaraja in Buleleng, and Negara in Jembrana.

Kain prada textiles are decorated with gold designs of flowers or birds. The patterns are outlined on plain coloured cloth, and the area spread with glue for adhering gold leaf. Today, cheaper gold paint is used, and more often than not glue is silkscreened onto the fabric and artificial gold leaf applied. These cloths are mostly worn by dancers and participants in religious ceremonies but are also used for making ceremonial parasols and dance fans, and for decorating shrines. Today, most *kain prada* is silkscreened on polyester in Sukawati in Gianyar and Satria in Klungkung.

In batik, wax designs are carefully applied on to plain white cloth which is then immersed in dye. This is repeated for other parts of the design with different dyes, the waxed parts resisting the colours. Finally, the cloth is boiled

Shadow puppets for sale in Sukawati village.

to remove the wax, revealing the multi coloured patterns beneath. Balinese-style batik pieces are very colourful with waxed outlines and hand-painted dyes that feature big designs and even cartoon characters. A major centre of production is at Tampaksiring in Gianyar. The more traditional batik on sale is produced in Java.

METALWORK

Works in silver and gold were once associated with royalty, whose family members wore heavy gold and silver headdresses, belts, bracelets, earrings, anklets and necklaces as symbols of their high status. Even the handles of some *keris* (daggers) were and still are made of gold in the shape of mythological figures and studded with gems.

Kamasan in Klungkung is the production centre for traditional jewellery, *keris* handles, ritual vessels and offering bowls.

Numerous workshops in Celuk in Gianyar, produce huge quantities of gold and silver jewellery in traditional and new designs. The Balinese are very quick to pick up on introduced ideas and copy what they know will sell, with some smiths collaborating with foreign jewellery designers living in Bali.

Keris and gamelan making are highly technical, demanding skills handed down in families. Forging a *keris* involves repeated folding and fusing of different metals to produce a blade that can wield supernatural force if ritually empowered. The only *keris* foundry is at Kusamba in Klungkung.

Many workers are needed to produce the bronze keys and gongs of a gamelan musical ensemble. The coordinated hammering requires quick action by an experienced team. Foundries operate in Tihingan in Klungkung, Blahbatuh in Gianyar, and Sawan in Buleleng.

PAINTING

The oldest known Balinese paintings, kept at Pura Besakih today, are of a lotus flower and of the Hindu elephant-headed deity Ganesha on two wooden boards dating from the 15th century. Paintings from the 19th century show episodes from Indian epics and other literary sources along with astrological signs. They were commissioned by palaces and temples as decorations and painted with natural pigments on cotton cloth primed with rice starch. Often the paintings were unsigned, for the painter was a craftsman working for the glory of the gods and not for himself.

The traditional painting style is derived from the two-dimensional *wayang kulit* (leather puppets) with strict iconography in facial details, dress and skin colours. Today, works are still made in Kamasan in Klungkung, where the descendants of artists who worked for the nearby Gelgel court use traditional materials and techniques. Other similar styles using manufactured paints are done in Kerambitan in Tabanan, Bedulu and Pengosekan in Gianyar, and Tejakula in Buleleng.

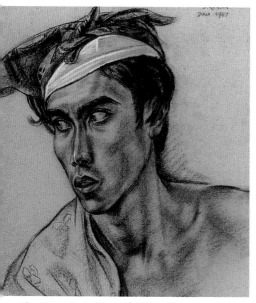

Painting by Rudolf Bonnet (1895–1978).

⊘ THE PITAMAHA SCHOOL

The Pitamaha (Great Vitality) artists' association was formed in 1936 in Ubud by its royal family along with Balinese and Western artists. It had branches in Denpasar and many villages. Painters, sculptors and metal-smiths were members. Its primary goals were to maintain a high standard of art by providing guidance and critique, and to guarantee its members' livelihoods by organising exhibitions and sales of their works locally and abroad. Pitamaha was disbanded in 1942 when Japanese forces invaded Bali during World War II. Many paintings and wood sculptures made by Pitamaha artists can be seen today at the Museum Puri Lukisan in Ubud.

NEW PATRONAGE AND STYLES

When the Dutch dismantled the old system of royal patronage in the early 20th century, there was a real danger that the arts would also decline. Ironically, tourists played a large part in preventing this by becoming new patrons. Balinese artists drew upon traditional forms and techniques, elaborating on them and experimenting with new ideas and expressions. As there was no local market for their creations, they were essentially producing exotic colonial images of Bali for the newly emerging tourist market.

Since Balinese artists created new works to replace deteriorating ones, a great degree of repetition existed. However, Balinese art was not at all static: paintings from Sanur and Singaraja created during the late 1800s show some perspective and more naturalistic figures and scenery. The artists were also beginning to paint single scenes from everyday life, a concept they borrowed from traditional astrological and agricultural charts.

While some Western artists had a hand in steering the Balinese in a different aesthetic direction, some claims have been overstated. During the 1920s and 1930s, Westerners like Walter Spies from Germany and Rudolf Bonnet from Holland settled in Ubud and promoted the village as the cultural centre of Bali. Spies and Bonnet are often credited with setting the tone for modern Balinese

confrontations. And in 1936, the Pitamaha school of art emerged (see box).

Yet another style developed in the early 1960s in Penestanan near Ubud. Under the guidance of Dutch-born artist Arie Smit, who had become an Indonesian citizen, a group of young Balinese created a distinctive and naive painting genre known as the Young Artists style, which showed daily and ritual life in strong oil colours with dark outlines. In the 1970s, paintings of flora and fauna were produced in Pengosekan, while miniatures developed in Keliki to the north.

Ceiling paintings at Bale Kerta Gosa, Semarapura.

art. However, experimentation with new and different media and styles had been going on among Balinese artists since the 19th century, and claims that the Europeans influenced the content of Balinese art are debatable.

Over the years, several styles of painting emerged. Ubud-style painting was characterised by naturalistic polychrome figures in landscapes and everyday scenes such as harvesting and presenting offerings. Another centre of painting developed at Sanur, where artists tended to work with ink on paper to show marine subjects from their area. At a third centre in Batuan south of Ubud, the painting was characterised by half-puppet, half-naturalistic figures in ink and pastel colours depicting daily scenes and supernatural

In Mas, master mask maker I Wayan Muka (tel: 0812-391 2902; 0361- 974 530) carves decorative masks preferred by tourists as well as ones used in ritual dances. Ask him to demonstrate some of the characters for you and be amazed at how he is transformed.

Places to see quality art in the Ubud area are Neka Art Museum, Museum Puri Lukisan and ARMA Museum & Resort. Taman Werdhi Budaya Art Centre in Denpasar also has a good collection of artworks.

GIFTS TO DEITIES AND DEMONS

On pavements, under trees, inside cars and at shrines, these exquisitely crafted offerings are ephemeral works of art.

Banten (offerings) are gifts to deities to ask for blessings and to give thanks, or as payoffs to demons to keep them appeased and away. Flowers, palm leaves, fruits, rice and meat are all assembled into ephemeral works of art, and nearly every village has its own unique style.

Offerings are very visible, like the graceful *penjor* bamboo poles, or personal, like the daily *jotan* of a few grains of cooked rice sprinkled with salt on small squares of banana leaves. For special ceremonies, a towering *sarad* has hundreds of colourful rice-dough figures representing the cosmos, while *sate tungguh* is its counterpart, made from the meat, innards and heads of pigs.

Presenting an offering requires incense, holy water and prayers. The physical parts of the offerings are eaten, regarded as *lungsuran* (leftovers) from the deities; those made to demons are discarded. Offerings are used only once and must be newly created each time.

Women carrying offerings to temple for a ceremony on their heads.

A roast pig lies among offerings for a temple festival. Pork or chicken along with rice, fruits and other sweets complement each other by symbolising male and female aspects of life. After the invisible essence of the food is offered to the deities, humans eat the physical remains.

A decorative bowl contains an artistic arrangement of fruits, hard-boiled eggs, sweets and rice cakes, while a 'crown' with streamers formed from young coconut leaves holds flowers and other essential ingredients.

A Balinese woman buying marigold flowers for offerings at Ubud's market.

The offerings industry

An average household spends at least half of its income on offerings. However, much of the offering eventually becomes part of the household's meals. Creating offerings is an act of devotion, but if there is no time to make them or if more elaborate forms for special ceremonies are needed, they can be purchased in the market or ordered in advance from a *tukang banten* (offerings expert). They are usually members of a priest's household who have gained the skills and knowledge from their families. Another path to becoming a *tukang banten* is to learn the art during preparations for religious events.

One can easily purchase the simple *canang* (coconut leaf tray) that is used in everyday offerings or more complicated *jejaitan* (stitchery), which are created from trimmed palm leaves held together with bamboo pins. Truckloads of young coconut leaves from east Java arrive daily in Balinese markets for this specific use. Today, metal staples and plastic string replace bamboo pins and thread, and coloured paper is used instead of dyed leaves. Purists disapprove, but perhaps it is better for offerings to go in this direction than to disappear completely.

Household canang offering. This is the most commonly used daily offering. A circular tray fashioned from young coconut leaves holds flowers and fragrant shredded leaves, beneath which lie a few symbolically important betel nuts.

...aking morning offerings to the sea at Padang Bai. ...alinese believe that demons symbolising disorder dwell ...neath the sea, and offerings must be made to prevent ...sasters such as earthquakes.

Scuba diving the 'Liberty' wreck, near Tulamben.

OUTDOOR ACTIVITIES

Bali isn't all about temples and culture. Those looking for thrills and spills will find opportunities to dive, snorkel and surf in sparkling seas, paraglide over hills, climb volcanoes, bike through the countryside, or tee off at golf courses.

Blessed with wide open spaces, sparkling seas and an equable climate, Bali is the perfect place to take part in your favourite outdoor sport. The range on offer is astounding and covers both land and sea sports, with a number of specialist adventure tour companies offering exciting excursions such as river rafting, mountain cycling, jungle trekking and four-wheel-drive expeditions. Most companies provide a door-to-door pick-up and drop-off service, and most activities are child-friendly.

> *An exhilarating rafting excursion on the Telaga Waja River will please those who want more of a rush from their white-water ride. Rated Class IV, this journey covers 14km (9 miles) and takes about three hours.*

DIVING AND SNORKELLING

Bali is the ideal location for diving among some of the world's finest tropical reefs. The water is warm and the marine life is abundant. Reputable dive schools, dive resorts and operators offer facilities, equipment and tuition for every PADI course from beginners' discovery dives to the highest recreational level. With a great choice of both easy and challenging world-class sites, speciality courses include drift dive, night dive, deep dive and underwater photography. Programmes for children are available too; the PADI Bubblemakers programme offers underwater adventure combined with lots of fun and games for children aged 8–12.

Bali's premier dive site is around the wreck of the *Liberty*, at Tulamben on the east coast. Located 40–50 metres from the beach, the

Surfing at Kuta, a good place for beginners.

wreck is 30 metres (100ft) below the surface at the deepest point, with 50 percent of the structure relatively undamaged.

It is the habitat of numerous underwater species, including the rare pigmy seahorse and ghost pipefish. Black tip reef sharks, dolphins and whales bask in nearby waters and the stark volcanic coastline borders a majestic coral garden with a 70-metre (230ft) drop-off.

The reefs around Pulau Menjangan on the northwest corner of Bali have drop-offs ranging from 60–80 metres (200–250ft). The sea here is incredibly calm, protected from winds and strong currents by the Gunung Prapat Agung peninsula. This is where 10-metre (30ft) long toothless whale sharks have been sighted, and where whales and dolphins migrate via the Bali Strait between Java and Bali.

Other popular sites include the Amed area on the east coast, and Nusa Penida island on the southeast where the visibility is superb; this is also the seasonal habitat of the *Mola mola* (also known as the giant Ocean Sunfish), which is the world's largest bony fish. In addition to day trips, live-aboard trips take divers further afield to explore the waters around neighbouring islands.

SURFING

Bali is renowned as one of the great surfing meccas of the world, offering more than 20 top-quality breaks. The peak surf season is April to October when the southeast trade winds blow offshore and the full force of the southern ocean swells hit the reefs around Kuta, Nusa Dua and the Bukit Badung peninsula. These are great draws for veteran surfers, and the breaks found at Padang Padang, Balangan and Uluwatu, with its famous entry cave, are world-class barrels.

For novices and surfers of intermediate ability, there are plenty of mellow beachbreaks. With a little bit of local knowledge, it's still possible to find great surf locations without huge crowds. There is a good choice of well-managed surf schools, offering adults and children the opportunity to experience the thrill of the waves, while learning board handling, surf etiquette and safety tips. Surf camps and 'surfaris' are available for those who wish to discover secret surf spots with local professionals. Bali is also the starting point for nearly all Indonesian surf trips with charter boats departing for G-Land (in East Java), Lombok, Sumbawa, and more distant areas like East Nusa Tenggara and North Sumatra.

DOLPHIN-WATCHING

If you prefer to stay dry, dolphins can also be viewed at Lovina, on Bali's north coast. At sunrise, primarily during the dry season (May–October), the dolphins gather and play in large schools just beyond the coral reefs off the scenic black sand bay. For a nominal fee, dolphin-watchers can go out with the fishermen in tiny, traditional *jukung* fishing boats and be treated to the breath-taking spectacle of these graceful mammals vaulting out of the water in a remarkable aerial display.

PARAGLIDING

A number of paragliding clubs operate from the Bukit Badung peninsula, taking off from the cliff top 80 metres (250ft) above Timbis beach on the southernmost tip of the island. Harnessed to these amazing non-motorised inflatable wings and using only the wind as a source of power, it is possible to soar like an albatross over remote beaches, coral reefs, turquoise waters, luxury hotels and Hindu temples; the views of the ridgeline are spectacular. Experience is not necessary as tandem flights can be

Try jet-boating at Nusa Dua, for a high-speed adrenaline rush.

arranged with professional instructors and the latest equipment. Full certification courses can also be organised for those aiming for pilot rating. The trade winds blow consistently from the southeast from June to September, making this ridge flyable on most days.

GOLF

Bali's five golf courses are all open to non-members.

The Handara Golf and Resort in Bedugul is located in the caldera of an ancient volcano and is considered to be one of the most beautiful golf courses in the world. This 18-hole, par 72 playground was created by Peter Thompson against a dramatic backdrop of towering mountains, pristine forest and the peaceful Danau Buyan. The refreshing temperature at this high altitude averages 10 degrees below Bali's coastal regions and is the perfect climate for golfing. Bali National Golf Club in Nusa Dua has three sections offering unique environments throughout the 18-hole course. In Badung, Bukit Pandawa Golf and Country Club is an 18-hole championship-calibre course. Other options are the New Kuta Golf Course at Pecatu, which commands splendid ocean views from its signature

hikes through rice fields, jungle, rainforests and national parkland, to challenging mountain treks in the dry season.

Recommended is the two-hour sunrise trek to Gunung Batur, which has erupted more than 20 times during the last two centuries. The 1,717-metre (5,632ft) high volcano comprises a set of cones resting in the centre of a gigantic caldera with an adjacent crescent-shaped lake. The trek begins around 4am, offering a clear view of Danau Batur Lake, the peaks of Gunung Abang and Gunung Agung, the distant sea and

Hiking on Batur volcano's caldera.

hole, no. 15; and the Bali Beach Golf Course at Sanur, a 9-hole course.

HORSE RIDING

There are several stables and equestrian resorts on the island offering riding adventures through rice fields, villages, forests and along beaches. All treks are accompanied by personal guides; lessons can be arranged and instruction is of a high standard. Most stables provide a good selection of well-trained horses with varying temperaments and sizes to suit all ages and levels of experience.

TREKKING AND MOUNTAIN CLIMBING

The island's geographical diversity allows visitors the opportunity for everything from gentle

even Gunung Rinjani on neighbouring Lombok. The strange landscape is punctuated by bizarre hillocks and a series of craters with jets of white steam puffing out of small holes. At the summit, trekkers might be served a breakfast of baked bananas and hard-boiled eggs cooked in the natural heat belching from the belly of the volcano.

After the descent, the hot springs on the lakeshore at Toya Bungkah are a welcome treat and perfect for easing aching limbs. Climbers are advised to take a guide; a local cartel actively discourages independent trekkers by not allowing people to hike alone. 'Official' fees for guides are exorbitant, starting around Rp 800,000 per person. However, much cheaper deals can be negotiated at some of the homestays and restaurants beside the lake. Before agreeing to take on a guide, ask to see his license, which is required.

At 3,014 metres (9,796ft), Gunung Agung in east Bali is Bali's tallest and holiest mountain with its resplendent summit dominating much of the island. There are two routes up the volcano, generally undertaken at night so that trekkers can reach the top in time to experience the sunrise. A guide is essential.

From Besakih, the ascent to the summit takes around seven hours and does not require any technical climbing skills or special equipment apart from a good pair of boots and a torch. The shorter route takes about three hours and begins at the large market temple of Pura Pasar Agung near Selat. This route leads to the rim of the crater and offers a clear view of towering Gunung Rinjani on neighbouring Lombok. A permit is not required, but climbing the mountain is forbidden when major religious events are being held at Pura Besakih, generally in April.

Taman Nasional Bali Barat (West Bali National Park) offers exceptional trekking with the bonus of magnificent panoramas in this

Cycling through paddy fields, Tegalalang.

☉ PROTECTING PARADISE

The paradise that was Bali has reached a breaking point. Lack of education among the local people coupled with a burgeoning tourism industry have changed the island irrevocably, particularly its coastal ecosystems. Among the many organisations that have been established to take action, the Denpasar-based Coral Triangle Center for Marine Conservation (tel. 0813-940 0400; https://savingoceans now.com) is doing something about the problem. Using creative methods such as shadow puppets and eco-games to spread the message about concern for oceans, it is a learning centre that's open to everyone, including tourists.

region watered by clear streams and traversed by trails. More like a forest than a jungle, walks lasting from two to nine hours can be arranged to suit physical requirements. The routes are often steep but relatively easy, although some areas are cross-country with no clear paths and, at times, it is necessary to crawl through undergrowth and use paths frequented by wild pigs and deer.

Visitors to the national park must apply for a permit and be accompanied by a guide. Arrangements for one-day permits and guides can be made at the park headquarters in Cekik (tel: 0365-61060; 7.30am–3.30pm), the ranger station at Labuhan Lalang or the Department of Forestry (PPHA) office in Denpasar.

Nature enthusiasts will also enjoy trekking through the tropical, almost primeval, rainforest that borders Danau Buyan and Danau Tamblingan, close to Bedugul. The pathways through the forest are narrow and the undergrowth is around 2 metres (7ft) high, but in the dry season it's not difficult to negotiate the route. Hidden temples lie in sunlit clearings within the trees, and trekkers may see deer, black monkeys and squirrels. From the lakeside, it is possible to arrange to be rowed across the tranquil waters by one of the local villagers in a *pedau akit,* a traditional double canoe.

BIRDWATCHING

Taman Nasional Bali Barat (West Bali National Park) is home to 110 different species of birdlife and is one of only two places where the Bali starling can be found in the wild. (The other is on Nusa Penida.) Extremely rare, this is the only surviving bird endemic to Bali, and is one of the world's most endangered species.

Within the boundaries of the reserve in the bay near Gilimanuk are several island sanctuaries for sea birds. Two species of tern nest in large numbers on the sandbanks at the entrance of Teluk Lumpur (Mud Bay) while brown boobies and lesser frigate birds roost on Pulau Burung further to the east.

The inland forests around Bedugul and Gunung Batukau are also abundant with birdlife, and magnificent kingfishers are a common sight along the island's many river banks.

MOUNTAIN BIKING

Specialist adventure tour companies offer exciting mountain biking tours. Starting at around 1,100 metres (3,600ft) above sea level, each tour is an exhilarating descent through farms, hamlets and lush valleys, past ancient temples and beautiful rice fields. The bike tours include a number of stops, allowing participants to sample some of the indigenous fruits and spices, and absorb the beauty of the terrain. Knowledgeable guides will point out places of interest and the variety of crops cultivated in these mountainous areas, while explaining the history of the land, the culture and its people. Some tours incorporate a visit to a typical Balinese compound home before concluding with an Indonesian buffet lunch.

WHITE WATER RAFTING

White water rafting is an action-packed journey through class II and III rapids, against an awesome backdrop of pristine rainforest, towering gorges, emerald rice terraces and dramatic waterfalls on the Ayung, Telaga Waja (Karangasem) and Unda rivers. There are quite a number of operators, and the more reputable ones have good safety standards with professional and experienced guides piloting the rafts. Welcome hot showers at the end are followed by a gourmet buffet feast.

Whitewater rafting.

CRUISING

Bali offers numerous ocean cruise options on luxury catamarans and yachts, including day trips around the islands of Nusa Lembongan, Nusa Ceningan and Nusa Penida, with plenty to see, not least the giant fruit bats at Bat Rock. These trips include lunch, snorkelling at Crystal Bay, a visit to a seaweed farming village on Nusa Ceningan, and activities such as snorkelling, sea kayaking and banana boat rides at Nusa Lembongan.

OTHER ACTIVITIES

Other outdoor activities include windsurfing, water skiing, fishing, ecotours, four-wheel drive and bike tours, bungy-jumping and more, all of which can easily be arranged in Bali.

Kamasan-style paintings adorn the ceiling of Bali Kerta Gosa in Semarapura.

ARCHITECTURE

The order of the cosmos defines how a traditional building is laid out and constructed in Bali. Some of these ideas have inspired contemporary styles that borrow from European design, often embellished with lush, spectacular gardens.

For centuries, all Balinese buildings have been laid out according to the principles of sacred space. Even in prehistoric times some kind of orientation was used. Ancient megalithic stones, for example, are oriented towards one of the island's main volcanoes. An important concept is the *kaja* (upstream) axis, the high direction where deities and ancestors reside, and the low *kelod* (downstream) direction of demonic forces. In south Bali, *kaja-kelod* is a north–south orientation, but on the northern side of the island, it refers to south–north instead. Another axis is *kangin-kauh* (east–west) based on the rising and setting sun, associated with life and death. At the centre of these four cosmic directions lies the human realm.

The Balinese traditional reverence for mountains was further developed by Indian influences during the 11th century. In Hindu-Buddhist cosmology, the sacred mountain Meru is at the centre of the universe and is the abode of the deities. This idea was embraced by the Balinese, who used the island's highest volcano Gunung Agung as their Mount Meru.

The Hindu-Buddhist concepts also give everything its allotted place in the universe, implying that any transgression of this natural order will lead to disharmony or disaster. The Hindu-Buddhist cosmos is divided into upper, middle and nether worlds. Architectural structures and their layouts follow this orientation with the roof as heaven, the middle section the earth, and the foundation the underworld.

THE HOUSEHOLD COMPOUND

Traditional Balinese houses, from village to court, are built within a walled courtyard or series of courtyards with mostly uncovered

The pink sandstone temple, Pura Beji, in Sangsit.

earth. Most Balinese feel more at home when surrounded by walls made of mud, brick or stone. Entry is through a small, covered gate with a niche in each side for offerings. Just inside the gate is an *aling-aling* (privacy wall) that obscures the interior from outside view. More importantly, it prevents evil spirits from entering since they cannot turn corners.

Within the enclosed compound are several *bale*, open-sided or walled pavilions found throughout most of Southeast Asia. Instead of being raised off the ground on posts, in Bali they are built on platforms of mud, brick or stone. The wooden pillars of a traditional pavilion must be erected in the same way as the tree grew so that it stands 'upright'. To determine which end is which, a rope is tied around the middle point of the lumber; when raised, the denser root end is heavier.

Pavilions have specific uses and are laid out according to the Hindu-Buddhist idea that the household compound is like a human body. The *sanggah* or *merajan* (family temple) is at the most sacred *kaja-kangin* (mountain-east) corner, the highest ground and equivalent to the head. The ritual *bale dangin* (eastern pavilion) is where birth ceremonies, tooth-filings and weddings occur. Bodies of the deceased

Bale Kambang, the "floating pavilion", at Taman Gili, Semarapura.

Measurements for a compound are taken from the owner. The layout is based on the length of the owner's foot and outstretched arms, thereby creating a home in harmony with him.

---

are placed here before cremations or burials. This pavilion and the central courtyard are the torso and navel.

The arms are the *bale daja* (north pavilion) which is reserved for the elders or married couples and where the family heirlooms are stored, and the *bale dauh* (west pavilion) where unwed

members stay. The *paon* (kitchen) is the stomach, while the *lumbung* (granary) and *bale delod* (pavilion towards the sea) for sleeping are the legs. The *lawang* (gate) represents the genitals, the garbage pit the anus. There may also be an area outside of the compound allocated to pig pens, coconut and fruit trees, and enjoyed by free-ranging ducks and chickens. This section of land, where in addition you might find the *semer* (well), is separated by a low wall, marking the border between the human quarters and the animal quarters. The layout of the compound is the same for a poor or wealthy family; only the materials used would differ.

Traditional carpentry joints are fitted together without nails, but wooden wedges are pounded in to hold them snugly. This gives buildings flexibility during earthquakes, allowing them to sway instead of collapsing. Interiors can be rather dark due to tiny windows or absence of them, and the only furnishings might be a simple bed, cabinet or table. Traditional thatched roofs used to be composed of dried grass panels, but clay tiles and metal shingles are commonly used today.

TEMPLE ARCHITECTURE

Since they are the residences of deities, temples follow stricter principles of spatial organisation compared to a household. The mountain and eastern sides are deemed most sacred. The stepped terraces of ancient sacred sites can still be seen in such temples as Pura Besakih on Gunung Agung, Pura Samuan Tiga in Bedulu (Gianyar), Pura Luhur Batukau in Tabanan, and Pura Kehen in Bangli.

A public temple, one not within a family compound, is called a *pura*, a Sanskrit word meaning 'fortress or walled enclosure'. In Bali there are tens of thousands of temples for clans, holy springs, irrigation, villages, regions, and the entire island. Within a village there usually are *kahyangan tiga* (three sacred spaces): *pura puseh* (temple of origin) dedicated to Brahma, god of creation; *pura desa-bale agung* (temple of the village and great pavilion) for Wisnu (Vishnu), god of life; and *pura dalem* (temple of the dead) near a cemetery, dedicated to Durga and her consort Siwa (Shiva), deities of death and reincarnation.

A temple's *jaba* (outer courtyard) is a public area outside the entrance and is often not walled. Performances occur in a large open-sided *wantilan*. In one corner of the outer walls surrounding a temple's other courtyards may be a *bale kulkul*. The hollow wooden logs hanging in this tower-like structure are struck to signal the arrival and departure of deities.

Entry into a temple is through a *candi bentar* (split gate) in one of the walls, which looks like a slender triangle vertically cut in half with the parts separated. They may be related to memorials for ancient ancestral worship. The *candi bentar* may also symbolise the splitting of the

shrines) are used for offerings. Just as in domestic structures, an *aling-aling* (privacy wall) prevents evil spirits from entering.

INNER SANCTUM

Even if the temple is built on level ground, the *jeroan* (inner courtyard) is usually set slightly higher. Rows of shrines or *pelinggih* (sitting places) line the east sides, with pavilions elsewhere. Most shrines are made of square brick and stone pillars topped by a small wooden enclosure with a thatched roof made from *alang-*

Pura Besakih, Bali's most important place of worship, also known as the 'Mother Temple'.

material world, allowing entrance to the spiritual realm. The walled *jaba tengah* (middle courtyard) has more pavilions, such as a *bale gong* for the *gamelan* music ensemble, and other structures where offerings may be prepared or where puppet performances may be presented.

The entrance to a temple's inner courtyard is often through a covered gate known as *candi kurung*, *kori gelung* or *kori agung*. It usually has steps on both sides of the doorway. Above the opening, the terrifying face and long-nailed hands of Boma frightens away evil forces. He is the son of Wisnu and Ibu Pertiwi (Mother Earth), and symbolises uncultivated fertility. Stone demons guard both sides of the gate for the same purpose, and *apit lawang* (gate-flanking

alang (jungle grass) or black *ijuk* (sugar palm fibre). If present, the most outstanding feature is the towering *meru*, a pagoda-like shrine symbolising the Hindu-Buddhist cosmic mountain after which it is named. The more important the deity, the more tiers or roofs on the *meru*, but always in odd numbers from 3 to 11.

Another important shrine introduced during the 19th century is the *padmasana* (lotus throne) for Sanghyang Widi Wasa, the Supreme Deity of Universal Order. Located in the most sacred *kaja-kangin* corner, this tall stone seat represents the cosmos. The base is carved with the foundation of the universe: the tortoise Bedawang Nala entwined by the two serpents Basuki and Anantaboga.

Receding levels represent the different layers of heaven, and are topped by an open throne. During temple ceremonies, the deities descend to occupy objects that are placed in their shrines. Sacred relics, normally safely stored away, are also brought out for this purpose.

Most prayers are not directed towards this Supreme Being but rather to his manifestations as the temple's deities. Unlike Indian and ancient Javanese Hindu-Buddhist temples, Balinese places of worship do not have enclosed buildings for people to pray. Instead, praying is done seated on the ground in front of shrines, rain or shine, day or night.

CONTEMPORARY ARCHITECTURE

The Balinese are known for borrowing ideas from other cultures, both East and West, and blending them together in unique ways. Chinese influences (see page 47) are visible in some temple structures and in the concept of household pavilions facing a central courtyard. Some palaces blend European and East Asian elements, as in the Dutch-style Bale Maskerdam

Bamboo construction used for modern design at Manjangan Dynasty Resort's Pasir Putih Beach Club.

⊙ GARDEN OF EDEN

Although arguably all five-star resorts and villas and even many of Bali's lower-priced accommodations have beautiful gardens, the landscaping at Vilhara Dharma Giri, a Buddhist temple and meditation centre in Pupuan, Tabanan Regency, stands out as spectacular. Relatively small, each plant from the towering cedars and yews that suit higher altitudes to bonsais in shallow pots placed on pedestals serves a distinctive purpose. A lotus pond near a meditation pavilion reachable by a curved pathway and a small, arched bridge bring a sense of serenity appropriate for such a place. Alcoves bedecked with birds nest ferns complete the tranquil ambiance.

and Chinese-style Bale Pemandesan at the Puri Agung Karangasem palace in Amlapura.

During the 1920s, German artist Walter Spies built himself a Balinese-style bungalow with bamboo walls and thatched roof in Ubud. Soon after, Belgian artist Adrien-Jean Le Mayeur de Merpres made his studio home on Sanur beach in a walled compound with pavilions set amidst gardens. But until more visitors began staying longer, most were content to live in traditional compounds. Gradually some of them built their own homes, combining the best of local architecture with their own sense of whimsical design.

Today, many expatriate homes and holiday rental villas have imaginative fusions of styles and materials while still retaining the fundamentals of traditional Balinese form and function (although by the same token there are quite a few ill-considered architectural hybrids).

Thatched bamboo bungalows have attracted visitors ever since the first hotel in this style opened on Kuta beach in the 1930s. Colonial authorities, who built more European-style accommodation unsuitable for the tropics, dismissed them as unsanitary 'native huts'.

During the 1980s, the trend was towards the florid, with grand lobbies, soaring roofs and ornamented surfaces. In the 1990s, designs became more sparse, with luxurious suites using textured stone walls, marble floors and natural materials for furnishings. Foreign architects such as Australian Peter Muller (the Oberoi in Seminyak and Amandari in Ubud) championed the use of natural materials such as rough stone and unfinished wood. Retaining the Balinese architectural aesthetic, they enclosed the traditional pavilions with big picture windows. In smaller places interiors were left whole but verandahs were added, hidden from view by surrounding walls like a traditional compound. Since the turn of this century, designs have taken yet another step deeper into nature. Relaxing in Manjangan Dynasty Resort's Pasir Putih Restaurant & Bar is similar to sitting in a bamboo forest, while Fivelements Retreat's Sakti Dining Room resembles an enormous thatched-roof lodge that might be found in a five-star forest.

GARDENS AND LANDSCAPING

The average Balinese traditionally did not have need for a home garden as plants could thrive anywhere in the vicinity; and the open central courtyard of a home was usually kept free of plants, since the area was used for ceremonies. Surrounding walls deliberately kept the civilised compound safe and separate from the natural and wild world outside. Although a few wealthy Balinese or royalty built pleasure pavilions in artificial ponds, such as Taman Tirtagangga and Taman Ujung in east Bali, they were mostly influenced by European ideas. A few older temples, such as the beautiful moat-surrounded Pura Taman Ayun in Mengwi, are unusual.

The expatriate community probably introduced landscaping as an integral part of embellishing hotels and homes, but things really began to change during the 1990s when local authorities began road side tree plantings to spruce up villages for competitions. More Balinese who worked in hotels with landscaped gardens also brought the idea home. This created a minor industry in ornamental plants, with rice fields near Sanur and Mas growing all sorts of flowering trees, decorative shrubs and potted plants.

Many domestic compounds now have attractive gardens with grassy areas, flower shrubs, bonsai plants and paved walkways. Private homes allow for more integrated contact with

Dragon statues at the entrance of Vihara Dharma Giri temple in Pupuan.

nature in smaller spaces. Even temples have received the same attention, although some over-zealous devotees have unfortunately covered many dirt courtyards with concrete to keep worshippers dry during rain – but roasting them on a sunny day.

Today, any hotel that lays claim to Balinese architecture must have lots of grassy lawns, flowering plants and shrubs along meandering paths, fishponds with fountains, tropical trees shading intimate pavilions, and even bathrooms open to the sky, complete with interior mini-gardens. Some have gone for a more natural look by keeping as many original trees as possible and building around them.

Carrying firewood and coconuts through rice paddies.

Pura Taman Saraswati water temple, Ubud.

Carrying out a melasti (cleansing ceremony) on Kuta beach.

BALI

A detailed guide to the island, with the principal sites
clearly cross-referenced by number to the maps.

*Taman Ujung water
gardens, near Amlapura.*

Some of the most overused clichés in travel writing have
been used to describe Bali: exotic, seductive, enchanting,
magical. Although these adjectives succinctly convey the
charms of this island and less florid praise would seem
inadequate, after a while they lose their power to convince
– leaving the writer with a real dilemma.

For a tiny island in the world's largest archipelago, Bali
has an astonishing diversity. The southern part, Badung
Regency, the urban and commercial centre of Bali, is where
most visitors play and party, mainly in the beach towns,
stretching from Kuta, Legian and Seminyak northwest along the coast to
Canggu.. Yet south Bali is not without redemption, for behind
the blatant commercialism lie some of the island's most
traditional aspects. In Gianyar and Bangli Regencies, the
contours become softer, the villages smaller and the culture
more unfettered. Bali's earliest kingdoms carved out realms
in these fertile lands and left behind a legacy of ancient temples. Ubud especially is a magnet for culture, with many of
its surrounding villages specialising in some form of the arts.

Klungkung and Karangasem Regencies in the east are
areas of striking contrasts, dominated by the island's highest mountain, Gunung Agung. Isolated villages, still conservative by nature, continue to maintain artistic traditions
and ancient customs. The northern coast of Bali falls within
Buleleng Regency, and is predominantly agricultural, growing everything from spices to grapes. Mountains almost
meet the sea on narrow black-sand beaches washed by calm waves.

*Pura Ulun Danu Bratan,
Bedugal Regency.*

In western Bali, Jembrana Regency and part of Buleleng, is more
sparsely populated than other areas yet culturally diverse; at times dry, at
times lush and ignored by most travellers. A national park with rare wildlife anchors this part of the island. Bali's eighth regency, Tabanan in the
southwest, was once home to royal dynasties, and is Bali's rice basket, its
sloping plains watered by crater lakes nestled under hulking volcanoes.

Take time to explore the many contrasts of this beautiful island; as well
as a stunning landscape you will find an intense spirituality, and a warm,
gentle, friendly people who refer to tourists as *tamu* – 'guests'.

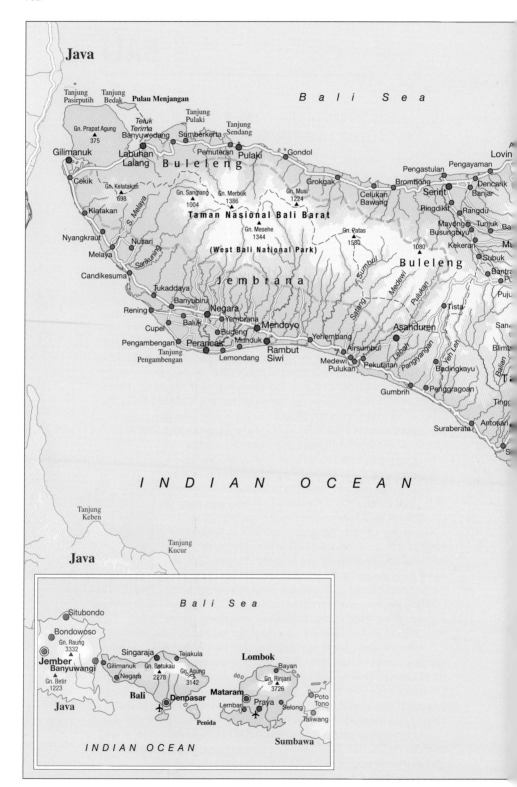

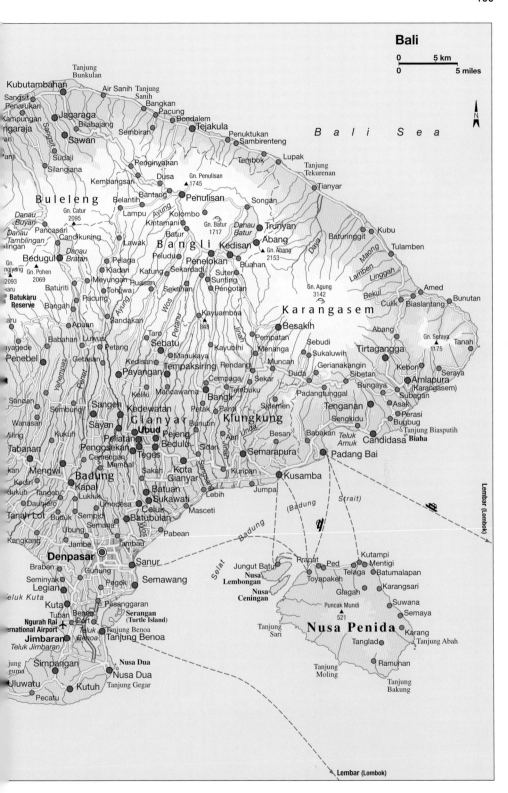

Bali

0 — 5 km
0 — 5 miles

B a l i   S e a

Kendongan fish market Jimbaran.

SOUTH BALI

Balinese cosmology considers the sea to be inauspicious. Yet it is on the sandy beaches of South Bali that most travellers end up, and where the widest choice of hotels, restaurants, bars and shops are found. Culture hounds who search hard enough will also find a sprinkling of temples, markets and museums here.

Southern Bali is the first stop for most visitors when they arrive on the island. And it's not surprising. The best beaches are to be found here, anchored by a tourism infrastructure that caters to every creature comfort, from luxury beachfront resorts and fine restaurants to trendy bars and pampering spas. While the area's bustling beaches by day and non-stop bar-hopping and dancing after hours can prove all too frenetic for a restful holiday, this part of Bali is without doubt one of the island's great draws.

The **Badung** district is the location of Ngurah Rai International Airport and the capital, Denpasar, a typically busy Indonesian city. South of Denpasar are Bali's beachside tourist enclaves: Kuta, Legian, Seminyak, Canggu and Jimbaran along the southwestern coast, and Sanur, Nusa Dua and Tanjung Benoa on the southeast stretch. South Bali covers just one-tenth of the island but is Bali's most heavily populated area.

DENPASAR

A growing metropolis of nearly 900,000 people, **Denpasar** ❶ (meaning "North of the Market", which indicates how much the city has grown) is a perennially busy city of winding alleys, illogical one-way streets, pungent smells and home to more cars per capita than Jakarta, Indonesia's capital. If your mind has been

Surfer on Kuta Beach.

unwinding on the beach, it may well be jerked back into reality in Denpasar. There are more than a few jewels to be found in Bali's capital city, most of them within a short hop of each other.

TAMAN PUPUTAN

At the corner of Jalan Udayana and Jalan Surapati is **Taman Puputan** Ⓐ (Puputan Square), a large grassy open space commemorating the last battle between the king of Badung and the Dutch militia in 1906. Thousands of Balinese warriors armed only with *keris*

Ⓞ Main attractions
Museum Bali
Denpasar's markets
Museum Le Mayeur
Pura Luhur Uluwatu
Jimbaran Beach
Waterbom Park
Seminyak's restaurants
Pura Tanah Lot

**Maps on pages
106, 108, 112,
114, 118**

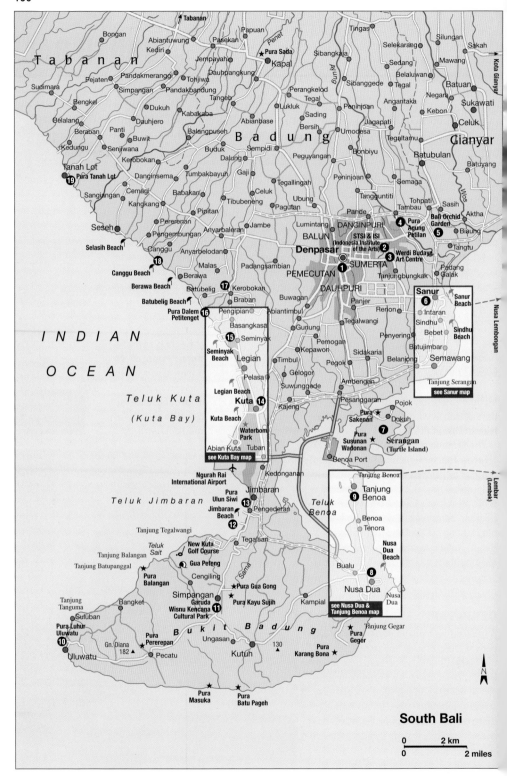

South Bali

0   2 km

0   2 miles

(daggers) and spears charged against a line of Dutch soldiers in a tragically heroic sacrifice. They died either by their own hands or by Dutch bullets in a Balinese ritual known as *puputan*. Today, the slaughter of the estimated 600 to 2,000 Balinese is commemorated with the large bronze statue of an adult and two children going to battle armed with bamboo staves, spears and daggers. A solemn ceremony is held here every 20 September to commemorate the tragic event. The space gets busy around sunset and on weekends when people gather to relax and socialise.

At the northwest corner of the square, at the main intersection of Jalan Veteran and Jalan Surapati, is **Catur** Muka , a great statue with four faces and eight arms. Erected in 1972, it represents Hindu gods of the four main directions: Iswara or Ishvara (east), Brahma (south), Mahadewa (west), and Wisnu or Vishnu (north).

MUSEUM NEGERI PROPINSI BALI

On the east side of the field is **Museum Negeri Propinsi Bali** ❸ Bali Provincial

State Museum), more simply known as **Museum Bali** (tel: 0361-222 680; Mon–Thu 8am-3.30pm, Fri 8am–12.30pm; fee). Established in 1932 by the Dutch government, the displays present a comprehensive history of Bali's social and cultural development from prehistoric times to the early 20th century. Items are presented without specific dates of origin, but fortunately English-speaking guides are on hand.

The museum is notable for its fine architecture. The *candi bentar* (split gate) entrance, courtyards and *bale kulkul* (warning drum tower) are reminiscent of a temple, while displays are housed in palace-style buildings echoing architecture from different parts of Bali. Unfortunately, part of the collection is wasting away in storage due to lack of exhibition space and proper care.

The main **Gedung Karangasem** at the back resembles the palaces of east Bali. Inside are prehistoric Neolithic stone implements and sarcophagi, and Buddhist and Hindu bronzes, along with implements for hunting, gathering and farming. Look for the ornate

Statue in Puputan Square.

Exterior of Museum Negeri Propinsi Bali.

Temple deity at Pura
Jagatnatha.

carrying cases for fighting-cock spurs. There are also wonderfully carved antique doors and animals that were used as supports for posts in pavilions.

Gedung Buleleng to its right belongs to the northern palace style and has impressive displays of beautiful wedding costumes, dance masks and ritual items such as tooth-filing implements and human effigies made from silver pieces, and Chinese coins used in death rites. The windowless **Gedung Tabanan** to the right, in the palace style of southwest Bali, displays mainly traditional textiles inside.

PURA JAGATNATHA

Adjacent to the museum is **Pura Jagatnatha** (daily daylight hours; donations welcome). Built in 1953, the temple is dedicated to Sanghyang Widi Wasa, the Supreme Deity of Universal Order, who is manifested as Bali's many Hindu gods and goddesses, local spirits and divine ancestors. Have a look at this deity in a gilded relief at the very top of the only shrine inside, a towering white *padmasana* (lotus throne) that

The padmasana shrine
at Pura Jagatnatha.

symbolises the Hindu-Buddhist universe. Supported by a tortoise entwined by two serpents, the receding platforms represent the levels of heaven on the cosmic Mount Meru.

Temple festivals held here on every full and new moon days have the atmosphere of a holiday celebration. Check exact dates with the Bali Tourism Board office (see margin tip).

DENPASAR'S MARKETS

Pasar Badung (Badung market) (daily 24hrs), Bali's largest traditional produce market, is found west along Jalan Gajah Mada opposite the Badung River. Stalls sell fruit, vegetables, meat, seafood, spices, cooking utensils, ritual paraphernalia, clothing and much of everything else.

Across the Badung River is **Pasar Kumbasari** (daily 8am–5pm), another sprawling market jammed with stalls selling clothes and handicrafts, as well as small eateries hawking local food. You can spend hours wandering around the market's dark and stifling interior, but keep a

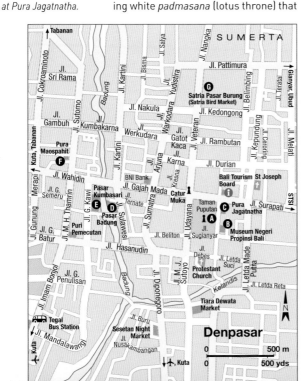

close eye on your belongings. Bargaining is recommended.

Nightlife in Denpasar revolves around the three huge *pasar malam* (local night markets) that operate at Pasar Badung, Pasar Kumbasari and **Pasar Kereneng**, near the bus station off Jalan Kamboja further east. Connected by a bridge, Pasars Badung and Kumasari and their pavements are illuminated at night, making them an attractive setting filled with food stalls and vendors. On weekends and holidays the riverwalk is crowded with local people enjoying the camaraderie of friends.

PURA MAOSPAHIT

Although a bit out of the way but still within walking distance, **Pura Maospahit** ➍ (daily daylight hours; donation) on Jalan Sutomo is the oldest temple in the city. It dates from the 14th century when invaders arrived from the East Javanese Majapahit (also called Maospahit) Hindu kingdom to conquer Bali. Extensively damaged in 1917 by an earthquake, most of this brick temple has been rebuilt, although the section at the back still has some of the original architecture. A shrine with real deer antlers is dedicated to the deity of Majapahit. The entrance to the temple is flanked by large brick bas-relief figures of the mythological Garuda bird and the giant warrior hero Bima from the Hindu *Mahabharata* epic.

PASAR BURUNG

Head north on Jalan Veteran and continue past the historic Grand Inna Bali Beach Hotel, which was built by the Dutch in 1927 and still retains its colonial atmosphere in spite of traffic zooming by outside. Further north at the entrance at Puri Satria is the **Pasar Burung Satria** ➏ (Satria Bird Market; daily 8am–3pm), which sells birds of all kinds along with puppies and other small mammals, tropical fish, reptiles, and even fighting crickets. Animal lovers are advised to avoid this place; the creatures are kept in cramped cages and tiny aquariums.

STSI AND ISI

About 2km (1 mile) east of downtown Denpasar on Jalan Nusa Indah **are Sekolah Tinggi Seni Indonesia** ➋ (STSI, high school) and the **Indonesia Institute of the Arts** (ISI, university; tel: 0361-227 316; Mon–Fri 8am–2pm). While the high school was founded in 1967, a university curriculum was added in 2003. College-level students here study traditional dance, music, puppetry and visual arts, as well as the choreography of new classical styles and contemporary interpretations of traditional art forms.

The campus' **Lata Mahosadhi Art Museum** exhibits every sort of gamelan ensemble known. Another building features new works by students and faculty members in the visual arts programme. Visitors to the institute may watch the classes in progress and see the museum and gallery displays. Seek permission from the institute's secretary at the main office.

Tip

Across Jalan Surapati from Pura Jagatnatha is the Bali Tourism Board (Mon–Sat 9am–5pm, tel: 0361-235 600).While the staff may not be very helpful, they do have a useful schedule of events happening in the city and other places in Bali.

Selling flowers in Pasar Badung to be used as offerings.

Close-up of a legong dancer – one of the many dances taught at Denpasar's Sekolah Tinggi Seni Indonesia.

Learning shadow puppetry at the Indonesia Institute of the Arts (ISI).

TAMAN WERDHI BUDAYA ART CENTRE

Just south of the arts institute is the **Taman Werdhi Budaya** Art Centre ❸ more simply known as the **Bali Art Centre** (tel: 0361-227 176; Mon–Thu and Sat 7.30am–3.30pm, Fri 7.30am–1pm). Set among lush gardens and lotus ponds, Bali's main visual arts are represented in this large complex, including painting, woodcarving, shadow puppetry, silverwork, weaving, dance costumes and even some remarkable ivory carving. This is also where the annual Bali Arts Festival takes place (see box).

PURI AGUNG KESIMAN AND PURA AGUNG PETILAN

On the main road from Denpasar to Gianyar stands **Puri Agung Kesiman** (no entry), the residence of one of three royal families that once ruled the Badung kingdom. The towering gates and high brick walls are typical of the southern architectural style. Peer through the gates for interesting glimpses of royal life.

Just east of the palace and on the same side of the main road is **Pura Agung Petilan** ❹ (daily daylight hours; donations welcome), an important temple for many Balinese. The slender red-brick gate is beautifully proportioned while inside the bare courtyard are several meeting pavilions for the deities, one of them with a cave-like opening in the base housing stone figures of the underworld – the tortoise and serpents that support the cosmos. During ceremonies here, villagers bring their sacred images, along with Barong and Rangda masks, in colourful, noisy processions. After praying, scores of men, women and even children become violently possessed, circling the cockfighting pavilion outside while stabbing themselves with sharp daggers without doing physical harm.

BALI ORCHID GARDEN

Heading east, the main road from Tohpati to Sanur is lined with many shops growing and selling all kinds of ornamental plants and flowers that have become popular among the Balinese

⊘ BALI ARTS FESTIVAL

Constructed to showcase Balinese art and culture, the Taman Werdhi Art Centre is a facility used by students during the year, but from mid-June until mid-July it comes alive as the focal point for the annual Bali Arts Festival. Kicking off with a gigantic parade, performers from Bali, other Indonesian islands and abroad gather here to share their love of the arts. Open stages and outdoor pavilions host vocal, musical and dance events, and visual arts are displayed. Stalls featuring local dishes and handicrafts pack the building, which is always crowded during performance times. Be aware that many of the performances are held at night and empty seats can be difficult to find.

for their homes. The **Bali Orchid Garden** ❺ (tel: 0361-466 010; www.bali
orchidgardens.com; daily 8am–6pm)
offers a more organised experience for
orchid lovers. The garden is located at
the junction of the bypass road and the
coastal road at Padanggalak. A huge
variety of orchids that bloom throughout the year are on display, and many
of them are for sale. Organised tours
are available but call ahead to ask first.

SANUR AREA

During the 1930s, **Sanur** ❻ was little
more than a tucked-away beach with
barely a hotel to its name. Its guileless
charm attracted modest interest from
a handful of foreign artists who settled
here. By the 1950s, the first cluster of
bungalows in Sanur had been built,
attracting international travellers.

A Sukarno-era project and something
of an eyesore, the 10-storey **Grand Inna
Bali Beach Hotel** at the northern end
of Sanur beach was built with Japanese
reparation money given to Indonesia for
hardships suffered during World War II.
When the hotel first opened in l966, it
was a source of wonder to the Balinese,
with its running water, electricity and
lifts. It was Bali's only high-rise structure at the time. Gutted by a fire in 1992,
it was refurbished and re-opened two
years later.

Meanwhile, other hotels have followed in its wake, and the beach
front is lined by establishments with
access roads crowded with kiosks
selling tourist souvenirs. A wise government regulation forbidding buildings taller than a coconut palm (or
15 metres/50ft) has allowed Sanur to
retain its modest character. But while
the rule remains in the books, new
construction seems to have found
creative ways around the law.

Still, the area has managed to retain
its heritage as a community headed by
brahmana (caste of high priests) and as
a centre of black magic. Offshore looms
the **Nusa Penida island** (see page 159),
home of Ratu Gede Mas Mecaling,
the great fanged lord of supernatural
forces. Violent trance performances
still occur during festivals at temples
beside Sanur's luxury hotels.

> ⊙ **Tip**
>
> If staying in Bali on an
> extended holiday, learn to
> speak Bahasa Indonesia
> at the Indonesia Australia
> Language Foundation
> (tel: 0361-225 243;
> www.ialf.edu) in Denpasar.
> Programmes include
> two-week intensive
> courses suitable for
> learning levels from
> beginner to advanced.

Fishing boat on Sanur beach.

Pura Sakenan on small Pulau Serangan island.

Museum Le Mayeur occupies the former home of a famous Belgian artist.

Sanur's golden-sand beach is calm and shallow, leaving great swathes of sandy mud and coral stretching for hundreds of metres at low tide, when the water can recede to your waist (and sometimes knees). When the tide is high, however, Sanur offers windsurfing and sailing, along with the numbing drone of jet skis.

MUSEUM LE MAYEUR

There are few historical sites in Sanur. The only surviving place from the romantic, artistic years of the 1930s is that of the Belgian painter Adrien-Jean Le Mayeur de Merpres (1880–1958), who moved to Bali in l932 and lived here until his death. **Museum Le Mayeur ⓗ** (tel: 0361-286 201; Sat–Thu 8am–3.30pm, Fri 8.30am–12.30pm) is found just on the beach north of the Grand Inna Bali Beach Hotel. Inside its walls are tropical gardens full of statues, luxuriant gold and crimson carvings, and Le Mayeur's paintings, mostly of his wife, Ni Polok, a renowned *legong* dancer whom Le Mayeur married when she was only 15 years old. Ni

Polok bequeathed the property to the government after she died in 1985. The paintings are not in mint condition, due to the salty air, but the atmosphere of the Balinese-style home-studio is like a time capsule of tropical tranquillity.

PURA SEGARA

Just south of the Grand Inna Bali Beach Hotel is **Pura Segara ❶** (daily daylight hours; donation), an unusual temple made entirely of coral that is dedicated to the goddess of the sea. Some of the statues and shrines are painted in bright (and rather tacky) colours. Profits from the restaurant at the front, which serves tasty seafood in an idyllic setting, are ploughed into supporting the temple and its surrounding community.

PURA BELANJONG

At the southern end of Sanur is **Pura Belanjong ❶** (daily daylight hours; donation). This temple houses the island's oldest example of writing, known as Prasasti Belanjong, set on an inscribed 177cm (70ins) tall stone pillar. Dating from AD 913 but found only

in the early 1930s, the pillar is not much to look at but is significant because of the two forms of writing it contains, in Old Balinese and in Sanskrit, which indicate the presence of Hindu influence three centuries before the arrival of Java's Hindu Majapahit court.

PULAU SERANGAN

Pulau Serangan , a tiny island, very nearly abuts Bali's east coast near Benoa Harbour. A hot, dry and rather inhospitable speck of land, it's main attributes are surfing off its east coast and a Turtle Conservation & Education Centre. Perhaps the centre's commitment to breeding is retribution for days gone by when green turtles nested here. But the beaches were filled in as a result of a grandiose project to turn the island into a tourist resort that ultimately failed. The centre itself is not large place, but the work they do here is necessary. In addition to habitat destruction, turtle meat has long been favoured by Balinese gourmands. In addition to providing much-needed conservation education, the centre also cares for rescued turtles. Visitors are invited to help feed them, and for a reasonable fee can adopt a hatchling that will be released into the sea.

On the northwest end of this island is **Pura Sakenan** (daily daylight hours; donation), a small but very important temple for Balinese people. Although not much to look at in terms of architecture, the ceremony here on the Sunday after Kuningan attracts worshippers from all over south Bali. Sacred Barong and Rangda masks are brought, and many people become possessed by spirits.

BUKIT BADUNG

Connected to the mainland by a low, narrow isthmus, the craggy limestone **Bukit Badung** (Badung Hill) peninsula rises almost 200 metres (660ft) above sea level. Fondly called The Bukit, cacti thrive on this arid land, with

some areas used for grazing cattle. Good surfaced roads meander across the peninsula bringing development to the area, and scenic vantage points afford breath-taking vistas of Bali with the peaks of distant volcanoes poking above clouds, turbulent waves churning below coastal cliffs and dramatic sunsets over the ocean.

This is also where you will find the up-market beach resort areas at Nusa Dua and Tanjong Benoa on the east coast, and Jimbaran on the west coast, each studded with luxury hotels and resorts. South of Jimbaran are the beaches that draw surfers from the world over with their renowned barrels and surf breaks.

NUSA DUA

Strung out on the eastern coast of Bukit Badung, **Nusa Dua**  (Two Islands) is a slightly clinical paradise in a ribbon-wrapped package. A purpose-built luxury hotel enclave sprawling in the middle of a coconut grove and alongside a white sand beach, it caters mainly to the up-market traveller,

⊙ **Tip**

The stretch of Nusa Dua beach where the Grand Hyatt and Ayodya Resort are located is much wider and nicer than the stretch where the Melia Bali sits, all the way to the Nusa Dua Beach Hotel.

Tree on the beach at Sanur.

Keep a close eye on the monkeys when visiting Pura Luhur Uluwatu – their cuteness can be deceptive.

Banana boat ride at Nusa Dua, just one of the many water sports on offer.

especially those seeking refuge from the pushy hawkers found elsewhere – they are banned from Nusa Dua, although they continue to flock to its edges. Thin on local ambience, it was built during the 1980s on land that was deemed unsuitable for agriculture by the local government, which was intent on separating tourists from locals.

Today, five-star luxury hotels complete with in-house dining, entertainment, and sports facilities line the lovely white-sand beach; one stretch of it, separated by a tiny spit of land, is even prettier and less crowded than the other (see margin tip).

There are a number of independent restaurants in the area including a stretch of decent eateries at Pantai Mengiat near Bualu village, and more at the Bali Collection mall, which is home to a range of shops and a department store.

TANJUNG BENOA

For many years **merely a fishing village, Tanjung Benoa** (Harbour Cape), on a long peninsula off the easternmost end of Bukit Badung, was overlooked by developers. This oversight has actually worked to the benefit of the area, which still retains its traditional Balinese village atmosphere. Hotels incorporating local building styles and materials line the shore. The white-sand beach can be disappointingly calm as the waters are sheltered by a ribbon of coral reefs in the distance. It is, however, ideal for water sports. Although Benoa village doesn't have any grand sights, a walk north up the peninsula will reveal a multicultural community, dating from its years as a trading centre, reflected in the Hindu, Buddhist, Islamic and Christian religious sites.

Both Tanjung Benoa and Nusa Dua are now accessible via a new scenic highway, a tolled causeway bridge stretching across the Gulf of Benoa, 12.7 km (8 miles) in length and completed in 2012.

PURA LUHUR ULUWATU

At the western tip of Bukit Badung peninsula, where rocky precipices

Nusa Dua and Tanjung Benoa

0   2 km
0   1 mile

Teluk Benoa

TANJUNG BENOA

Bali Mandara Toll Road

TERORA

Jl. Pratama

Badung Strait

The Tanjung Benoa
Bali Reef Resort
Novotel Benoa
Novotel Bali Benoa
Bali Khama
Sadara Boutique Beach Resort
Hotel Nikko Bali
Benoa Beach

MUMBUL

Jl. By Pass Ngurah Rai

Conrad Bali

Bali Tropic Resort & Spa
Sol Beach House Benoa
Club Med Bali
Nusa Dua Beach   Sofitel Bali
Hotel & Spa   Nusa Dua
CELUK   The Westin Nusa Dua
The Laguna

WISMAKAMPIAL-
PERMAI

Jl. Siligita

Jl. Keruksetra

BUALU

Melia
Bali

Jl. Raya Bualu Ungasan

BUALUINDAH
PANDE

Jl. Srikandi

Grand Hyatt Bali

NUSA DUA

Aman Villas at
Nusa Due

The Balé

Ayodya Resort
Bali

The St Regis Bali Resort

SAWANDAN
KELOD

Jl. Nusa Dua Selatan

The Mulia Nusa
Dua Bali

INDIAN OCEAN

Hilton Bali Resort

drop almost 100 metres (330ft) to the turbulent ocean below, is **Pura Luhur Uluwatu** , or Temple above the Headstone (daily daylight hours; charge). This small but very important sacred site sits on top of a dramatic promontory; the short path left of the temple leads along the cliff top to breathtaking views.

Originally dating from the 10th century, Pura Luhur Uluwatu is one of the major sea temples revered by many Balinese. The legendary 16th-century Javanese priest Danghyang Nirartha helped to establish this temple, and it is said that he achieved enlightenment here.

The temple's *candi bentar* (split gate) is flanked by carvings in the shape of wings. The entrance to the second courtyard is an arched gateway guarded by statues of Ganesha, the elephant-headed god revered as the remover of obstacles. The innermost sanctuary is off limits to those who are not praying. Beware of the aggressive monkeys residing here.

Part of the temple actually fell into the sea during the early 1900s, which was an omen of the impending destruction of the royal courts that soon followed. More recently, lightning struck some shrines during the late 1990s, again an omen of the economic and political troubles that befell Bali and Indonesia in 1998. The temple was renovated soon after these events.

SURFING BEACHES

Just north of the temple, the western end of The Bukit is well known among surfers. Due to the dangerous reefs and strong currents, however, only experienced riders should attempt the tricky waves that swell from April to September. Viewers can watch the action from the shore, but the beaches are not ideal for swimming.

Among the famous surfing beaches stretching along the dramatic northwest coast of the peninsula are **Uluwatu**, **Suluban**, **Padang Padang**, **Impossibles**, **Bingin**, **Dreamland** and **Balangan**.

GWK CULTURAL PARK

Return to the middle of Bukit Badung and head north, turning right at the

Bukit Badung's famous surfing beaches are best tackled by more experienced surfers.

Pura Luhur Uluwatu is perched on a dramatic cliff side.

Waxing a surfboard on Kuta beach.

entrance road to the **GWK Cultural Park**  (tel: 0361-700 808; www.gwkbali.com; daily 8am–9pm; fee), officially **Garuda Wisnu Kencana Cultural Park**. This grandiose project was originally conceptualised in the early 1990s and was finally completed and inaugurated in 2018, albeit not as originally planned.

The focal point of the 60-hectare (148-acre) site is an enormous statue of the Hindu god of life, Wisnu (Vishnu), riding upon half-man, half-bird Garuda, symbolic of freedom and respected in Indonesia. Looming toward heaven at a total of 120 metres (294ft), if counting the pedestal that contains an observatory, it is clearly visible when arriving at Bali's airport. The original statues of Wisnu and Garuda, which were never completed and have stood in a virtually empty lot for nearly 30 years, stand guard in a plaza used for cultural performances. Much of the park is flanked by steep limestone cliffs, some of them beautifully carved, and can be traversed by bicycles and Segways available on-site. There are restaurants and shops as well as several venues for events.

JIMBARAN

North of Bukit Badung is the stretch of beach known as **Jimbaran** ⓬, an exclusive luxury resort area that hugs the coast south of Kuta. This lovely crescent-shaped bay bordered by grey-sand beaches is pounded by the same thundering surf as Kuta. Its southern end is anchored by the deluxe Four Seasons Jimbaran, from where the Ngurah Rai International Airport is clearly visible (but thankfully not close enough to hear the noise of jets landing and taking off).

Go to the beach early in the morning to watch fishing boats bringing in their daily catch. The village is justly celebrated for its open-air restaurants that open around sunset right on the beach, all serving delicious and freshly grilled seafood.

PURA ULUN SIWI

Just across from the main market in Jimbaran village is the stately **Pura Ulun Siwi** ⓭ (daily daylight hours; donation), a large *banjar* (irrigation society) temple dominated by a towering *meru* (pagoda). Inside, the shrines are oriented to the west, in the direction of the former kingdom of Mengwi that once owned the sacred site, the holy mountain Gunung Batukaru (see page 197) and the distant Gunung Semeru, far away in East Java.

THE SOUTHERN BEACHES

Frequently referred to simply as "Kuta", the Kuta Bay area is actually made up of several villages stretching from Tuban (where the airport is located) north through Kuta, then to Legian and Seminyak. As young partygoers and increasing traffic began taking over, solace-seekers began looking for quieter beaches further north. Inland at Kerobokan, villas began to appear, and Canggu has emerged as the newest scene for beer-swilling surfers. In addition, starred resorts now reach up the coast as far as Tanah Lot.

TUBAN

South of Kuta village is **Tuban**. The atmosphere here is less frantic with many large family-oriented hotels, restaurants and attractions. In contrast to Kuta, nearly all lodgings have direct access to the beach.

The hotels along this stretch are mainly mid-range to expensive. If looking for budget accommodation, head to Kuta proper. For a shopping excursion, visit the beachfront **Discovery Mall**. Fully air-conditioned, the three storey mall has two department stores, global lifestyle branded boutiques, local retailers, beachside cafés, and more.

WATERBOM PARK

Along Jalan Kartika Plaza in Tuban is the **Waterbom Park** (tel: 0361-755 676; www.waterbom-bali.com; daily 9am–6pm, closed Nyepi day) with spiralling slides, thrilling ramps, a meandering river and play areas, along with restaurants and a spa. Even though lifeguards are on duty, adults must accompany children under 12 years old. It can get crowded later in the day and especially at weekends with long queues, making it best to go early and avoid weekends. Be prepared to climb a lot of steps to get to the top of the rides, but it is well worth it. Lockers and towels can be rented.

KUTA BAY

The Kuta area comprises Tuban at its southern end and continues north into Kuta proper, then Legian, Seminyak and Kerobokan. In reality, however, the borders in between these villages are invisible, as one area merges into the other.

The original **Kuta** ⑭ villagers were farmers, fishermen and metal-smiths. Very few visitors today are aware that in former times Kuta was also a leper colony and slave station, with poor soil. Cynics might suggest that there are parallels to be drawn with the hordes that flock today to this tourist enclave for the combination of sun, sand, sea, and surf. For many, Kuta is a veritable garden of pleasures, while others decry its plunge into rampant commercialism.

Danish entrepreneur Mads Lange (1806–56) was the first to put Kuta on the map in 1839 when he opened a

A quieter moment on Kuta beach, usually a hotbed of tourists and commercialism.

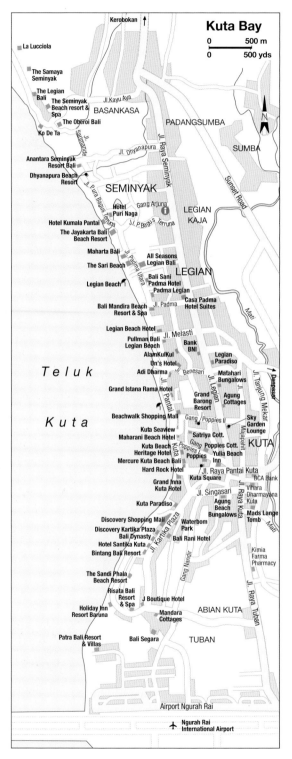

Kuta Bay

0 ——— 500 m
0 ——— 500 yds

Kerobokan

La Lucciola

The Samaya Seminyak

The Legian Bali

The Seminyak Beach resort & Spa

The Oberoi Bali

Ko De Ta

Jl.Kayu Aya

BASANKASA

PADANGSUMBA

SUMBA

Jl. Raya Seminyak

Jl. Dhyanapura

Anantara Seminyak Resort Bali

Dhyanapura Beach Resort

SEMINYAK

Jl. Pura Bagus Teruna

Hotel Puri Naga

Gang Arjuna

Jl.P.Bagus Terruna

LEGIAN KAJA

Sunset Road

Hotel Kumala Pantai

The Jayakarta Bali Beach Resort

Maharta Bali

The Sari Beach

Legian Beach

Jl. Padma Utara

All Seasons Legian Bali

Bali Sani

Padma Hotel

Padma Legian

LEGIAN

Mati

Bali Mandira Beach Resort & Spa

Jl. Padma

Casa Padma Hotel Suites

Legian Beach Hotel

Jl. Melasti

Pullman Bali Legian Beach

AlamKulKul

Un's Hotel

Adi Dharma

Bank BNI

Legian Paradiso

Jl. Benesari

Matahari Bungalows

Jl. Tanjung Mekar

Denpasar

Teluk

Jl. Pantai

Grand Istana Rama Hotel

Grand Barong Resort

Agung Cottages

Kuta

Beachwalk Shopping Mall

Gang /Poppies II

Sky Garden Lounge

Kuta Seaview

Maharani Beach Hotel

Kuta Beach Heritage Hotel

Mercure Kuta Beach Bali

Hard Rock Hotel

Satriya Cott.

Gang Poppies I

Poppies

Poppies Cott.

Yulia Beach Inn

Jl. Maaspahit

KUTA

Jl. Raya Pantai Kuta

Kuta Square

BCA Bank

Grand Inna Kuta Hotel

Jl. Singasari

Agung Beach Bungalows

Jl. Raya Kuta

Vihara Dharmayona Kuta

Kuta Paradiso

Mads Lange Tomb

Discovery Shopping Mall

Discovery Kartika Plaza

Bali Dynasty

Hotel Santika Kuta

Bintang Bali Resort

Jl. Kartika Plaza

Waterbom Park

Bali Rani Hotel

Kimia Farma Pharmacy

Gang Nandir

The Sandi Phala Beach Resort

Risata Bali Resort & Spa

Holiday Inn Resort Baruna

J Boutique Hotel

Mandara Cottages

ABIAN KUTA

Jl. Raya Tuban

Patra Bali Resort & Villas

Bali Segara

TUBAN

Airport Ngurah Rai

Ngurah Rai International Airport

---

trading centre that soon developed into a thriving port. In 1937, an American couple, Robert and Louise Koke, built the first bungalow-style hotel on the beach, attracting many visitors until the Japanese forces invaded in February 1942 during World War II.

Kuta once again fell into obscurity until the advent of mass tourism during the 1970s. At first, villagers looked askance at the nearly naked foreigners romping on the beach, a place which the Balinese traditionally viewed as close to the underworld. But they saw profits to be made and so converted their homes into cheap *losmen* (guesthouses) for tourists.

Both Balinese and tourists can be found along the broad sandy beach day after day, swimming, surfing – the waters off Kuta are among the best places to learn this sport – sunbathing and strolling. Countless touts hawking cheap souvenirs roam the beach while women offering nail painting, hair braiding and massages huddle beneath umbrellas and trees. Inland Kuta is packed with a jumble of bars, souvenir shops, surf shops, tattoo parlours, travel offices, accommodation, restaurants and fast-food joints. Unregulated street hawkers are an increasing annoyance, and the congested streets and confusing one-way traffic is mayhem, banishing all traces of an island paradise. Still, if one stares out to sea and forgets the commercial swirl behind, the legendary Kuta sunset – when the conditions are right – is just as beautiful as it was a century ago.

Crime has escalated, so don't get too starry-eyed and romantic on the beach at night. On 12 October 2002, bombs planted by Indonesian Muslim terrorists exploded at two packed nightclubs, killing more than 200 people, mostly foreign tourists. A memorial across the street from the bomb site at Sari Club opened in late 2002. The area was slowly recovering when three bombs exploded again barely three years later on 1 October 2005, one at a busy restaurant in Kuta Square and two on Jimbaran Beach. A further 20 people died in these attacks.

SHOPPING AT KUTA

Shopping options abound along Kuta's main street, **Jalan Legian**, and just about every side street all the way up to **Jalan Melasti**. At its southern end, near the Bemo Corner (Stasion Bemo) Jalan Legian-Jalan Raya Kuta intersection, you'll find the **Matahari Kuta Square**, a crowded, bustling shopping area centred around a department store, Matahari department store. Jalan Pantai Kuta and its slew of commerce then continues north, parallel to the beach, taking in the open-air Beachwalk Shopping Mall Center (https://beachwalkbali.com) with its eco-friendly design incorporating a wide choice of shops and restaurants, the digital-format **Cinema XXI**, and the **Museum Kain** displaying rare batik cloth, changing exhibitions and events.

LEGIAN

North of Jalan Melasti, the loud and obnoxious chaos of Kuta drops off perceptibly. The beach at **Legian** is the main centre of activity; although a bit more sedate than Kuta, don't expect it to be completely free of traffic and commercialism. This is the preferred beach for many of Bali's expatriate population, although increasingly, residents are turning to the charms of Seminyak beach. For an extreme adrenaline rush, **5GX Bali Reverse Bungy** is on Jalan Legian between Kuta and Legian opposite Sky Garden Rooftop Lounge.

   Jalan Legian is packed with opportunities to spend money. At the lower end are T-shirts and souvenirs, but nearing Seminyak, posh boutiques begin to appear. Do this on foot and stop for a cool beverage and a snack as necessary.

SEMINYAK

Further north is hip **Seminyak ⓖ**, blessed with a wide sandy beach and thundering surf to frolic in. This once

Surfboards for rent at Kuta. The waters here are among the best places to learn surfing, but it is believed that the god of the sea claims at least one victim each year. Women who live here leave canang (coconut leaf tray) offerings at the high-tide mark daily to pacify spirits.

Making lace in Seminyak.

◷ Tip

For maximum serenity, it's best to visit Pura Tanah Lot during the early morning hours. This way you'll avoid the hordes of tourists in search of the legendary sunset backdrop of the temple. In the evening, some strategically positioned cafés along the cliff top, just where the best sunset views are, charge inflated prices.

distant Kuta suburb is both the home of exclusive hotels like The Legian and The Oberoi Bali, and chic beach side restaurants like La Lucciola and Ku dé Dé Ta, both favoured by expats. Accommodation ranges from modern budget hotels to primarily top-range hotels and villas.

Seminyak's **Jalan Kayu Aya** (Laksmana) and **Jalan Abimanyu** (Dhyana Pura) are both action-packed streets: the former has a clutch of restaurants ranging from Italian to Japanese, together with a collection of enticing boutiques, while the latter is home to a string of live music bars, gay bars and clubs. A number of chic home furnishing and decor stores have also flourished along **Jalan Raya Seminyak,** in recent years, selling sell silk cushion covers, coconut-wood artefacts and lamps made of indigenous materials.

PURA PETITENGET

Basically a Seminyak suburb, the main point of interest in Petitenget is **Pura Dalem Petitenget** ⓰ (daily daylight hours; donation), a small but key temple by the beach where many ceremonies are held. It was built in honour of a visit by the 16th-century Javanese priest Danghyang Nirartha, who came to Bali to escape from the then encroaching Islam. He left his box of betel-chewing ingredients here, which explains the name, 'Temple of the Awesome Box'. During the late 1990s, a nearby sacred tree fell on the temple and damaged its structures, which had to be rebuilt. Although the temple looks new, it has a rather haunting atmosphere because of its lonely location.

KEROBOKAN

The main road does not run near the coast, so getting to places along the southwest shore is via long but paved access roads through rice fields. As development has crept further up along the coast, the next village in line becomes the scene for future speculation. **Kerobokan** ⓱ now has a growing number of fine restaurants, furniture and antique stores, lavish expatriate homes and exclusive villas for holiday rentals, with the added attraction of a rural atmosphere. Most villa rentals include the service of housekeepers, chefs and personal butlers.

CANGGU

Further up the coast are beaches at **Batubelig** and **Berawa**, followed by **Canggu** ⓲, a dark sand beach blessed with great ambience in what is becoming a fast developing area, favoured by expatriates, and presenting a wide choice of restaurants and cafés. It's also a popular surfing spot, now dominated by surf camps and surfing schools accompanied by the cafes and beer stops that wave-riders frequent. More beaches at **Batu Mejan**, **Pererenan** and **Selasih** in various stages of development stretch all the way up to Tanah Lot.

Football at sunset, Legian beach.

PURA TANAH LOT

Although located across the Badung border in the Tabanan Regency, (see page 191), **Pura Tanah Lot ⑲** (daily daylight hours) is more easily reached from south Bali. Located on a picturesque rocky islet just off-shore and with its shrines and tufts of foliage spilling over the cliffs, the temple is reminiscent of a Chinese painting. Sadly, the endless rows of souvenir stalls on the approach road diminish both the image and mood.

The founding of Pura Tanah Lot is attributed to the 16th-century high priest Danghyang Nirartha, who fled to Bali from Java to escape invading Islamic kingdoms. During his travels, he was attracted to a light emanating from a point on the west coast where he stopped and meditated. Villagers became entranced with Nirartha and began studying with him. However, a local leader became jealous and challenged the high priest. Unperturbed, Nirartha simply moved the place where he was meditating to the sea, thus giving its name – 'Temple of the Land in the Sea'. He tossed his sashes into the waves, where they were transformed into venomous sea snakes, which still dwell in caves located in the base of the temple. The sacred snakes are considered to be living guardians of the temple that prevent evil forces from trying to enter.

There are many other temples scattered around the area, among them **Pura Batu Bolong** (Temple of the Perforated Stone) that sits on a rocky outcropping with waves surging through a large opening below.

Visitors are not allowed into Pura Tanah Lot but can get a dramatic view of it from the opposite coast, especially at sunset (see margin tip).

Nearby **Pan Pacific Nirwana Bali Resort** has an excellent Greg Norman-designed golf course (open to the public), with spectacular views of rice fields, the ocean and Pura Tanah Lot.

From Tanah Lot, the beaches continue west to Tabanan (see page 191) and onwards into West Bali (see page 181).

Introduced to Asia by the Portuguese and Spanish, chillies are frequently planted between paddy fields. They range from plump and fiery to slender, milder ones, and appear in most typical Balinese dishes.

Pura Tanah Lot is a major tourist magnet.

📷 BALI BEACH ACTIVITIES

As well as surf, sand and sun, beaches offer impromptu shopping, outdoor massage and a variety of sports.

Bali's beaches are unfortunately not blessed with the archetypal white sands and gin-clear aquamarine waters that one associates with tropical island havens, in fact many of its beaches have black or grey sand due to the volcanic origins of the island. The only true white-sand beaches are the surf beaches on the south of the Bukit Peninsula, as well as Nusa Dua, Tanjung Benoa and Sanur.

The beaches at Kuta, Legian and Seminyak on the southwest coast have grey sand but make up for it with thundering surf, fabulous mango-streaked sunsets and a broad, flat expanse of shore that is perfect for long walks and sports such as volleyball, frisbee and soccer. They're a hive of activity, with people surfing, swimming and sunbathing while warding off the hawkers. At around four or five o'clock in the afternoon, especially on Sundays, Balinese families join the throng; their children paddle naked in the shallows and build sandcastles more reminiscent of miniature Taj Mahals than of Norman fortresses.

Sanur is bounded by a 5-km (3-mile) long shoreline within a gentle reef-sheltered lagoon. Swimming is safe off this golden-sand beach, and surfers can take a boat out to the nearby reef. Head to Tanjung Benoa for jet-skiing, water-skiing, windsurfing, wakeboarding, parasailing and Flying Fish – an experience involving a floating bed being dragged behind a speedboat, causing it to fly up in the air.

A dive instructor at Pulau Menjangan. The coral reefs around Pulau Menjangan in northwestern Bali teem with rich aquatic life.

Surfer on Kuta beach. The breaks and barrels off the south coast attract surfers from around the world.

Parasailing is a popular activity at Tanjung Benoa and Nusa Dua beaches. Not for the faint-hearted, 'fliers' take off and land on the beach strapped to a parachute and hooked to a speedboat, which pulls them into the air. Suitable for ages 10–65 (maximum weight 80 kg), either single or tandem flights can be arranged. Kids must fly with an instructor. Wind direction and weather conditions are closely observed before going aloft.

Sanur beach is popular with tourists due to the golden sand and lack of waves. The town is relaxed and offers an abundance of restaurants and accommodation options.

he beach at Tanjung Benoa – the slender peninsula that ts into the bay north of Nusa Dua – is the domain of ater sports operators.

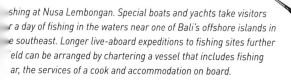

shing at Nusa Lembongan. Special boats and yachts take visitors r a day of fishing in the waters near one of Bali's offshore islands in e southeast. Longer live-aboard expeditions to fishing sites further eld can be arranged by chartering a vessel that includes fishing ar, the services of a cook and accommodation on board.

Holy spring at Pura Tirtha Empul, Tampaksiring.

UBUD AND SURROUNDINGS

Gianyar Regency, to which Ubud belongs, is Bali's undisputed cultural enclave. This is where to find artists' studios and galleries – together with lush rice fields, ornate temples and ancient historical sites. Ubud is where visitors gravitate to when they want to escape the tourist hordes of the south.

Driving northwards from Denpasar into Gianyar Regency, the cacophony of south Bali recedes a little, depending upon exactly where one is headed. Shrines and temples dot landscapes of verdant rice paddies, soothing one back to sanity. The richly cultural Gianyar region was home to ancient kingdoms, extending from the centre of Bali down to the southern coast.

Gianyar has given the island much of its reputation as a centre of creativity, born literally from the incredible fertility of its spring-fed, lava-enriched soil. With such bountiful harvests, the people had time to cultivate their artistic talents; the result is a high level of aesthetic excellence that extends even to the commercial arts and crafts industry. Ubud is one of Gianyar's main tourist centres and is easily accessible from all parts of the island.

DENPASAR TO UBUD

The roads leading to Ubud are lined with countless villages, once isolated but nowadays nearly indistinguishable from one another in the continual sprawl. Non-stop driving might take just over an hour from Denpasar, but doing so would be a great pity as many villages along the way specialise in some kind of art form and are usually worth lingering at.

A stone carver at work in Batubulan.

BATUBULAN

The first large village of note upon entering Gianyar Regency is **Batubulan** ❶ (Moonstone), stretching for about 2km (1 mile) and distinguishable from urban Denpasar only by the numerous *paras* stone-carving shops lining the road sides. *Paras* is composed of compressed clay and volcanic ash found in nearby ravines. It's so soft and porous that the tropical climate wears it down, making it necessary for temple carvings to be replaced every few decades. Men usually carve

 Main attractions
Taman Burung Bali Bird Park
Celuk
Ubud Market
Neka Art Museum
Monkey Forest
Herons roosting at Petulu
Tegallalang
Elephant Safari Park
Gunung Kawi
Pura Kehen at Bangli

Map on pages 126, 132

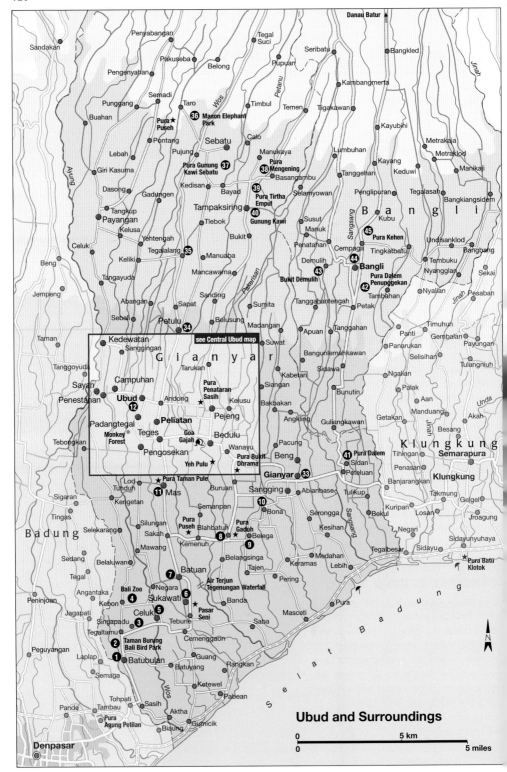

Ubud and Surroundings

0 — 5 km
0 — 5 miles

in groups, copying in stone what their ancestors carved before them, and increasingly, what appeals to visitors.

BALI BIRD PARK AND RIMBA REPTILE PARK

North of Batubulan is **Bali Bird Park** ❷ (tel: 0361-299 352; www.balibirdpark.com; daily 9am–5.30pm). Paved paths lead through landscaped gardens where more than 1,000 specimens of over 250 exotic bird species live in well-designed aviaries. It is dedicated to the protection of mostly Indonesian birds; the park was the first to breed the endangered *jalak putih* (white Bali starlings) in captivity.

Ticket includes entry to the adjacent **Rimba Reptile Park**, which is home to one of the biggest collections of rare reptiles and amphibians in Indonesia, all living among lush tropical gardens.

SINGAPADU

Continue about 1km (.5 mile) north on the main road and turn right at a T-junction into **Singapadu** ❸ (Fighting Lions) village. Numerous wood-and-stone

carving shops are interspersed among the houses, but the village is more famous for producing some of Bali's talented musicians and dancers. Take time to visit one or more woodcarvers while you're in the area.

BALI ZOO

Further along the road in Singapadu, on the left, is the family-friendly **Bali Zoo** ❹ (tel: 0361-294 357; www.bali-zoo.com; daily 9am–6pm). This 3.5-hectare (9-acre) landscaped zoo is where you will find birds and animals, including the beast after which Singapadu was named. *Singa* (lion) refers to the two royal brothers who *padu* (challenged) each other for the right to rule.

CELUK

From Singapadu, turn right at the T-junction and travel east to **Celuk** ❺ (Cove), synonymous with silver- and goldsmiths, and one of the wealthier villages in Bali. Shops along the way, less crowded and often cheaper than those along the main road, offer all kinds of sterling silver and gold

Batubulan is noted for performances of the Barong and Rangda dance. Tourists are brought in by bus from Ubud to see this dramatic struggle between good and evil.

Barong masks and costumes in the old royal palace, Puri Saren Agung, which hosts traditional dance performances nightly.

Tip

Bali Zoo has a lot more in store for visitors besides simply gazing at amazing animals. You can have breakfast with an orangutan, give an elephant a mud bath or experience nocturnal creatures at night. You can even opt for a package tour that includes a revitalisation treatment.

jewellery and decorative objects. Stop to have a look in the artisan workshops which are usually small and dimly lit rooms crowded with workers, some not even in their teens. The intricate details obtained from using simple hand tools are amazing. As with most Balinese crafts, silversmithing is largely an art passed down from one generation to the next.

SUKAWATI

From Celuk, head east, then north to **Sukawati** ❻ (Beautiful Joy), once the centre of a powerful kingdom during the 18th century. *Kain prada* cloth, gold-leafed by hand in the past, is silk-screened by the metre by Sukawati's villagers for costumes and shrines, and made into lovely temple parasols and dance fans. Look out for the road side shops selling these items.

Sukawati, however, is more famous for producing some of Bali's best *dalang* (puppeteers), who make their own *wayang kulit*, or leather puppets, delicately carved from thin cattle hide and then painted (see page 71). The

Shadow puppet in the making, Sukawati.

dalang's work is very complicated and it takes years to master the craft. A number of puppeteers live in **Banjar Babakan** neighbourhood behind the market.

Sukawati's **Pasar Seni (Art Market)** (daily 9am–7pm) is a big two-storey building at the centre of town. Although it is filled with hundreds of stalls selling every imaginable kind of arts and crafts, there is an equal number of vendors hawking clothing and knick-knacks outside, who can be aggressive. Items vary in quality, but all are much less expensive than at the larger art shops and even at stalls in Kuta. Bargaining is expected.

BATUAN

Another 1km (0.5 mile) north of the Sukawati market is **Batuan** ❼ (Boulder), where some of the finest *topeng* masked dancers (see page 68) in Bali live. This dance is an essential part of most religious events. Full of anecdotes and bawdy jokes, and depicting a wide range of different characters, a good dancer can completely engage onlookers.

A more modern dance with its roots in Batuan is the Frog Dance, performed by children wearing frog masks and costumes. It is usually done only for tourist shows at hotels. The music is a unique ensemble of jew's harps, reeds, flutes and drums.

Batuan is also known for its distinctive style of painting, which evolved in the 1930s. Using mainly black or dark green ink, Batuan painters fill their canvases with dense scenes drawn from everyday life – villagers, ceremonies and the supernatural. Quite often, modern and quirky elements are introduced into these traditional Balinese scenes, like surfers and long-nosed Western tourists pointing long camera lenses at everything.

Another of Batuan's attractions is the **Pura Puseh** (daily daylight hours; donation). The temple dates back to the 11th century and has many fine carvings. Regular performances of *gambuh* (see page 70) are held on the 1st and 15th of every month (7–9pm). Although efforts have been made to revive this dance form (there are fewer than a dozen remaining venues on the entire island), it is not popular among the Balinese because of its slow pace, archaic language that is not understood by many, and near absence of humour.

BLAHBATUH

After another 2km (1 mile) north up the main road to **Sakah**, turn right at the big, ugly statue of Brahmarare (Brahma as a Baby) to **Blahbatuh ⑧**. Here is the temple of **Pura Gaduh** (daily daylight hours; donation), associated with Kebo Iwo, the legendary giant from the 14th-century Bedulu kingdom. After entering the temple, have a look at the main gate's balustrades, with carvings of women performing some rather erotic acts with horses.

In a pavilion is a huge stone head said to be in the likeness of Kebo Iwo. According to legend, Gajah Mada, prime minister of the Javanese Majapahit kingdom, realised he couldn't conquer Bali as long as Kebo Iwo was alive. Gajah Mada then hatched a plan. Knowing the giant was a bachelor because no woman could match his size, Gajah Mada had a huge female puppet constructed with a warrior hidden inside to trick Kebo Iwo into thinking that she would become his wife. Gajah Mada told Kebo Iwo to dig a well for his future house, which the eager giant did with his bare hands in the porous limestone. When he was deep down inside, still unable to find water, Gajah Mada ordered his soldiers to fill in the hole, burying him alive. With his dying breath, Kebo Iwo swore that since he was covered with chalky white dust, he would return as a giant albino *kebo* (water buffalo), the animal in his name, and subjugate the Javanese for 300 years. The curse came

true with Dutch colonial rule of Java from the 17th to 20th centuries.

While in Blahbatuh make a stop to visit **Sidha Karya Gamelan Foundry** (tel: 0361-8942 798). Here, you can see men pump the bellows to fire up the heat for metal forging. Others use large mallets to hammer the heated bronze into the desired shapes for musical instruments. Instrument cases also are carved and gilded here. An entire *gamelan gong kebyar* (costing over US$10,000) may be purchased; orders must be placed far in advance.

BELEGA, BONA AND MAS

On the back road 1km (.5 mile) east from Blahbatuh is **Belega ⑨** village, where bamboo furniture of all sorts is produced. Another 1.5km (1 mile) northeast is **Bona ⑩**, which specialises in products woven from dried fan-palm leaves. Bona is also the place where the dramatic *kecak* dance was born (see page 70).

From Bona, continuing another 2km (1.25 miles) northeast will lead to **Gianyar** town, the capital of Gianyar

Batuan's delightful frog dance is mainly performed by children.

Dressed up for a temple festival in Ubud.

Gamelan gongs at the Sidha Karya Gamelan Foundry.

Belega is a centre for bamboo furniture production.

Regency. Otherwise, backtrack to the Brahmarare statue near Sakah and head north to **Mas** (Gold), best known for its intricate woodcarvings and masks. Today, Mas also hosts a large number of workshops producing teak furniture. A string of galleries and souvenir shops line Mas' main road and side alleys for the next 3km (2 miles). One of the best-known artists for new designs in masks here is **Ida Bagus Anom Suryawan** who has a woodcarving workshop and showroom, Astina Mask Gallery, along the main road (tel: 0813-3844 8444; 8am–6pm; www.balimaskmaking.com). He has carved masks for pantomimes as well as performance artists from all over the world and his distinctive yawning masks have been widely copied throughout the island.

On the west side of the main road near the main market in Mas is **Njana Tilem** Museum (tel: 0361-980 707; Mon 1pm–5pm, Tue–Sun 10am–5pm, closed Nyepi Day, fee). The late Ida Bagus Njana and his son Ida Bagus Tilem were two of Bali's most talented wood

sculptors. Many of their innovative and intricate pieces are on display along with a large collection of antique pieces.

Many of the inhabitants of Mas are *brahmana*, the priestly caste who trace their roots back to Danghyang Nirartha. This 16th-century Javanese high priest founded **Pura Taman Pule** (daily daylight hours; donation), located just beyond the field north of the market and named after the *pule* tree (*Alstonia scholaris*) which is used for making masks.

UBUD

The name **Ubud** comes from the Balinese word *ubad* (medicine) because of the healing properties of plants growing by the Campuhan River on the western end of town. Blessed with a picturesque location that inspired the arts, Campuhan village (now an extension of Ubud) became the adopted home of Western artists like Walter Spies and Rudolf Bonnet in the 1920s.

During the 1930s, together with a local nobleman named Cokorde Gede Agung Sukawati, they founded an artists' association known as Pitamaha (see page 78). This initiative inspired a renaissance, transforming the sleepy Campuhan village into a centre of artistic activity. The masses that followed in the ensuing decades naturally led to commercialisation, but the money from tourism has benefited the arts here.

A few minutes away from the main road souvenir outlets, art galleries, cafés and persistent dance performance ticket salesmen lies a gentler, calmer Ubud unaltered by the tourists zooming about on their rental scooters. However, this is fast disappearing: like Kuta in the south, neighbouring villages have lost some of their geographical distinctiveness to Ubud's expanding sprawl.

Bearing in mind the size of Ubud and its population of around 74,000, the vast range of accommodation and restaurants competing for the

attention of tourists – not to mention the rampant commerce – may seem overwhelming. Visitors hoping to escape the area entirely will do well to head for the surrounding villages – like Campuhan, Sayan, Peliatan or Pengosekan – which provide better opportunities for experiencing life in a Balinese village community.

Ubud's favourable location makes it an ideal base for excursions. Athletic types can visit some of the oldest temples on the island or explore the delights of the local countryside on foot or by rented bicycle. The area is crisscrossed by a network of narrow but mostly well-constructed roads, linking the many villages in the vicinity of Ubud with each other.

CENTRAL UBUD

The main east–west artery is **Jalan Raya Ubud**; the centre of town is where it intersects with the north–south **Monkey Forest Road** (Jalan Wana Wana). Most of the following sights can be covered by starting at the main market, Pasar Ubud, in the centre of town.

PASAR UBUD

Located at the crossroads of Jalan Raya Ubud and Monkey Forest Road is the main market, **Pasar Ubud (Ubud Market)** ⓭. The complex is a two-storey building, with an annex just to the right if facing it from Monkey Forest Road. At the back is a fresh produce market (daily 6am–2pm), while the side facing the main road is stocked with clothing, fabrics, handicrafts and souvenirs, and is aimed more at tourists (daily 9am–5pm). It's best to avoid shopping here when buses laden with tourists are here.

PURI SAREN AGUNG

Across the road from the market is **Puri Saren Agung (Ubud Palace)**, the palace of the royal family that ruled from the late 1800s until World War II. Most of the buildings were designed by

I Gusti Nyoman Lempad (1862–1978), Bali's most famous architect, artist and carver, and were erected following a devastating 1917 earthquake. There are 15 pavilions inside available for guests who want to experience life in a Balinese palace (Puri Saraswati Bungalows, tel: 0361-975 164; www.purisaraswatiubud.com). The front courtyard is open to the public during daylight hours, and traditional dance performances are held here every evening at 7.30pm; tickets are available at the courtyard reception desk in the afternoons. Be sure to dress modestly for palace performances. Just across the road is the unremarkable **Pura Desa**, which is the main place of worship for the people of Ubud.

PURA TAMAN SARASWATI

Back on Jalan Raya Ubud, turn right at the corner; next to the Lotus restaurant is a path leading to a large pond of pink lotuses. Behind the sculpted animals, out of whose mouths gush water, stands **Pura Taman Saraswati** (sarong and sashes are available on site), the

Statue at Puri Saren Agung, the former palace of the Ubud royal family.

Pasar Ubud (Ubud Market).

Batik scarves for sale at Ubud Market. Gianyar region has a major centre of batik textile production at Tampaksiring.

Lotus Garden Temple of Saraswati, the Hindu goddess of learning, knowledge and the arts. This architectural masterpiece was designed by Balinese architect and artist I Gusti Nyoman Lempad. Inside is an incredible stone throne to Saraswati carved by the master himself.

YAYASAN BINA WISATA

Close to the intersection along Jalan Raya Ubud is **Yayasan Bina Wisata** (Tourism Development Foundation; tel: 0361-973 284; daily 8am–8pm). Tasked with the job of preserving Ubud's natural and cultural beauty in the face of mass tourism, the foundation strives to unify the needs of both visitors and local people. Visitors are asked, for example, to respect the local ceremonies and wear traditional clothing when appropriate, and are encouraged to learn more about the special qualities of Ubud.

The multilingual staff are helpful in answering questions and planning journeys. A message board has details of performances and ceremonies in the area and tickets to dances can also be bought here.

THREADS OF LIFE

Around 100 metres west of the main Jalan Raya Ubud and Monkey Forest Road intersection heading north is **Jalan Kajeng**, a side street paved with blocks bearing the names of local people and places. Continue a little further up to the interesting **Threads of Life** (tel: 0361-972 187; www.threadsoflife.com; daily 10am–7pm) on the right, where beautiful natural dyed and handmade ikat textiles from throughout the archipelago are on display and for sale. The centre encourages traditional weaving skills using natural dyes and collaborates with expert weavers from 12 Indonesian islands. They also offer five-day workshops on fibre arts using natural dyes at their botanical garden and dye studio.

MUSEUM PURI LUKISAN

A short walk west of Pura Taman Saraswati is the **Museum Puri Lukisan ⑭** (tel: 0361-975 136; daily 9am–6pm). Descend

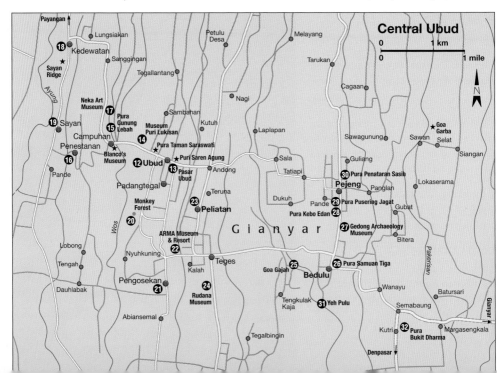

a long flight of stairs and up again to a peaceful setting of beautiful gardens and lotus pools. Opened in 1956 (and renovated in the mid-1990s), the excellent collection showcases the richness of traditional and modern Balinese art.

The main building features Balinese paintings and sculptures from the 1930s, including works by the Pitamaha artists and fine drawings by the great I Gusti Nyoman Lempad, whose fluid classical scenes gained him the most recognition.

A second gallery displays works by the Young Artists from the 1960s as well as traditional and contemporary paintings. A third building is mainly used for temporary exhibitions. Would-be purchasers of serious art will find this place a useful introduction to the principal genres of art practised in Bali. Some of the paintings on display are for sale.

NEKA ART GALLERY

Stay on the main road, Jalan Raya Ubud, and turn left (north) a few metres to the **Neka Art Gallery** (daily 8am–5pm; tel: 0316-975 034), one of the first to open in Ubud in 1967. Individual galleries feature the different styles of Balinese painting. Be sure to go up to the top floor where a special room displays works by the famous Dutch-born Indonesian artist Arie Smit; another section has contemporary Balinese and Indonesian paintings. All the works here are for sale, unlike in the associated Neka Art Museum (see page 134).

WEST FROM UBUD

Although some of these sights are within walking distance from the centre of town (on a cool day), the roads are narrow and congested with traffic. Your accommodation can hire a car with a driver for you.

CAMPUHAN AND PURA GUNUNG LEBAH

Jalan Raya Ubud, heading west from Ubud's main crossroads, leads to the **Campuhan River** (Confluence of Two Rivers) and **Campuhan** village, a spiritually powerful site. Just down a small

⊙ Tip

Ganesha Bookshop, at the corner of Jalan Raya Ubud, near the post office, has shelves jam-packed with an incredible range of books on Indonesian topics, music CDs and arts and crafts. Used books can be brought here and sold or exchanged for other things. It is open daily from 9am–6pm; tel: 0361-970 320; www.ganeshabooksbali.com).

Pura Taman Saraswati.

The entrance to Blanco Renaissance Museum.

road is the important **Pura Gunung Lebah** (daily daylight hours; donation) the Low Mountain Temple, dedicated to the goddess of Danau Batur. Extensively renovated during the early 1990s, this picturesque temple is believed to have been the 8th-century residence of the legendary Javanese priest Resi Markandeya. Several important purification rituals take place here, especially the bathing of sacred temple relics and the dispersing of ashes of the cremated dead.

BLANCO RENAISSANCE MUSEUM

The late Spanish artist Antonio Blanco (1911–99) built a garden home-studio with a towering *meru* (pagoda) at the top of a steep driveway on the left just after the short Campuhan Bridge. The flamboyant Blanco is most well-known for his rather erotic paintings of his favourite models: his Balinese wife and their daughter. Blanco was also a poet of sorts, and often combined verses into his visual art.

Just behind the home is the **Blanco Renaissance Museum** (tel: 0361-975

502; daily 9am–5pm; www.blancomuseum.com; fee). Adorned with gold painted statues and stained-glass windows, it displays many of his drawings and paintings.

PENESTANAN

Up a steep road just on the left is **Penestanan** . This area arose from obscurity when the Dutch-born Arie Smit, who lived and worked here as an artist, encouraged some local youths during the early 1960s to paint. With Smit's encouragement and freedom of choice on subject matter and style, the artists produced imaginative, naive-style scenes of village life and rituals that became eventually known as the Young Artists style. This genre uses oil paints thinned with turpentine for a matte effect, applied in flat, bright areas of colour with dark outlines. Lighting and shadow are absent, there is little perspective, sometimes no facial features, and decorative foliage dominates the scenes. Although there is no one main Young Artists studio in Penestanan, its streets are dotted with numerous galleries selling these works.

NEKA ART MUSEUM

Another 1km (.5 mile) further up the main road along Jalan Raya Sanggingan is the **Neka Art Museum** (tel: 0361-975 074; www.museumneka. com; Mon–Sat 9am–5pm, Sun noon–5pm; fee). Housing one of the finest collections of art on the island, it was founded in 1976 by former school teacher Suteja Neka, one of Indonesia's foremost art connoisseurs. The collection is housed within several Balinese-style buildings set amid gardens. Hundreds of artworks are chronologically displayed and well-documented with descriptive labels in English (and Japanese), providing an excellent background to the development of painting in Bali. The multilingual staff are both friendly and knowledgeable.

Lush gardens at Museum Puri Lukisan.

The Balinese Painting Hall contains Balinese works ranging from the classical narrative *wayang* (puppet) style to the Ubud and Batuan styles. The large Arie Smit Pavilion is devoted to the work of this Dutch-born artist along with works by his students of the Young Artists school, plus contemporary Balinese art in a wide range of styles.

Works by Indonesian artists, some of whom have lived in Bali, are displayed in the Contemporary Indonesian Art Hall, while the East-West Annex has works by foreign artists like Miguel Covarrubias, Rudolf Bonnet, Han Snel and Donald Friend. A special display features black-and-white photographs of Bali during the late 1930s and early 1940s, taken by Robert Koke, an American who built the first hotel on Kuta beach. The important Lempad Pavilion has one of the largest collections of drawings by I Gusti Nyoman Lempad, Bali's most renowned artist. Adding to the atmosphere are numerous traditional and modern sculptures in wood and metal scattered throughout the galleries and grounds.

Views from the open-air café are spectacular and overlook a lush river valley. The museum has an extensive research library, large bookstore and a gift shop. A wide selection of high-quality paintings are for sale at Neka Art Gallery (see page 133).

Door detail at the Neka Art Museum. The museum is one of Bali's finest in terms of quality of work. Try to visit before noon when bus loads of tourists take over the place.

KEDEWATAN, PAYANGAN AND SAYAN

From Sanggingan, the main road climbs some 3km (2 miles) north to **Kedewatan** ⓲ (Divine Place), a village blessed with outstanding views and sweet rambutan fruit trees. This area and **Payangan**, further north and more rural, is where you will find a clutch of ultra-expensive luxury resorts like Amandari, Alila Ubud and Como Shambhala Estate. Even if you can't afford to stay here, have a meal at any one of the hotels' highly rated restaurants and sneak in views of breathaking architecture.

South of Kedewatan is **Sayan** ⓳. This village hugs the edge of a beautiful gorge with the **Ayung River** tumbling through the valley below. The scenery

An odalan (temple festival) at Pura Gunung Lebah.

⏱ Tip

White-water rafting down the Ayung River is more exciting during the rainy season from Nov–Mar. The two best operators are **Sobek** (headquarters in Denpasar): tel 0361-729 016; www.bali sobek.com, and **Mason Adventure Tours**: tel: 0361-721 480; www.mason adventures.com.

here is some of Bali's most dramatic. One of the best ways to take in the area's stunning beauty is on a white-water trip down the Ayung River (see margin tip). The Canadian ethno-musicologist Colin McPhee (1900–64), who documented Balinese gamelan music, built his home here during the 1930s. A more modern intrusion is the lovely Four Seasons Sayan resort, with a reception area resembling a space pod.

SOUTH FROM UBUD

Monkey Forest Road (Jalan Wanara Wana), going south from the centre of town and all the way down to Pengo-sekan village, is an almost continuous stretch of shops, art galleries, restaurants, hotels and guesthouses. At the beginning of the 1980s, it was just a quiet village street, but now it demonstrates all too clearly the extent to which rapid development has taken a toll on the Ubud environment.

PONDOK PEKAK LIBRARY

Just down Monkey Forest Road on the east side of the football field is the

Macaques in Monkey Forest, regarded as sacred by the Balinese.

Pondok Pekak Library and Learning Centre (tel: 0361-976 194; daily 9am–9pm). For a small fee, users can borrow books from the only children's library in Bali and from a general section. There is a restaurant and a breezy upstairs reading room. Courses in Balinese art and culture are offered, and the centre also has a children's music and dance group staging regular performances, and a club for expatriate women.

MONKEY FOREST

Continuing your walk south will bring you to Ubud's well known **Monkey Forest ⓩ** (www.monkeyforestubud.com; daily 8.30am–6pm), best done early morning or late afternoon when the sun isn't so scorching. Follow a paved path in the forest and be sure to conceal your cameras, jewellery, keys, sunglasses or any other shiny object, for the mischievous and fearless macaques will snatch them and run off in a flash. The Balinese regard the monkeys as the sacred descendants of the monkey general Hanoman. Forest

guards are on hand to make sure the sacred forest is respected. It's best not to feed the monkeys as they can become aggressive.

Descending the steps into the forest, past the sacred *waringan* tree, you reach the cemetery and eerie **Pura Dalem Agung** (Great Temple of the Dead), dedicated to the goddess of death, Durga. She often takes the form of the widow-witch Rangda.

Nearby **Padangtegal** (Grassy Fields) village is home to many of Ubud's painters, and has a number of pleasant guesthouses fronting lush rice fields.

PENGOSEKAN

As Monkey Forest Road bends east, turn right at the Y-junction and head south to **Pengosekan ㉑**. Villagers here make beautiful baskets from dried *lontar* (fan-palm) leaves. The leaves are first buried in the ground to produce different shades of brown before being spirally plaited into traditional basket shapes. Pengosekan is also known for its particular style of painting, dense with birds, butterflies and blossoms.

ARMA MUSEUM & RESORT

At a T-junction in Pengosekan, turn left to the main entrance of the **ARMA Museum & Resort ㉒** (tel: 0361-976 659; www.armabali.com; daily 9am–6pm). Opened in 1996 by art dealer Anak Agung Rai, the grand buildings are set in landscaped grounds. The upper floor of the main gallery is dedicated to Balinese paintings, some of them from the 1930s.

The lower floor features classical *wayang* (puppet) style works from the early 1900s, antique textiles and contemporary Indonesian art. Labels are in English, Indonesian and Japanese.

Another building displays works by famous artists, including the only paintings on Bali by the Javanese Raden Saleh and the German Walter Spies. Paintings by other foreign-born artists who lived and worked in Bali

are shown too. The museum also promotes the performing arts with regular dance presentations and a children's gamelan music and dance group (check website for details).

PELIATAN

Continue west on the main road, and turn left to enter **Peliatan ㉓** village, which gained international fame for its *legong* dancers who took New York and Paris by storm while on tour during the 1950s. Today, the daughters of these performers, along with their cousins and friends, continue the tradition. The original dancers were all trained under the discerning and critical eyes and ears of the late Anak Agung Gede Mandera. For decades, Gung Kak, as he was affectionately called, groomed both dancers and musicians alike, and his legacy lives on today in Peliatan. One of the few all-women gamelan troupes *(gamelan wanita)* in Bali rehearses here; many of them are relatives of Gung Kak.

At the main crossroads, stop for a look at **Puri Agung Peliatan**, the palace

Woodcarving at the Rudana Museum.

Waiting to Dance (1983), by Abdul Aziz, at Neka Art Museum.

UBUD WALKS

If you're weary of crowds and yearn to get out to see some of the countryside for a bit, here are three easy walks that begin and end in central Ubud.

Setting off early in the morning or late afternoon when it's cooler is a good idea. Bring along a bottle of water, insect repellent, sunscreen and a hat.

CAMPUHAN RIDGE WALK

Easy to accomplish, the Campuhan Ridge walk is northwest of Jalan Ubud Raya. It's about a 2 km (1.25 mile) stretch of partially paved paths and roads that can be done in less than one hour unless you stop along the way for a snack to take in the views at one of the *warung* (food stalls) along the way.

The path begins at the Warwick Ibah Luxury Villas & Spa in the centre of Jalan Ubud Raya. There's a

Ducks in a rice paddy near Ubud.

sign there pointing to the ridge, so follow that path down some stairs that lead to Pura Gunung Lebah. After the temple veer off to the right and you're on the Campuhan Ridge Walk trail. While sauntering along you'll pass tree-dotted hills with the Campuhan River below, and rice fields toward the end of the trail. Turn around and retrace your steps to return to Ubud's main street.

KAJENG RICE FIELD WALK

This walk takes you through Kajeng village, past rice fields, guesthouses and art shops and, after passing a forested irrigation canal, loops back to Ubud. How long it takes depends on how many stops you make for a cool drink or a snack along the way. Less than two hours should be sufficient.

A logical beginning point is off Jalan Ubud Raya at Jalan Kajeng near Pura Taman Saraswati. Follow the signs to Sweet Orange Warung on Jalan Subak Juwuk Manis. (Side note: Sweet Orange is a good rest stop that features Balinese family recipes prepared with ingredients from the chef's own gardens.) Alternatively, if you've had enough for one day, at the fork that leads to Sweet Orange turn right instead of left and head back to Ubud. If you continue on Jalan Subak Juwuk Manis, it will lead you back to Jalan Raya Ubud.

JALAN SUBAK SOKWAYA WALK

This sojourn is an easy walk through rice fields with two excellent food choices. It takes only 15–20 minutes one way, but is rewarding for the fresh air and scenery.

From the Ubud Market, go west on Jalan Raya Bisma to Pura Dalem Ubud, then watch for signs to Sari Organik café. Turn into that steep road, which leads to the paddies. Amid amazing farm land is a large round building with a bamboo roof. That's Café Pomegranate, owned by two Japanese brothers who combined skills to create this little slice of heaven with good food and amazing sunsets. Keep going straight through the rice fields and you'll come upon Sark Organik, famed for its vegetarian and vegan cuisine. Sari Organik is open for breakfast if you need an excuse to start your walk early in the day. Bring a torch if planning to have dinner at either place as there are no lights to help you find your way back home.

of the royal family. The *kecak* dance is held in the front courtyard every Saturday night (6.45pm-8.15pm).

RUDANA MUSEUM

From Peliatan, continue south on the main Mas–Denpasar road to the **Rudana Museum** ㉔ (tel: 0361-975 779; daily 9am–5pm; fee). Opened in 1995, it is owned by Nyoman Rudana, a local politician and art enthusiast. There are over 400 pieces of fine art and sculpture exhibited here. Start at the top floor of this three-storey museum, which features works in the traditional Balinese styles. The first and the lower floors display works by well-known Indonesian contemporary artists, including a big display of exquisite wooden sculptures. Regular exhibitions are held here, with the biggest one in August to commemorate the museum's anniversary.

EAST OF UBUD

East of Ubud is a region heavy with ancient archaeological sites and old temples. The history and origins of some of these sites are vague, adding to their mystery. Most of them are concentrated in **Bedulu** and **Pejeng**, once the realm of Bali's earliest kingdom. Most of the sites can be done on a day trip out of Ubud, but pick and choose the ones that most interest you as there are too many to squeeze into a single day. Temples in each cluster are within walking distance of each other, but getting to some of those further away requires transport. Many small *warung* along the way sell snacks and bottled water, but eating places are almost non-existent here.

GOA GAJAH

Follow the main road south out of Ubud and head east towards Gianyar. Stop in Bedulu at the **Goa Gajah** ㉕ (Elephant Cave; daily 8am–5pm; fee), which is recognisable by the many stalls flogging cheap souvenirs to tourists on its approach road. Dating

back to the 11th century, reference to a Lwa Gajah (Elephant River) in Bali, the supposed dwelling place of a Buddhist priest, is made in a 14th-century Javanese court poem.

At the entrance of the cave are six large stone figures, spouting water from pots held at their bellies into two holy pools. The heads and torsos once stood in front of the cave before the bathing pools were excavated by Dutch archaeologist, J.C. Krijgsman in 1922.

To the left of the man-made cave is a 1,000-year-old statue of the demonic goddess Hariti, who once devoured children but later converted to Buddhism and became their protector. The Balinese call her Men Brayut, the woman who had 18 children. Villagers pray here to be blessed with offspring of their own.

Just above the cave entrance is a monstrous head with its hands appearing to push apart its fanged gaping mouth. The demonic face, with bulging eyes and large earplugs, is a Boma figure that frightens away evil. All around it are fantastically carved animals and humans running away in fear.

> **Tip**
>
> There are elements of both Hinduism and Buddhism found at Goa Gajah, derived from the 8th to the 14th centuries. The cave may be an early precursor of the Hindu-Buddhist character that to a large degree defines Bali today.

Pura Dalem Agung at Monkey Forest.

Tip

During the full moon in April or May, dozens of villages bring their deities to visit Pura Samuan Tiga during a 13-day temple festival. There are ceremonial dances, ritual battles with hundreds of devotees, and long processions of offerings.

The dark and musty interior contains several niches, which may have been sleeping places or meditation alcoves. At the left end of the T-shaped corridor is a four-armed statue of the elephant-headed god of obstacles, Ganesha, son of Siwa (Shiva). At the cave's right end are three *lingga* (phalluses), the attribute of Siwa, carved from a single block of stone.

Outside on the other side of the cave are a series of shrines, plus a small one in the middle of a pond fed by a holy spring. A flight of stairs by the towering *kepuh* (kapok) tree leads down to the river, where lie the remains of a Buddhist shrine carved in bas-relief and another meditation niche near a small bathing place. There were once a few seated Buddha statues; only a headless one remains as the other statues were stolen in 1992.

PURA SAMUAN TIGA

Continuing east, a left turn at the T-junction leads to **Pura Samuan Tiga** 26 (Tripartite Meeting Temple; daily daylight hours), one of the most important temples in Bali. In the late 10th century, the Balinese religion lacked cohesion. A number of separate sects were in constant conflict with each other, and so a meeting was held at this temple to merge the three elements of Shivaism, Buddhism and animism, which is still practised today. Pura Samuan Tiga was also the state temple of the Bedulu kingdom from the 9th to the 14th centuries.

Unusual among temples is the descent upon entering it. Built on terraces, the immense complex looks like a small village of gates, shrines and pavilions, most of which were refurbished during the mid 1990s. A trio of stone *meru* (pagodas) for the deities of the lakes, material wealth and sea are shaded by a huge banyan tree. Down by the river is a sacred spring.

GEDONG ARCHAEOLOGY MUSEUM

From Pura Samuan Tiga, head out west to the main road, turn right and go uphill about 500 metres to visit **Gedong Archaeology Museum** 27 (tel: 0361-942 354; Mon–Thu 8am–3pm; Fri 8am–noon). There are four buildings on this site which display megalithic and Bronze Age artefacts from all over Bali, including huge stone sarcophagi from 300 BC; look out for the turtle-shaped ones that were found in Bangli.

PURA KEBO EDAN

A little further uphill on the other side of the road towards Pejeng is **Pura Kebo Edan** 28 (Crazy Buffalo Temple; daily daylight hours; donation). Inside the temple is an engaging figure over 3 metres (10ft) tall. Restored in 1952, the Pejeng Giant, whose face is covered by a stone mask with horns and fangs, is depicted trampling on a wide-eyed and dead demon. More notable, however, is the giant's pierced penis, which swings to the left, a sign of the "left-handed" practices of the Tantric Bhairawa cult who used magical and perhaps even erotic practices in their worship of the Hindu god Siwa (Shiva) in his terrifying form.

Women taking offerings to the Pura Dalem Puri temple.

Everywhere around the temple are carved stone skulls, demons and the temple's namesake figures of water buffaloes with their heads crazily turned back on their bodies.

PURA PUSERING JAGAT

Further north on the main road, turn left at the next side road to the **Pura Pusering Jagat ㉙** (Navel of the World Temple; daily daylight hours; donation). Inside is a shallow oval pit in the ground, the 'navel' that gives rise to the temple's name. Offerings placed here are said to miraculously appear at Pura Penataran Agung Ped on the offshore island of Nusa Penida, home to Ratu Gede Mas Mecaling, the great fanged lord of supernatural forces. A cylindrical vessel called Naragiri (Mountain of Men) is carved with the story of the deities and demons churning the ocean of milk to produce the elixir of immortality. The reliefs are rather worn, but the vessel is sacred and miraculously produces holy water during the temple's anniversary ceremony during the full moon in July.

PURA PENATARAN SASIH

Another 100 metres north on the other side of the main road is **Pura Penataran Sasih ㉚** (State Temple of the Moon; daily daylight hours), which was the state temple of the ancient Pejeng kingdom from the 9th–14th centuries. The shrine contains many carvings from this time but the oldest and most impressive artefact is the **Moon of Pejeng**. This great 190cm (75in) bronze gong in the shape of an hourglass drum dates back to Indonesia's Bronze Age, which began in 300 BC. It is said to be the largest kettle gong in the world. The head is decorated with eight stylised faces and other motifs, indicating that the relic originated from the Dong Son culture, which was based in the Tonkin region of present-day northern Vietnam.

Legend has it that the gong was a wheel of the chariot that carried the moon on its nightly journey across the sky. One night, one of the wheels fell and landed in a tree. A thief was disturbed by the brilliant light, so he climbed up and urinated on it in the

Working on the Tegalalang rice terraces where the subak irrigation system is used.

The entrance to Goa Gajah.

Dyed cotton threads ready for weaving into endek fabric. Gianyar Regency is a major centre for this type of weaving.

Artefacts at Museum Purbakala.

hope of extinguishing it. The wheel exploded and lost its shine, and the thief lost his life from the blast. A piece of the base broke off when it fell to the ground. The gong is never sounded, even during the temple's anniversary ceremony in the full moon in February, which features beautiful offerings, sacred dances and ritual battles.

YEH PULU

Head back about 1km (.5 mile) south and then east along a paved path that goes through scenic rice fields to **Yeh Pulu** ③ (Rice Container Water Temple; daily daylight hours). Aside from a statue of the elephant-headed god Ganesha, the carvings in deep bas-relief show scenes from daily life. They begin with a *kakayonan*, the cosmic tree of life that is the first to appear in a *wayang kulit* (shadow puppetry) performance. Next to it is a man gesturing in welcome. Other scenes include that of a woman at her house, some men on horseback, a boar hunt, and a woman pulling at the tail of a horse with a rider.

Some scholars say that they tell the story of Kresna (or Krishna) as a youth, but this tale of the Hindu god was not known in Bali when the bas-reliefs were carved during the 14th century. Locals say the legendary giant Kebo Iwo carved them with his fingernails.

A small temple at the end has a holy spring with *yeh* (water) trickling out of a small stone shaped like a *pulu* (traditional rice storage bin) in the middle, thus explaining the name of the site.

PURA BUKIT DHARMA

On the main road past Bedulu to Gianyar, turn right at the **Semabaung** junction, marked by a statue of a goddess surrounded by snakes. Head south to **Kutri**, where on the left side is **Pura Bukit Dharma** ② (daily daylight hours; donation). After visiting the temple, climb up the forested hill for some nice views and to see an ancient stone figure of the multiple-armed goddess Durga slaying a buffalo demon. She is believed to represent the Javanese queen Mahendradatta, wife of the Balinese king Udayana.

TAMAN BALI, BANGLI

GIANYAR

From Bedulu, travel east along the main road to **Gianyar** ㉝ (New High Priest Residence). Once the capital of a kingdom, it is now an overgrown town and the administrative capital of Gianyar Regency. Wander around the market and commercial centre. Try some of Gianyar's famous *babi guling*, a plate of spicy roasted pork, crispy skin and blood sausage served with mounds of rice; not for those who keep tabs on their cholesterol levels. A night bazaar with local food and wares begins around 4pm in the parking area of the market.

The speciality of this area is the *endek* cloth (see page 77) that the Balinese use as part of their traditional temple attire. There are a number of factories that hold informal tours, and it's intriguing to watch the process of turning white threads through a complex dyeing process into patterns of vibrant colour.

At the centre of town is **Puri Agung Gianyar**, the palace of the local royalty. In the late 1800s, the Dutch saved Gianyar from attack by its hostile neighbours and made it a protected state. During Indonesia's war of independence from 1945–9, the royal family supported the Dutch. The palace is well maintained but not open to the public, so peer through the gates for some views.

NORTH FROM UBUD

Escape from the hustle and bustle of Ubud by heading north for scenes of natural beauty and the Tampasiring area, where a cluster of ancient temples is the main focus of interest.

PETULU

About 6km (4 miles) north of Ubud is **Petulu** ㉞. Every morning at dawn, huge flocks of *kokokan* (white **Javan pond herons** and **plumed egrets**) fly off in search of food and then noisily return to roost at sunset (around 6pm). Thousands of them cover the trees like snow and splatter the roadsides with their droppings, so view them from a safe distance. Locals say that the birds are manifestations of souls of people killed in the aftermath of the failed Communist coup against

The best place to see the kokokan, or white egrets, of Petulu is to bag a table at one of the nearby viewing stations, order a drink, sit back and watch the spectacle at sunset.

The Moon of Pejeng shrine at Pura Penataran Sasih.

Koi carp reside in the spring-fed pools at Pura Tirtha Empul.

Posing in front of one of Yeh Pulu's rock wall carvings.

the Indonesian government in Jakarta in 1965. Soon after some 100,000 people connected with the Jakarta coup were massacred in Bali, the egrets mysteriously appeared in Petulu in 1966. It's a spectacular sight, as the flocks of birds fill the sky before landing, squabbling over prime perches and turning the tree tops white. Village tradition dictates that the birds should not be disturbed during their roosting, but you can sit at a simple viewing platform, and drink cold Bintang beers or soft drinks as you watch.

TEGALALANG

Back on the main road, another 7km (4 miles) north in the wood carving village, **Tegalalang** ㉟ (Grass Fields), are pretty rice terraces worthy of a stop. A winding river valley is carved into steep embankments, and the long-stemmed *padi Bali* (indigenous Balinese rice) is grown here. Workshops and simple wholesale outlets line the road for 5km (3 miles), selling all sorts of wooden handicrafts and bamboo wind-chimes at half the price you'd pay in Kuta.

MASON ELEPHANT PARK

Continue north past Pujung to **Taro** where children will enjoy the family-friendly **Mason Elephant Park** ㊱ (tel: 0361-721 480; www,masonadventures. com; daily 9am–6pm; fee). The first elephants here were rescued from the effects of deforestation in Sumatra, and their breeding program has been successful. At the park, visitors are able to touch, hand feed and interact with these amazing creatures. Rides are offered, although animal welfare bodies strongly advise against encouraging these. The 27-room **Mason Elephant Lodge** at the park offers visitors the chance to interact more closely with the elephants through a longer stay (www.masonelephantlodge.com).

PURA GUNUNG KAWI SEBATU

Return on the road towards Pujung and turn left into **Sebatu** (One Stone), following it all the way to **Pura Gunung Kawi Sebatu** ㊲ (daily daylight hours). This picturesque temple, with colourful shrines and pavilions, is dedicated to the goddess of Lake Batur. Water cascades

down a cliff and fills a sacred pool with a shrine in the centre. In the front of the temple, the water gushes out from spouts into two pools that were previously used for bathing. Newer bathing pools (for men and women) have been constructed nearer the exit, and there is an extra charge to use these.

PURA MENGENING

The main road through Sebatu continues 3.5 km (2 miles) to **Tampaksiring**, the centre for intricate carvings in coconut shells and cattle bones. Filigreed designs of mythological figures, animals and plants are painstakingly cut into these fragile materials.

Continue across the main road, and nearby on the right is a side road that leads to **Pura Mengening** ❸ (daily daylight hours; donation), which has a holy spring to one side. A reconstructed stone *candi* (temple) similar to those found in central Java from the 9th century, dominates the inner sanctum. This may be the commemorative shrine of the 10th-century Balinese King Udayana.

PURA TIRTHA EMPUL

Further up the main road in Tampaksiring is another holy spring at **Pura Tirtha Empul** ❸ (daily daylight hours), bubbling up through black sand within a sacred enclosure inside. It is the source of the Pakerisan River. The Balinese believe that the spring was created by the Hindu god Indra, who pierced the earth to create *tirta* (holy water) in order to revive his soldiers who were poisoned by the demon king Mayadanawa. The temple was built during the 10th century, and the waters gushing through its many spouts are said to have magical curative powers. People often journey here from near and far to purify themselves in the pools after presenting a small offering to the spring's deity. Sacred Barong dance masks and costumes are also spiritually recharged here.

GUNUNG KAWI

Back on the main road and 1km (.5 mile) downhill, turn left and go east to the end of the small road. A very long flight of steep stone steps descends to the ancient site **Gunung Kawi** ❹ (daily

Pay heed to signage at all Balinese temples and shrines.

Rice terraces at Tegalalang.

Statue at Pura Kehen.

daylight hours), an amazing complex of rock-hewn *candi* (shrines) facades and monks' alcoves nestled in a scenic valley overlooking the Pakerisan River.

Dating back to the 11th century, the carvings are remarkably preserved royal memorials for members of Bali's Warmadewa dynasty. One theory holds that the main group of five *candi* across the river honours King Udayana, his queen, Mahendradatta, his concubine and his two sons. Another theory suggests that they honour Udayana's son Anak Wungsu, who ruled Bali during the 11th century, and his wives.

Next to these five monuments are a cluster of niches and rooms hewn out from solid rock. Footwear must be removed before you enter, so be careful of the rough ground. Just outside is a more usual type of Balinese temple with open-sided pavilions, shrines and carved gates. South of this temple is an isolated group of stone meditation alcoves.

Holy springs at Pura Tirtha Empul.

Four more *candi* on the west side of the river are for queens or royal concubines. A tenth one with monks' cells stands alone some distance away

through the rice terraces, and may have been for a high court official. Ask the vendors at souvenir shops lining the staircase for directions.

BANGLI

The road heading north from Gianyar town leads to **Bangli Regency**, a former kingdom founded in the 18th century by a prince from Klungkung in east Bali. From Bangli, it is possible to travel all the way north to Gunung Batur.

PURA DALEM SIDAN

Head east out of Gianyar and after 2km (1 mile) is the turn-off that leads to **Peteluan**. Go uphill and continue 1km (.5 mile) to the **Pura Dalem** ❹ (Temple of Death) at **Sidan**. The *kulkul* (wooden gong) tower is bedecked with bas-reliefs showing underworld demons punishing sinners. The carved gate is equally magnificent. Across the road are some nice views of rice terraces above a river valley.

PURA DALEM PENUNGGEKAN

Further uphill, you shortly come to a large stone gateway marking the

entrance to Bangli Regency. Continue for another 7km (4 miles) to a Y-junction. The left side goes uphill into Bangli town. Around 400 metres up on the right side, going out of town, is **Pura Dalem Penunggekan** ⓬; either walk to this Temple of Death from the road going into town, or visit it on your way out. The outer walls of the temple are carved with vivid scenes of sinners being punished in hell.

BUKIT DEMULIH

Continue further west and at a Y-junction veer left and follow the road, turning right at the crossroads to **Bukit Demulih** ⓭ (Hill of No Return). Be warned that it may take a while to find the right vantage point, but when you do it makes the 500-metre (1,600ft) climb well worth it: the view of central Bali from the top is superb. In fact it's all so peaceful and relaxing that you won't want to leave – as the name indicates.

BANGLI

The capital of **Bangli Regency** ⓮, which is also called **Bangli**, stretches out for over 3km (1.75 miles) and is a pleasant, laid-back mountain town with the towering *meru* (pagodas) of temples and palaces lining the main road. Take some time to explore the local market. Dried palm-leaf crafts are the speciality here.

PURA KEHEN

At the northern end of town, less than 1.5 km (1 mile) from the centre of Bangli, turn right at a T-junction and continue east to **Pura Kehen** ⓯, (daily daylight hours; donation), a 13th-century terraced mountain sanctuary and the state temple of Bangli. A long flight of stairs leads up to a towering gate. An enormous banyan tree with a hut for a *kulkul* (warning drum) below it shades the first courtyard, where the walls are inlaid with pieces of Chinese porcelain. The highest level has a 11-tiered *meru* (pagoda) to Siwa (Shiva) and an elaborately carved throne with three compartments for the Hindu trinity Brahma, Wisnu (Vishnu) and Siwa (Shiva). From here, the main road continues 15km (9 miles) uphill to **Gunung Batur volcano** and its adjacent lake.

The terraced mountain sanctuary at Pura Kehen.

GUNUNG BATUR AND SURROUNDINGS

Aboriginal Balinese known as the Bali Aga reside on the shore of Bali's largest freshwater lake, Danau Batur, located at the base of the active volcano Gunung Batur. On a clear day, the viewpoint at nearby Penelokan offers magnificent panoramas.

◎ Main attractions
Gunung Batur
Danau Batur
Penelokan
Batur Volcano Museum
Pura Ulun Danu Batur
Pura Puncak Penulisan

Map on page 149

As the road climbs steadily out of **Bangli** town, the terrain gradually changes from thick bamboo forests to open windswept slopes. Temperatures drop perceptibly and visibility is often reduced by dense mists that roll in during the late afternoon. Colourful fruit stalls line the final approach to the crater rim overlooking the active volcano **Gunung Batur ❶**. At 1,717 metres (5,600ft), the volcano sits in a vast caldera measuring 11km (7 miles) in diameter and 200 metres (600ft) in depth. Following a minor eruption in

2000, it sends out clouds of ash from time to time. Legend tells of Siwa (Shiva) dividing the mythological Hindu Mount Meru and placing the two halves in Bali as Agung and Batur. To the **southeast, Gunung Abang** towers at some 2,150 metres (7,065ft). It is best to visit this area before noon when the rolling mists descend.

At the foot of Gunung Batur lies **Danau Batur ❷**, Bali's largest freshwater lake measuring 7km (4 miles) long and 2km (1 mile) wide. Its depth has never been measured, but this is the source of the rivers and springs for the entire eastern half of Bali, and irrigates most of the island's fertile rice fields. Few people swim in the calm but chilly waters, although it's not forbidden.

PENELOKAN

The road uphill from Bangli finally emerges at Gunung Batur's crater rim at **Penelokan ❸** (Looking Place). Ribbons of black lava ripple down the sides of Gunung Batur, while Danau Batur resembles a blue or silver sheet of glass – depending on the time of day. The hawkers here can be aggressive and persistent. If arriving during daylight hours, note that entrance fees are charged for a vehicle and each passenger; this allows you access to the entire Gunung Batur

Worshippers making offerings at Pura Ulun Danu Batur.

area. Keep the tickets while travelling around the area and show them at checkpoints to avoid being charged again.

While here, you might like to visit **Batur Geopark Museum** ❹ (Jl Kintamani, Penelokan, tel: 0366-51186; Mon–Fri 8am–4pm; Sat–Sun 8am–2pm; fee), where you can learn all about the secrets and mysteries of volcanic phenomena through various panels, interactive games and computer simulations as well as three 20-minute film shows (for groups) in the theatre. Kids love it. The museum was opened after this region was accepted as a Unesco Global Geopark.

PURA ULUN DANU BATUR

Follow the main road 4km (2.5 miles) northwest along the crater rim to Bali's second most important temple after Pura Besakih, **Pura Ulun Danu Batur** ❺ (daily during daylight hours). This complex of more than 100 shrines sits on a spectacular and peaceful site overlooking the mountain and lake below. The rituals at this temple venerate Ida Betari Dewi Danu, the goddess

of Danau Batur, who blesses most of Bali with her water.

In 1917, Gunung Batur erupted violently and sent out powerful tremors, destroying thousands of homes and temples, and claiming more than 1,000 lives. Lava engulfed Songan village (see page 151) below the volcano but miraculously stopped at the foot of the temple at the northern end of the lake. The people took this as a good omen and continued to worship here.

In 1926, another eruption nearly buried the temple. This time, the villagers moved everything up to the crater rim and built the temple where it stands today. Towering gateways open into courtyards covered with black gravel. Rows of *meru* (pagodas) in the inner sanctum stand silhouetted against the open sky overlooking the crater. The main one in the middle is for the lake goddess; others flanking it are for deities of the mountains and royal houses.

KINTAMANI AND PENULISAN

Just beyond Pura Ulun Danu Batur lies **Kintamani** ❻ village. Inscriptions from

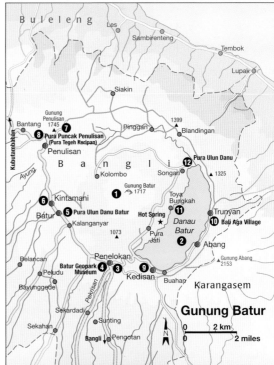

In 2019, Belgium-based Federation Cynologique Internationale listed the Kintamani dog, making it the first dog breed to be recognised internationally as native to Indonesia.

Effigy at Pura Ulun Danu Batur.

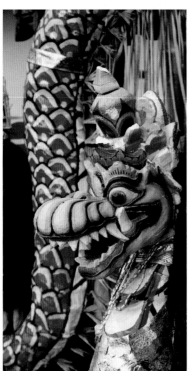

the 10th century indicate that this area was one of the earliest kingdoms. It is a rather plain town today, with hardly any evidence of its ancient glory. On every third morning (5–10am), the main street comes alive with a fresh produce market.

Continue 5km (3 miles) north along the main road to a forested area often enshrouded by clouds. On a clear day during the dry season (May–Oct), the vista from the viewpoint at **Gunung Penulisan** ❼, some 1,745 metres (5,780ft) high, takes in vistas of the northern coast, Lombok to the east, Nusa Penida island to the south, as well as Bali's three great mountains – Gunung Batur, Abang and Agung.

Closer to the road junction, a long flight of steps leads to **Pura Puncak Penulisan** ❽, also known as **Pura Tegeh Koripan** (daily during daylight hours). This is Bali's highest temple, a complex of terraced sacred sites. The sparse pavilions shelter sculptures of deities and royalty from the 11th to 15th centuries, including that of Batari Mandul, an 11th-century Chinese princess. If the clouds haven't descended

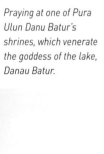

Praying at one of Pura Ulun Danu Batur's shrines, which venerate the goddess of the lake, Danau Batur.

yet, the views from here are incredible. For a different breath-taking sunrise, drive up to **Pinggan**, further east, for ethereal views, best between September and November when the morning fog places a haze over the village.

KEDISAN AND TRUNYAN

From Penelokan, a steep, winding road leads 3km (2 miles) downhill to **Kedisan** ❾, on the shore of Danau Batur where boats make the trip to **Trunyan** ❿, the Bali Aga (aboriginal Balinese) village known for its ancient ancestral rites. Trunyan is named after the *taru menyan* (fragrant tree) that grows in the nearby cemetery.

Departing from Balinese tradition, cremation is not practised at Trunyan; instead, the dead are left in open graves. There is no odour of decaying flesh due to the presence of the *taru menyan* tree, which produces a pleasant aroma, while its roots – beneath the bodies – bafflingly prevent putrefaction. If venturing to the shadowy *kubutan* or cemetery (situated about 500 metres outside the village, and accessible only

by boat), don't expect to see piles of dead bodies. Instead there are 11 open graves hidden by bamboo lattices. The most recent dead body replaces the oldest one, whose skull is cleaned and placed with others on a stone platform nearby. Secretive and protective of their customs, the villagers keep the 4-metre (13ft)-tall image of Dewa Ratu Gede Pancering Jagat hidden in a pagoda; tourists are forbidden to see it.

Proceed with caution if visiting Trunyan (there have been cases of boatmen wanting to renegotiate rates in the middle of the lake). Settle on a price for the boat from Kedisan to Trunyan, Kuban, Toya Bungkah and back to Kedisan.

Most visitors are discouraged by tales of touts demanding extortionate boat fares that increase halfway across the lake. However, the village is now accessible by a narrow, winding and incredibly-steep road; it is possible to negotiate the road by car but probably safer by *ojek* (motorcycle taxi), which can be arranged in Toya Bungkah. Be prepared to pay a steep donation of anything up to Rp 600,000 to the head of the village.

TOYA BUNGKAH

If skipping Trunyan, travel from Kedisan by the winding 7km (4-mile) road past an arid landscape strewn with massive lava boulders to **Toya Bungkah ⑪**, on the west bank of Danau Batur. (Watch out for trucks carrying sand and gravel.) Toya Bungkah is known for its hot springs, said to be imbued with medicinal properties. The free public bathing pools are divided into two sections, one specifically built for tourists encased by a wall. Alternately, take advantage of the pristine hot springs at **Toya Devasya Resort & Spa** (tel: 0819-3309 4796, https://toyadevasya.com).

PURA ULUN DANU

At the northern end of Danau Batur at **Songan** is the original **Pura Ulun Danu ⑫**, nearly engulfed by lava in 1926 but later rebuilt on the same site. Legend tells of a deity here who meditated underground and caused a great flood. The villagers prayed for the water to be channelled underground and it did so, eventually emerging again as the source of Danau Batur.

A shrine at Pura Tegeh Koripan - Bali's highest temple.

Capturing the sunrise from Batur mountain.

Seaweed farmers at sunset over Jungutbatu Bay, Nusa Lembongan island.

EAST BALI

In the Balinese world view, the east is an auspicious direction. Not surprisingly, Bali's pre-eminent temple, Pura Besakih, is here. Vestiges of former grandeur – such as the palace remnants at Taman Gili – remain, and there are startling black-sand beaches with hundreds of fishing outriggers moored onshore.

Neither as developed nor as rich as the southern part of the island, the eastern side of Bali has a different ambience, defined by its lava-strewn landscapes and high, bare hills ribbed with ancient rice terraces. Partly hidden by the eastern coastal ranges is the colossal cone of the active volcano **Gunung Agung**, which at 3,014 metres (9,796ft) high, dominates this drier, sparser side of Bali. The coastal strip along the eastern shore, lined with fishing and salt-producing villages and black-sand beaches, has become a tourist destination in its own right. Unfortunately, the gathering of coral to make lime for local construction has irreparably damaged some of the reefs and led to the erosion of many beaches, however diving is excellent further from shore. Further inland, a few villages, set in lush valleys, still retain their archaic traditions.

PURA BESAKIH

The access point to Pura Besakih is via **Menanga**. From here, follow the road another 5km (3 miles) as it ascends to **Pura Besakih** ① (daily daylight hours; www.besakihbali.com; donation). This is Bali's largest and most important place of worship, often referred to as the 'Mother Temple'. Opinions are divided on whether it's worth visiting, mainly because of the overt commerce (there are souvenir shops and

persistent vendors everywhere) and the hard-sell tactics of the 'official guides' (see margin tip page 155).

Pura Besakih began as an ancient terraced mountain sanctuary as early as the 8th century AD. Over time it was enlarged, until it grew to its present size of more than 80 public and one main temple with hundreds of shrines, most of which were added between the 14th and 18th centuries. From the 5th to the 17th centuries, Pura Besakih became the state sanctuary of the Gelgel dynasty. Today, the temple is

◎ Main attractions
Pura Besakih
Taman Gili
Nusa Lembongan
Tenganan
Pasir Putih Beach
Taman Ujung
Taman Tirtagangga
Pura Lempuyang
Amed
Tulamben Marine Reserve

Map on page 154

Visiting Pura Besakih.

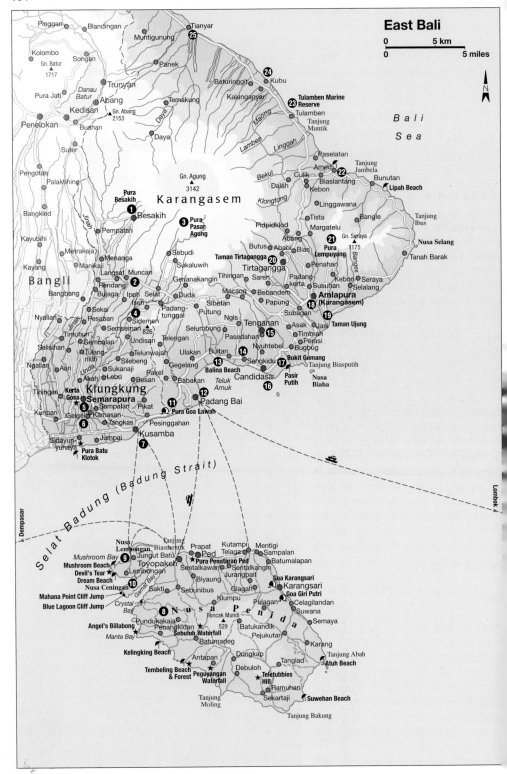

East Bali

Pinggan
Blandingan
Muntigunung
Tianyar
25
Kolombo
Gn. Batur
1717
Songan
Panek
Danau
Batur
Trunyan
Baturinggit
Kubu
24
Pura Jati
Kedisan
Abang
Temakung
Kalanganyar
23 Tulamben Marine
Reserve
Penelokan
Buahan
Gn. Abang
2153
Daya
Tulamben
Tanjung
Muntik

B a l i
S e a

Suter
Daya
Raselatan
Pengotan
Palaktihing
Jinah
Amed **22**
Tanjung
Jambela
Metrakaja
Pura
Besakih
Besakih
1
3 Pura
Pasar
Agung
Bekul
Culik
Biaslantang
Kebon
Bunutan
Lipah Beach
Bangkled
Pempatan
Linggawana
Kayubihi
Kayang
Menanga
Manikaji
Langsat Muncan
Sebudi
Sukaluwih
Butus
Pidpidklod
Ababi
Bias
Tista
Margatelu
Bangle
Tanjung
Ibus
Bangli
Rendang
Bujaga Ipah
2
Selat
Isen
Gerianakangin
Saren
Tirtagangga
20
Padang
kerta
21 Pura
Lempuyang
Gn. Seraya
1175
Nusa Selang
Bangbang
Sekai
Pesaban
Duda
Sibetan
Macang
Bebandem
Papung
Susuhan
Kebon
Seraya
Selalang
Tanah Barak
Nyalian
Timuhun
Semseman
Sidemen
826
Padang-
tunggal
Putung
Ngis
Selumbung
Pasedahan
Nyuhtebel
Subagan
18 **Amlapura**
(Karangasem)
Jasi
Kebon
Selalang
Perasi
Selisihan
Gembalan
Tulang-
niuh
Undisan
Telunwajah
Telengan
Tenganan
15
Asak
Timbrah
19 Taman Ujung
Ngalian
Aan
Sukanaji
Lebu
Pakel
Gegelang
Ulakan
Buitan
14
Sengkidu
Bugbug
Bukit Gumang
17
Tanjung Biasputih
Thingan
Akah
Besan
Babakan
13
Balina Beach
Teluk
Amuk
Candidasa
Pasir
Putih
Nusa
Biaha
Kerta
Gosa
Klungkung
Semarapura
5
Sampalan
Pikat
16
Kwripan
Gelgel
Kamasan
6
Tangkas
Pesinggahan
Padang Bai
11
12
Pura Goa Lawah
Sidayun-
yuhaya
Jumpai
Kusamba
7
Pura Batu
Klotok

Selat Badung (Badung Strait)

Dempasar
Lombok

Nusa
Lembongan
Tanjung
Biasmentik
Prapat
Kutampi
Mentigi
Mushroom Bay
Mushroom Beach
Devil's Tear
Dream Beach
Jungut Batu
Toyopakeh
9
Ped
Pura Penataran Ped
Sentalkawan
Sentalkangin
Telaga
Sampalan
Batumalapan
Nusa Ceningan
10
Lembongan
Biyaung
Jurangpait
Glagah
Klumpu
Klumpu
Sakti
Sebunibus
Ganaf Bay
Goa Karangsari
Karangsari
Goa Giri Putri
Mahana Point Cliff Jump
Blue Lagoon Cliff Jump
Crystal
Bay
Pulagan
Celagilandan
Suwana
8 *N u s a   P e n i d a*
Puncak Mundi
529
Batukandik
Pejukutan
Semaya
Angel's Billabong
Pundukakaja
Penangkidan
Sebuluh Waterfall
Batumadeg
Karang
Manta Bay
Dungkap
Tanglad
Tanjung Abah
Atuh Beach
Kelingking Beach
Antapan
Debuloh
Tembeling Beach
& Forest
Peguyangan
Waterfall
Teletubbies
Hill
Ramuhan
Suwehan Beach
Tanjung
Moling
Sekartaji
Tanjung Bakung

overseen by the descendants of the Klungkung royal family who are direct heirs of the Gelgel kingdom.

In 1917, Pura Besakih was almost levelled by a massive earthquake and was rebuilt. In 1963, however, the temple miraculously suffered minimal damage during the eruption of Gunung Agung (see box below), even though it is located only 6km (4 miles) from the crater.

PURA PENATARAN AGUNG

Within the complex is the all-important **Pura Penataran Agung**, built on a series of terraces. A long flight of steps leads to an austere *candi bentar* (split gate) made of granite. The setting is magnificent, with Gunung Agung's peak looming overhead and panoramic views of south Bali below. Non-worshippers are not allowed into the temple even if properly dressed, but you can see the inner sanctum through the gates or by walking around the complex and peering over the walls.

Inside the main courtyard, which interestingly is not the highest one, is a large *padmasana tiga* (triple lotus shrine) of dark volcanic stone with three high seats on a single base for enthroning three aspects of the supreme god: Siwa, Sadasiwa and Paramasiwa. Many Balinese interpret this shrine as the more familiar Hindu trinity of Brahma, Wisnu (Vishnu), and Siwa (Shiva). The other temples that make up Pura Besakih are not worth seeing, although each one has a symbolic importance.

The main festival at Pura Besakih, Batara Turun Kabeh, when 'the gods descend together', takes place during the full moon in March or April. Thousands of worshippers come by bus and truck loads from all over Bali during this 11-day event.

MUNCAN

Back on the main road and 2km (1 mile) downhill from Menanga, turn left at the T-junction in **Rendang** village to **Muncan ❷**. Follow the road as it winds 4km (2.5 miles) east through spectacular rice terraces. On the eve of the lunar-solar New Year in March, a special ceremony takes place in Muncan, when two large male and female figures fashioned from

Woman weaving songket, Sideman.

⊙ APPEASING THE GODS

In 1963, devotees at Pura Besakih were preparing for Eka Dasa Rudra, the greatest sacrifice that occurs only once every 100 years, when Gunung Agung began to rumble to life after over 120 years of being dormant. This was seen as a good sign, and activities continued. By the time the ceremony took place in March, thick columns of dark smoke were rising from the summit. Shortly after, Agung exploded violently. More than 1,600 people were killed and 100,000 were left homeless, most losing their livelihoods as entire villages were engulfed. To most Balinese, the eruption was punishment for doing the ritual at the wrong time. In 1979, a properly timed ceremony to mark the end of a Balinese century went without incident.

⊘ Tip

The easier way to climb up Gunung Agung is from Pura Pasar Agung, since the temple is already halfway up the slopes. This approach, however, does not reach the peak, which can only be done by a very difficult hike from Pura Besakih. Either way you should hire the services of a guide.

special trees enact an ancient fertility rite with a simulated public mating. Afterwards, the figures are thrown into the river; it is believed that using the river water to irrigate the rice fields will result in bountiful harvests.

PURA PASAR AGUNG

Some 4km (2.5 miles) east of Muncan, in **Selat**, a paved road winds 12km (7.5 miles) uphill through **Sebudi** and lava fields to **Pura Pasar Agung** ❸ (daily daylight hours; donation). This is the start point of one of the trekking routes up the mountain. Completely destroyed during the 1963 eruption of Gunung Agung (see box), the temple was rebuilt and expanded during the late 1990s. Located at the top of a long flight of stairs, the setting is spectacular with the summit of Agung up close and stunning panoramas of east Bali peeking out from the clouds below. Inside is a triple lotus shrine similar to the one found at Pura Besakih.

SIDEMEN

Back on the main road, just 1.5km (1 mile) west at **Duda,** turn south and

Pura Besakih – the long flight of steps leading to the granite split gate.

follow the road as it winds 12km (7.5 miles) downhill through scenic rice fields to **Sidemen** ❹. Travellers who miss the Ubud of the past before commercialisation set in have discovered this haven away from the madding crowds. Still idyllic, Sideman is an excellent base for exploring east Bali.

On one road outside the main village is accommodation – most of which are new – ranging from simple homestays to the luxurious, with other lodgings scattered elsewhere. If feeling lethargic – and rightly so – there is plenty to do in the village, such as cooking, silversmith, yoga, or meditation classes or strolling through paddy fields or forests. If hand-woven textiles are of interest, ladies weaving songket (traditionally, gold or silver thread brocade) and endek (weft-ikat cloth) are happy to demonstrate their skills. There are other centres for weavings in nearby villages. Simply ask where you're staying for schedules and guide recommendations.

SEMARAPURA (KLUNGKUNG)

About 11 km (7 miles) downhill from Sideman, follow the road into **Semarapura** ❺, the capital of **Klungkung** Regency.

During the late 17th century, the Gelgel kingdom, based in present-day **Gelgel** town (see page 158), lost a series of battles and allegiances. One of the king's ministers revolted and put himself on the throne, and a long battle ensued to regain it. In 1710, a new court was built at Klungkung because the old site at Gelgel was considered cursed. As the seat of the Dewa Agung, the highest of the Balinese kings, Klungkung Regency holds a special place in the island's history and culture; many of Klungkung's kings and noblemen supported and developed styles of music, drama and art that flourish today in Bali.

Just east of the main crossroads in Semarapura is the shopping area.

Explore the handful of antique shops on the main street and the multistorey **Pasar Klungkung** market (daily 6am–6pm) at the back for local items and wares. Towering over the town centre is the **Puputan Klungkung Monument**. This sombre black stone tower commemorates the massacre of the Klungkung royal family by the Dutch in 1908.

KLUNGKUNG PALACE COMPLEX

Today, the remains of the old palace are found across the street within the grounds of **Puri Agung Semarapura** (Semarapura Royal Palace) (daily 9am–5pm) grounds. **Bale Kerta Gosa** (Pavilion of Peace and Prosperity) to the right of the main entrance has exquisite examples of painting and architecture in the traditional Kamasan style.

In this Hall of Justice, different animal-headed armrests on the chairs indicate that the king (lion), his priests (bulls) and advisers (serpents) met here to consult on affairs of the realm. The ceiling paintings, arranged in several tiers, are in the Kamasan *wayang* (puppet figure) style, named after the village where artists still paint such works (see page 158).

Reading from bottom to top and going clockwise, they tell the story of *Bima Swarga* (Heavenly Bima) from the *Mahabharata* epic. The hero Bima searches for the souls of his parents in the underworld, battling first with demons and the god of hell, and then against the heavenly deities to allow their souls to enter paradise. Other levels show the *Tantri* animal fables, the story of the mythological Garuda bird, events caused by earthquakes, and the grisly punishments that await sinners in hell.

The adjacent **Bale Kambang** (Floating Pavilion), built in the middle of a pond, was used by the royal family as a place to rest and be entertained. The ceiling paintings show Balinese astrological signs along with the Buddhist tales of the Men Brayut family, with 18 children, and the bodhisattva *Sutasoma* battling demons.

SEMARAJAYA MUSEUM

On the left-hand side of the complex stands the red-brick gate of the **former palace**, now fenced-off as a shrine. According to local lore, the palace doors mysteriously sealed shut by themselves after the royal family was massacred, and no one has dared to open them since. Look for figures of Chinese, Portuguese and Dutch figures scrambling up the sides of the gate.

At the back of the grounds lies **Semarajaya Museum** containing artefacts of the Klungkung region such as old photos of the former court, and paintings and sculptures by the Italian artist Emilio Ambron (1905–96), who lived and worked in Bali during the 1930s.

TIHINGAN

Head 2.5km (1.5 miles) west out of town on the main road to the interesting

At the base of the Puputan Klungkung Monument are some statues of the Klungkung royal family who were massacred by the Dutch in 1908.

Bale Kambang, the "floating pavilion".

gamelan-making village, **Tihingan** (Bamboo). Families in this village keep furnaces burning to melt bronze for the keys and kettles of Balinese gamelan musical instruments. Go during the cooler morning hours when most of the work is done at the small foundries located behind homes. Listen out for rhythmic pounding – although as forging is not done every day, it's mainly a matter of being there at the right time. The wooden instrument cases which hold the gamelan keys are also carved and gilded here.

NYOMAN GUNARSA MUSEUM

From the Tihingan crossroads, head 2.5km (1.5 miles) downhill to the **Museum Seni Lukis Klasik** (Nyoman Gunarsa Museum) (tel: 0366-22256; daily 9am–4pm). The three-storey building houses a collection of traditional Balinese paintings, masks (look out for the giant Barong image), carvings and other antiques, including contemporary semi-abstract works by the late I Nyoman Gunarsa, founder of the museum (who hailed

A Kamasan-style painting.

from Semarapura) and other modern Balinese artists.

KAMASAN

About 2km (1 mile) south of Semarapura is **Kamasan**, where artists use natural pigments to illustrate episodes from Indian-Hindu epics, Javanese-Balinese romances, legends, and astrological and agricultural charts in the wayang (puppet-figure) style featured in Klunkung Palace buildings. Workshops are found along the main street; although Kamasan-style paintings are sold all over Bali, better quality works are found here at lower prices. One of the leading practitioners of this art form, I Nyoman Mandra, still lives in Kamasan.

Be sure to stop by the the school that he curates to see some fine examples of Kamasan painting. The school also holds classes in painting, dance and gamelan playing.

GELGEL

Just south of Kamasan is **Gelgel ❻** (pronounced ghell-ghell), the former

capital of the Klungkung dynasty. In the late 1400s and 1500s, the Balinese kings here wielded immense power during the golden age of art, culture and religion. Today there is little evidence of its former glory; the town feels more Islamic in character and is dominated by a large mosque. Exquisite handwoven *songket* (brocade with gold or silver threads) and *endek* (weft-ikat cloth) are made in many homes in Gelgel.

Gelgel's **Pura Dasar Bhuana** (daily daylight hours; donation) is a large and important temple for members of the *pasek* commoner clans. The temple has ancient megalithic stone seats and rows of beautiful *meru* (pagodas) built in the local style. During the full moon in October, dozens of villagers come here to take part in an extremely colourful temple ceremony.

KUSAMBA

Leave Semarapura town and head towards the coast at **Kusamba** ❼ where numerous colourful *jukung* or fishing outriggers with painted faces line the black-sand shores of its beach.

Apart from fishing, salt production is the other main activity in this region, evidenced by the thatched huts and wooden troughs lined up along isolated stretches of the beach near Kusamba and sections of the north-eastern coast around Amed and Tianyar. To produce salt, villagers splash seawater onto plots of sand, a process repeated many times. The dense salt-infused sand is then placed in conical wooden vats in the thatched huts and seawater is poured over it. Concentrated salt water filters into pots, and is then poured into long wooden troughs outside to partially evaporate into sludge. The wet crystals are then scooped into bamboo baskets to let the liquid drain out, then and left to dry completely.

NUSA PENIDA

Across from Kusamba to the south-east lie three sparsely populated islands which can be accessed by boat from Kusamba and Padang Bai or from Sanur and Benoa harbour in the south. The largest of the islands is **Nusa Penida** ❽ which covers 240 sq km (95 sq miles) and has a population of roughly 48,000 fishermen and seaweed farmers.

Originally a penal colony for the Klungkung kingdom on the mainland, Nusa Penida is dry and austere. Many of its inhabitants are considered to be experts in black magic, for this is the home of the great fanged lord of supernatural forces, Ratu Gede Mas Mecaling.

Nusa Penida's lack of development and diverse landscapes attract adventurous souls willing to gear down to a slower pace over unimproved roads. Day-trippers scramble up rugged hills to absorb amazing scenery, but truly experiencing the island takes more than a day. With several choices of accommodations, overnighting is recommended.

Boats from Nusa Lembongan drop passengers off at **Toyopakeh** in the

Producing sea salt near Kusamba.

Pura Segara, part of Pura Penataran Ped complex, Nusa Penida Island.

Seaweed cultivation and porters at Jungutbatu Bay, Nusa Lembongan.

north, where rental vehicles with drivers can be hired. Past **Sampalan** to the east, continue down the coast to **Goa Giri Putri** (Cave of the Mountain Princess) dedicated to Parwati, consort of Siwa (Shiva). Guides with pressure lamps wait at a small temple near the mouth of the cave. After a short but steep descent down a tiny opening with a low ceiling, the cave opens up to 15 metres (50ft) in height, where sunlight shines through a large opening. Be aware that this is a holy place and show the proper respect.Continuing south along the coast there are a series of beaches and viewpoints, some requiring great effort to ascend for spectacular panoramas – such as towering cliffs at **Atuh Beach** and crystal clear azure water reached via a steep staircase down to the sea at **Suwehan Beach**.Rounding the point there's more to see. Stop at **Teletubbies Hill** for unique cone shaped mounds, followed by a steep up and down climb on blue stairs to a pilgrimage temple and cascading pools that flow into the sea at **Peguyangan Waterfall**.

Expect to see a lot of tourists photographing a rocky outcropping resembling a Tyrannosaurus Rex at **Kelingking Beach**, but relief is nearby. At **Tembeling Beach** there is a patch of forest housing spring water pools used by Balinese-Hindus for ritualistic cleansings. You're welcome to take a dip in this isolated location remembering that the large pool is for men and the smaller one exclusively for women.

Manta Bay, further west is a prime snorkelling spot with a chance to swim with manta rays year-round. Then continue on to **Angel's Billabong**. If you're there at low tide a dip in the amazingly clear pools will reveal stunning topography below. Round out your sojourn with a snorkel or dive at **Gamat Bay**.

NUSA LEMBONGAN

Although much smaller at 10 sq km (4 sq miles), **Nusa Lembongan** ⑨, has attracted more visitors than its sister island in the past thanks to hard-core surf breaks going by names such as Shipwreck, Lacerations and

Playground. The long white-sand stretch of beach at **Jungut Batu** have long been a surfer haven and there is budget accommodation here. South of Jungut Batu at **The Bukit**, resorts and villas have appeared.

Mushroom Bay along the western coast is ringed with cosy guesthouses and boutique resorts, ideal for family stays, while beach clubs offer snorkelling and diving facilities for day trippers arriving on catamarans from Tanjong Benoa. Further south at **Sandy Bay** are deluxe resorts and fabulous sunsets.

Apart from diving, for which the waters around these islands are renowned, there is also a lively surf scene along the south coast at **Dream Beach** during the dry season and cliff jumping at **Devil's Tears**. Visitors can travel around the island (which is small enough to be covered on foot or mountain bike) to seaweed farms and mangrove swamps.

NUSA CENINGAN

East of Lembongan village, a 1km (.5-mile) suspension bridge, connects to the smallest island in the group, **Nusa Ceningan** ❿. Explorations of the major sites can be done in a day on foot. Of interest in the south are **Mahana Point**, a popular surf break, followed by the almost-empty **Secret Point Beach** and its shallow reef running the length of the beach. **Blue Lagoon** is an adrenaline junkie spot where the highlight is cliff jumping. Round out the day with a snack and an exhilarating zipline ride at **Driftwood Bar and Zipline**.

PURA GOA LAWAH

Back on the mainland, about 2.5km (1.5 miles) east of Kusamba is the 11th century bat cave temple **Pura Goa Lawah** ⓫ (daily daylight hours). Be forewarned that the hawkers here are extremely pushy. The walls of the cave literally vibrate with thousands of bats – their bodies packed so close together that the upper surface of the cave resembles undulating mud. Occasionally a python, believed to be a manifestation of the mythological underworld serpent Basuki, appears and feeds on

Interior of the Goa Giri Putri temple.

⏱ Tip

It's difficult to predict Tenganan's Usaba Sambah festival dates, but it is usually held at full moon in June or July. A similar but smaller festival occurs at the same time in neighbouring Tenganan Dauh Tukad village.

them. In 2004, one snake died and was respectfully cremated.

Lining the entrance are several small shrines covered with smelly bat droppings. The temple is very important for post-cremation rites: on the beach across the street, the soul is called in from the sea and a container is symbolically filled with seawater and brought to the cave. After rituals are performed, it's then brought to Pura Dalem Puri, which is part of the Pura Besakih complex (see page 153). The cave is said to extend via a lava tube all the way to Pura Goa, also in the Besakih complex.

PADANG BAI

Some 1.5km (1 mile) east along the road, a scenic point by the shore with huge regional symbols marks the exit from Klungkung Regency and the entrance to Karangasem Regency. A further 5km (3 miles) east is a T-junction; veering right leads to **Padang Bai ⑫**. This picturesque bay cradled by hills is the main port for the Bali–Lombok ferries and fast boats as well as the public boats to Nusa Penida. Passenger and cargo vessels, yachts and international cruise liners stop by here, and there is a range of tourist facilities. Beyond the ferry terminal is the white-sand **Bias Tugal Beach**, also referred to as *Pantai Kecil* (Little Beach). To get there, follow the road from the police station for 100 metres/yds up the hill, turn left at the sign for the beach, head up the steep hill and then descend via the hillside track through the bush. You'll be asked to pay a small fee to enter the road to the beach.

At a headland east of Padang Bai is **Pura Silayukti**, built in honour of the great Javanese priest Empu Kuturan, who lived in this area at the beginning of the 11th century. The temple occupies the site of his former home. From its vantage-location are good views of the bay below.

Beyond the temple on the other side of the headland are **Blue Lagoon** and **Teluk Jepun** (Japan Bay), both good for snorkelling and diving. At Blue Lagoon, the snorkelling areas

Local women preparing for a festival in Tenganan.

are easily accessible from the beach, while getting to the snorkelling sites in Teluk Jepun requires a short boat trip. The coral reefs are varied, as is the marine life, but the waters can be cold and cloudy at times. Diving trips can be arranged through local operators at Padang Bai.

BALINA AND MANGGIS

Beyond Padang Bai comes the broad sweep at **Teluk Amuk** (Amuk Bay), the site of a controversial oil terminal. At its eastern end, after the coastal road crosses an iron bridge, a track leads down to **Buitan** village and **Balina**  beach. Apart from simple guesthouses, this is where you'll find the fabled Amankila resort (which is blessed with a surprisingly picturesque sandy beach) and the more modest but still stylish Alila Manggis.

Nearby is **Manggis** fishing village, **Manggis**, which takes its name from the delectable mangosteen fruit (look for the giant statue of this purple-skinned fruit along the road).

SENGKIDU

Further east along the main road is **Sengkidu** ⓮. The **Pura Puseh** (daylight hours) temple has a colourful ceremony during the full moon in November with men in trance stabbing themselves with sharp daggers and hundreds of villagers joining in ritual dances. Small hotels and guesthouses line the beach at Sengkidu, which is another place that has been affected by erosion.

TENGANAN

Continue east on the main road and at a junction before Candidasa turn left up an asphalt road to a Bali Aga (aboriginal Balinese) village, **Tenganan** ⓯ (daily, daylight hours; donation). Surrounded by a wall, houses line both sides of a long, stone-paved terrace with ritual pavilions in the centre. Until the 1970s, Tenganan

was a closed society, visited only by the occasional ethnologist. An entrance fee is now charged, a sign of how much times have changed. The villagers practise unusual rituals, many of which date from Bali's pre-Hindu animist days. The dead, for instance, are not cremated in this village; instead, the bodies are buried naked face down.

By one account the inhabitants originally came from a pre-Majapahit kingdom in central Bali. But another legend from the 14th century tells of the king of Bedulu in Gianyar whose favourite horse ran away. He sent his subjects to search for it; some went east and found the corpse of the animal. When the king offered to reward them, they asked for the land wherever the decaying horse could be smelled. For several days one of the men led the court official around, yet the air remained pungent with the odour of rotting horse. When the tired official decided that too much land had been given up and left, the gleeful man who led him pulled out

Purchase a puppet as a souvenir from the walled village, Tenganan.

The harbour at Padang Bai.

Detail of pattern from geringsing fabric. The cloth is said to be imbued with magical properties.

Bale Maskerdam at the old palace complex, Puri Agung Karangasem in Amlapura.

a piece of smelly horse flesh hidden inside his clothes.

The village still owns these large tracts of land, making it one of the richest in this area. By tradition, the men do not work the fields but hire people from the surrounding areas to cultivate them in return for a share of the harvest. The men instead spend their time inscribing dried fan-palm leaves to make illustrated *lontar* (manuscripts), or crafting basketry from smoked *ata* (liana vines).

The village women weave the famous double-ikat cloth called *geringsing* (see page 77), which means "illness-free". A single high-quality cloth can take up to three years to complete. A finely woven piece can cost several thousand dollars, and they are in great demand by Balinese for rituals and by foreign collectors and museums overseas. In the village souvenir shops, you will mostly find inferior quality fabrics for sale at lower prices.

During ceremonies, girls wear geringsing and adorn their hair with golden flowers for ritual dances, accompanied by men playing the gamelan selonding, an archaic and rare music ensemble with iron-keyed metallophones.

In June or July during the annual Usaba Sambah festival, which lasts a month, creaky wooden *ayunan* (Ferris wheels) are set up and manually operated by men. Unwed village maidens ride these as part of ancient fertility rites; the turning symbolises the descent of the sun to the earth.

Another Tenganan practice during the Usaba Sambah festival is the *makare*, where men engage in a fight using thorny pandanus leaves, accompanied by *gamelan selonding* music. Both opponents must draw blood as offerings to the demons, warding off attacks with rattan shields. After the battles, the wounds are treated with a stinging mixture of turmeric and vinegar that, miraculously, leaves no scars.

If you have time, visit Tenganan Dauh Tukad (West Tenganan), for which you will see the turning signposted on the right as you drive back to the main road. This village was once part of

the original Tenganan but became separated by a river following a flood. Quieter and much less visited, West Tenganan is similar to East Tenganan but not bound by such strict *adat* (customary law) practices.

CANDIDASA

On the main road just past the Tenganan junction is **Candidasa** beachside resort area **Candidasa** ⓰, which has a wide range of hotels and restaurants and is a good base from which to explore eastern Bali. Unfortunately, the shore is blighted by ugly jetties protruding into the water, too little and too late to stop the erosion caused from years of unbridled coral removal for construction. As a result the beach here is very narrow, although golden and sandy. **Pasir Putih** beach, however, is gorgeous, blessed with soft silvery-white sand (access is via a steep rough track signposted "Virgin Beach", negotiable by car, which leads off the main road 6km/3.5 miles to the east of Candidasa).

Across from Candidasa's man-made lotus lagoon is **Pura Candi Dasa Candidasa** (daily daylight hours; donation), a 12th-century complex built on several levels on the hillside. One of the upper temples is for Hariti, originally a child-eating ogress who converted to Buddhism and became a protector of children. The Balinese call her Men Brayut, from the folktale of a mother who had 18 children. Women who want to conceive come here to pray and make offerings to her.

BUKIT GUMANG

After Candidasa, the road climbs and winds for 5km (3 miles) through the hills to **Bukit Gumang** ⓱ and you'll see monkeys hanging around the roadside. On every even-numbered year by the light of the full moon in October, the *perang dewa* (Battle of the Gods) takes place here. Thousands of people from four surrounding villages ascend 300 metres (1,000ft) to the peak, carrying

offerings of suckling pigs, which are then hung from frangipani trees. Men bearing images of the village deities in portable shrines fall into trance, causing the palanquins to collide and battle with each other.

From Bukit Gumang, the road descends to **Bugbug** (pronounced *boog-boog*), where long narrow lanes, wide enough only for a single person to pass through, run perpendicular to the village's one main road.

AMLAPURA

Continue along the main road to **Amlapura** ⓲, the capital of the Karangasem Regency. This former kingdom was founded during the weakening of the Gelgel court in the 17th century. By the late 18th and early 19th centuries, it was the most powerful state in Bali, and had extended its domain to neighbouring Lombok island.

Amlapura's main attraction is the old palace complex **Puri Agung Karangasem** (daily 8am–5pm), a fusion of European and Asian architectural styles and design dating back to the

Entrance to Puri Agung Karangasem.

Bali Aga women pounding rice the traditional way in Tenganan.

Water-lily pond in the water gardens at Taman Ujung.

Amed with Gunung Agung in the background.

turn of the 20th century. Now unoccupied, the main palace building with a wide veranda is the **Bale Maskerdam**, named after Amsterdam in Holland and in deference to the Dutch who allowed the king of Karangasem to retain his royal title and some of his powers in return for his cooperation. Inside is some furniture donated by the Dutch royal family. Opposite is the ornate **Bale Pemandesan**, a pavilion used for tooth-filing ceremonies and embellished with Chinese features. The third pavilion, **Bale Kambang**, appears to float in the middle of a large artificial pool. It was used by the royal family for relaxing and entertainment.

TAMAN UJUNG

The Karangasem kings created delightful water gardens to escape the heat of eastern Bali. **Taman Ujung** ⑲ (daily 8am–5pm), the "Eternal Happiness Park" at **Ujung**, about 8km (5 miles) south of Amlapura, is a vast complex of pools, pavilions and a long bridge with archways, all artistically moulded in concrete (see page 168) Built in 1919,

the water park was destroyed by an earthquake in 1976. After a drawn-out restoration, it reopened in 2004 and is once more worthy of a visit.

UJUNG TO AMED

From Ujung the road continues about 6km (4 miles) along the coast and uphill to **Seraya**. A vehicle with very good brakes (preferably a four-wheel-drive) is necessary, especially for continuing further along the northeastern coast to Amed. The views of the ocean along this route are magnificent, with black-sand beaches filled with hundreds of colourful *jukung* (outrigger fishing boats), and the route is worthwhile for those seeking adventure. From Seraya, it winds another 25km (15 miles) or so along a narrow road filled with sharp bends around the base of **Gunung Seraya** (1,175 metres/3,855ft), and on to **Amed** beach resort area. **Amed**.

TAMAN TIRTAGANGGA TO AMED

An easier and just as picturesque route to **Amed** continues 6km (4 miles) northwest of Amlapura to **Taman Tirtagangga** ⑳ (daily 8am–5pm; fee) the 'Water of the Ganges River' another royal water park. Local people flock here just before sunset to bathe in pools fed by natural springs gushing out from animal statues and fountains. Parts of this water park were destroyed by the Gunung Agung eruption in 1963 and subsequently repaired.

PURA LEMPUYANG

From Taman Tirtagangga, the road leads 4km (2.5 miles) to **Abang**, with spectacular views between two mountains, Gunung Agung to the west and Gunung Seraya to the east. Back in the late 1960s (or so the story goes), before electricity reached this part of Bali, a space satellite reported the observation of a blue beam emanating from earth; the precise location was plotted and the source confirmed as **Pura Lempuyang** temple ㉑ (daily daylight hours; donation).

Just east from the main road is a white structure nestled on the hillside: this is the split gate of the lower temple. Drive up to this point by turning right at Abang, and on a clear day you will see an amazing view of Gunung Agung, perfectly framed within the boundaries of the gate. The temple guardians – three pairs of colossal sea serpents, complete with scales and ferocious teeth – border a trio of towering steps, but this is only the beginning. Further on, a stairway of 1,700 steps winds through the forest up to the temple itself, 768 metres (2,520ft) above sea level. The intense spiritual energy of this place is almost tangible.

From Abang, it's another 14km (9 miles) along a winding road, forking right first at **Culik**, to Amed.

AMED

Although **Amed** ❷❷ refers to the fishing village, it is also the name given to a series of seven gravelly beaches tucked into coves and stretching several kilometres along the coast – Jemeluk, Bunutan, Lipah, Selang, Banyuning and Aas. Out to sea are views of Lombok while those inland are of Gunung Agung. All along the beach are colourful fishing outriggers and thatched huts where salt is produced. It is an idyllic setting and perfect for those who shun crowds. Village life is simple here, but there's enough tourism infrastructure in the way of small hotels and restaurants along the coast to keep visitors occupied for a few days. There are also ample opportunities for diving, snorkelling and mountain treks.

TULAMBEN

To reach the north-eastern coast, return to Culik and turn right. About 10km (6 miles) from Culik is **Tulamben Marine Reserve** ❷❸. Diving and snorkelling are the main activities at the site of the wrecked American navy cargo ship *Liberty*, which was sailing

in the Lombok Strait in January 1942 when it was torpedoed by the Japanese. In 2012 a Dutch cargo ship, the *Boga*, was sunk in the sea to create a coral reef at **Kubu**, just up the road from here. Unusual items, such as an entire Volkswagen Beetle, are in the storage area. Because of its depth, the Boga wreck is recommended for experienced divers only.

NORTHEAST COAST

A long stretch of well-paved road runs along the northeast coast, which still displays evidence of the 1963 Gunung Agung eruption in the form of dark lava flows on the mountain sides. It's a stark, raw and dramatic drive through mostly dry hills covered with scrub and lava boulders and punctuated by fan palm and coconut trees.

Along the way are **Kubu** and **Tianyar**, the salt-making villages **Kubu** ❷❹ **Tianyar** ❷❺, with wooden troughs for evaporating seawater lining black-sand beaches similar to those found at Kusamba. There is little of interest till you reach Tejakula (see page 172).

Colourful outrigger (jukung) boats on a black-sand beach at Amed.

Taman Ujung, a former royal summer retreat.

📷 WATER PARKS OF EAST BALI

Pools, pavilions and gardens, once the preserve of royalty, offer a welcome respite from the heat.

Water lilies at Pura Jagatnathna, Denpasar.

Taman Ujung Ujung, also known as Taman Sukasada Ujung (Eternal Happiness Park), was built in 1919 by the last Raja of Karangasem, Anak Agung Anglurah Ketut Karangasem. The water palace was formally used from 1921 as a place for the Raja to entertain as well as being a retreat for the royal family. It was shattered by an earthquake in 1976 but restored in 2004.

The renovated park isn't as atmospheric as the original but it is still extremely beautiful, graced with water-lily-filled reflecting pools, airy pavilions and bridges with decorative arches.

More evocative is **Taman Tirtagangga** (Water of the Ganges Park), built by the same king in 1948 and modelled after Versailles Palace in France. Chilly, natural spring water gushes out from spouts and fountains into large pools in which you can swim. Accommodation is also available in the park.

Taman Ujung. Previously used as a royal summer residence, the Bale Kambang (floating pavilion) sits in the midst of a large reflecting pond full of water lilies.

Fountain at Taman Tirtagangga. Water pours down the sides of an 11-tiered pagoda fountain and gushes out from the mouth of a large boar into a swimming pool.

Statue at Taman Ujung. A contemporary Balinese rendition of the Ganges river goddess Dewi Gangga, seen pouring water from her pot.

Inside a Pool Villa at Tirta Ayu Hotel & Restaurant.

Lodging at Tirtagangga

It's worth spending a relaxing night or two at Taman Tirtagangga, using it as your base to explore east Bali. The park itself is very pretty and is the perfect foil for the stunning surrounding landscape of hills and rice terraces. Guesthouses in the area have guides who can take you on interesting walks along back roads to remote villages.

Right on the grounds of Taman Tirtagangga, on the hill overlooking the park is Tirta Ayu Hotel & Restaurant. Three villas provide all the luxuries, and one has a private swimming pool. Their excellent restaurant serving Balinese and Western food is an ideal lunch stopover while touring or simply relaxing with a cool drink and a snack while soaking up the peaceful atmosphere of the gardens below. The hotel also offers spa treatments, if you're interested.

For booking details, contact: tel: 0363-22503, hoteltirtagangga.com.

Bull statue at Taman Tirtagangga. This is one of many whimsical figures with water pouring out of its mouth into the pools.

...athers cool off in the chilly waters of one of several pools ...ontinuously fed by a holy natural spring from the hill ...ehind Taman Tirtagangga.

Thundering Air Terjun Gitgit is best seen during the wet season.

NORTH BALI

North Bali is almost a world unto itself in terms of its people, terrain and architecture. You can linger at Lovina, a peaceful coastal resort, or head inland to the foot of lofty mountains where the cool highlands are speckled with waterfalls, serene lakes and temples, as well as coffee, clove and vanilla estates.

Geographically separated by a chain of towering volcanoes running from west to east across Bali, the northern part of the island is not only physically different from the south but has developed its own distinctive character over time. For centuries, the coastal communities of the north participated in the trade that traversed the calm Java Sea. The Dutch, too, conquered this part of Bali first in 1849, before moving south. All these have exposed the local Balinese population to outside influences, making them much more cosmopolitan as a result.

Some of the highest educated Balinese are from the north coast, partly due to the early implementation of a Western-style educational system by the Dutch. Modern Balinese literature also had its beginnings in the north. With a softer variety of sandstone available from local quarries, carvers have been able to create intricate stone carvings for temples. As a result North Bali temple carvings are more three-dimensional and exuberant than anywhere else on the island. The countryside, too, appears golden due to lower rainfall. Orchards of grapes, spices, coffee, cacao, and flowers for offerings replace the familiar rice fields, although non-irrigated rice is widely grown and prized by most Balinese for its delicious flavour.

Brahma Arama Vihara.

LES

Travelling from east Bali along the main north coastal route, turn left towards Les village, and follow the road for about a kilometre to a small junction, where there is a sign indicating a waterfall, and a parking area outside a small group of shops. From there the journey can only be continued by foot. Follow the beaten track south, away from the rice fields, for about 20 minutes. The spectacular, little-visited **Yeh Mampeh** (fee) ❶, meaning 'Flying Water', is Bali's highest waterfall.

⊘ **Main attractions**
Pura Meduwe Karang
Pura Dalem, Jagaraga
Lovina
Brahma Arama Vihara
Air Panas Banjar
Air Terjun Gitgit
Pura Ulun Danu Bratan
Bali Botanical Gardens
Danau Buyan and Danau
  Tamblingan

Map on page 172

Painting of a young Balinese man at Symon's Art Zoo in Alassari.

You can bathe in the shallow pool right beneath the torrent.

TEJAKULA

Further along the main road, **Tejakula ❷** was once only known for its traditional musicians and dancers and its quaint horse baths fed by a natural spring. However, nowadays a new attraction has been added: snorkelling and diving in areas such as Angel Canyon and Tangga Reef. With much to see ranging from large fish to critters, there are accredited dive centres and dive sites at Penuktukan, Tejakula and Bondalem, with the bonus of nice resorts and a beach club. Only 51km (32miles) northwest of Amed and 40km (25miles) southeast of Lovina, this area is a good base for snorkelling and diving from several beaches.

PURA PONJOK BATU

Further west about 12km (7 miles) along the coast is the dramatic **Pura Ponjok Batu ❸** (daily daylight hours; donation), perched on a scenic hillside overlooking the sea. The temple marks the site where the 16th-century Javanese high priest Danghyang Nirartha had stopped to admire the view when he saw a boat in trouble. He revived the unconscious crew with the waters from a spring that magically appeared on the beach. They were able to continue travelling even though the boat had no sail and the mast was broken. Just below the temple, a replica of the boat is found on a small rock battered by waves. West of the temple is Alassari Plantation Resort, offering gorgeous coffee field views and wellness therapies.

SYMON'S ART ZOO

At Alassari, another 3km (2 miles) west of Pura Ponjok Batu, is the funky **Symon's Art Zoo ❹** (tel: 0819-3430 1205; daily 9am–5pm), a fantasy homo-erotic land created by American artist Symon. Stop by to see his life-size sculptures and colourful paintings of young Balinese men and other pop art themes. Be sure to climb up to the top of the pagoda-like tower for stunning

Tejakula village with the old horse baths on the right.

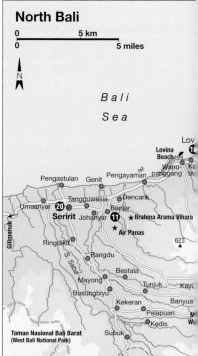

North Bali

0   5 km
0   5 miles

N

Bali Sea

Lov
Lovina
Beach
Wanu
Ke
panggang
bi
Pengayaman
Pengastulan   Genit
Tangguwesia   Dencarik
Umaanyar ⑳   Banjar
Seririt Johanyar ⑪   ★ Brahma Arama Vihara
Ringdikit   ★ Air Panas
S. Saba   Rangdu   623
Mayong   Bestala
Busungbiyu   Tunjuk   Kayt
Kekeran   Banyua
Pelapuan   N
Taman Nasional Bali Barat   Subuk   Kedis   W
(West Bali National Park)
Gilimanuk

views of the coastline and surrounding hills and then enter its base to see the Buddhist sanctuary filled with images and incense.

AIR SANIH

A further 5km (3 miles) west are the cool springs at **Air Sanih** ❺, also known as Yeh Sanih (daily daylight hours). The big spring-fed pool under spreading frangipani trees near the sea isn't terribly inviting but many local people flock here, especially around sunset, to swim or bathe. Accommodation, mostly budget-range places, and restaurants are available nearby if you decide to spend the night.

PURA MEDUWE KARANG

Just before the main road north from Gunung Batur meets the coastal road in **Kubutambahan** is a small side road towards the sea leading to **Pura Meduwe Karang** ❻ (daily daylight hours; donation). Built in 1890, the structure is filled with the elaborate carvings and decorations so typical

of northern-style temple architecture, often depicting scenes that are humorous, highly animated and even erotic in character. Fertility motifs abound, including portrayals of various erotic acts. Other carvings show demons and humans, including Dutch artist W.O.J. Nieuwenkamp (1874–1950) riding a bicycle with flowery wheels – look for it on the ocean-side wall of the main shrine in the temple's inner courtyard. At the start of the 20th century, Nieuwenkamp travelled everywhere in Bali by bicycle, sketching scenes of what he saw.

Pura Meduwe Karang literally means 'Temple of the Landowner', and it honours the deity of the crops of dry agriculture. Just as *subak* (irrigation) temples ensure harvests on irrigated rice fields, this temple assures blessings for plants grown on unirrigated land, including fruits, coconut and coffee.

JAGARAGA

Another 2km (1 mile) east in Bungkulan, turn (left) uphill at the main

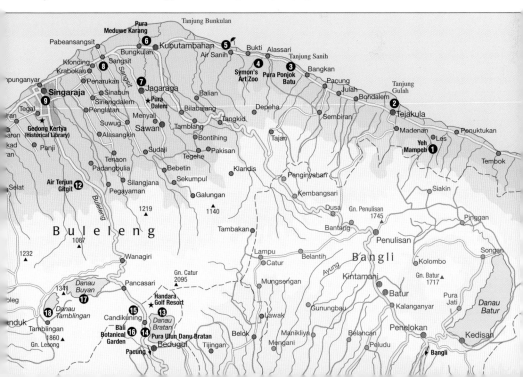

The Yudha Mandala Tama Independence Monument graces the waterfront at Singaraja.

Tourists set off for dolphin watching from Lovina beach.

T-junction and continue 4km (2.5 miles) inland to **Jagaraga** . This is the scene of the bloody 1849 battle between the Balinese and the Dutch, which killed off most of the village's population and ended several years of fighting between the two sides. Today, Jagaraga is more famous for its interesting **Pura Dalem** (Temple of the Dead; daily daylight hours; donation), where Siwa (Shiva), the Hindu god of destruction, presides. Highly animated bas-reliefs portray life before and after the Dutch arrival – armed bandits holding up two smug Europeans riding in an antique Ford car, World War II airplanes engaged in an aerial battle with some plunging into the sea, and a Dutch steamer sending out a smoky SOS signal while being attacked by a sea monster. Even the widow-witch Rangda and the statue of a dazed mother buried under a pile of children are carved with a sense of humour.

PURA BEJI

Back along the main northern coastal road in **Sangsit**  is the amazing

Pura Beji (daily daylight hours; donation) built of pink sandstone during the 15th century. At this *subak* (irrigation) temple dedicated to Dewi Sri, intricate carvings of *naga* (serpents) and symbols of water and fertility adorn the balustrades, with fantastic beasts, demonic guardians, jawless birds and fierce tigers peering out from the entangled flora. Rows of slender towers jut up from the temple terraces, forming a labyrinth of stone. To counterbalance the overpowering motifs, the temple courtyard is unusually spacious and planted with frangipani trees.

SINGARAJA

About 9km (6 miles) west of Pura Beji Sangsit is **Singaraja** , Bali's second largest town (after Denpasar) and the north's main commercial centre. In many respects, Singaraja is also the intellectual hub of the north, with two major universities. After the Dutch imposed direct colonial rule on the Buleleng kingdom in 1882, Singaraja became the capital and chief port

⏃ LAKE TRANSPORT

The pathways through the rainforest between lakes Danau Buyan and Danau Tamblingan lead to Pura Tahun, a temple with an 11 roofed *meru*. From here, you can arrange for one of the lake's attendants to row you across the tranquil waters in a *pedau akit*, a traditional double canoe – motorboats and water sports are forbidden here. The natural spring that feeds the lake provides water for drinking and the waters are also a rich source of fish, evident from the offshore fishing platforms. On the far side of Danau Tamblingan is Pura Gubug, the Farmers' Temple, dedicated to the lake goddess, and the tiny Munduk Tamblingan village where the locals rear cattle on the lotus that grows in the shallow water.

until 1953, when the administrative centre was moved to Denpasar in the south. But even before the Dutch showed up, Singaraja was an important shipping and trading centre. Today, Singaraja still has a bustling and cosmopolitan flavour. Its population comprises Balinese, Javanese, Arabs and Chinese.

Singaraja's port was destroyed by rough waves during the early 1990s and has now been restored. Nearby is the **Ling Gwan Kiong Chinese Buddhist Temple** (daily daylight hours; donation), dating back to 1873 and filled with colourful murals of deities and mythological figures. Further up the waterfront is **Yudha Mandala Tama Independence Monument**, which commemorates Indonesia's struggle against the Dutch from 1945 to 1949.

MUSEUM GEDONG KIRTYA

On Jalan Veteran just two blocks east of the **Singa Ambara Raja**, a large statue of the winged lion-king that symbolises Singaraja, is the historical **Museum Gedong Kirtya** (tel: 0362-25141; Mon–Thu 7am–2.30pm, Fri 7am–12.30pm; free). This repository of old books and Balinese manuscripts was established by the Dutch in 1928 – partly to compensate for their bloody conquest of Bali. It has a fine collection of *lontar*, traditional books made from dried fan-palm leaves cut into strips, inscribed and preserved between two pieces of wood or bamboo. Some works are relatively newer copies of older ones that have disintegrated due to humidity, fungus and insect damage. The *lontar* manuscripts cover literature, mythology, historical chronicles and religion. Some even have miniature drawings, which are masterpieces in the art of illustration. The museum also has several royal edicts inscribed on thin sheets of bronze dating from the 10th century, among the earliest written documents in Bali.

WEST OF SINGARAJA TO LOVINA

About 10km (6 miles) west of Singaraja is the low-key beach resort area **Lovina** ⑩. Stretching over 8km (5 miles)

Entrance to Ling Gwan Kiong Chinese Buddhist Temple in Singaraja.

Pura Beji is built from sandstone, unlike most other Balinese temples.

Canang sari (offering of flowers in a woven coconut leaf tray) at Air Panas Banjar.

Fishing boats on Danau Bratan.

of mainly black-sand beaches, the collective name Lovina (Lovely Indonesia) was given by Panji Tisna, the last king of Buleleng and a convert to Christianity, to the north coast's string of fishing villages with names like Kaliasem, Kalibukbuk, Anturan and Tukad Mungga.

Caressed by gentle waves, Lovina is well suited for families because of the rather laid-back pace and calm sea. Accommodation ranges from simple guesthouses to mid-range resorts with restaurants and other facilities, mostly located on both sides of **Jalan Raya Lovina**.

Nearly every hotel, guide or fisherman in Lovina offers dolphin watching tours, very early in the morning in motorised traditional jukung fishing boats. Occasionally no dolphins are sighted, but about 90 percent of the time dolphin-watchers are treated to the breath-taking spectacle of these graceful mammals vaulting out of the water in a remarkable aerial display. Diving and snorkelling are major activities in Lovina, although better options are found in the waters around Pulau Menjangan to the west.

BRAHMA ARAMA VIHARA

Continuing west from Lovina, turn left at Dencarik and continue for about 3km (2 miles) to **Brahma Arama Vihara** (tel: 0361-92959; daily 8am–6pm) in **Banjar** ⓫. This striking Thai-style Theravada Buddhist temple, with its bright orange roof and colourful statues of Buddha and other figures, was founded in 1958 by a Balinese monk and rebuilt in 1971. The views down to the coast are stunning, and visitors are welcome as long as they dress modestly, lower their voices and walk quietly and barefooted.

AIR PANAS BANJAR

From Brahma Arama Vihara, it's another 3km (2 miles) to **Air Panas Banjar** (daily 8am–6pm), a natural sulphuric spring with slightly warmer than tepid water cascading out from the mouths of carved naga (serpents) into two pools. You can get a free massage from the water gushing out from the higher spouts at the third pool. There are changing rooms, toilets and a restaurant on site.

SOUTH OF SINGARAJA TO GITGIT

About 11km (7 miles) south of Singaraja, take the turn-off on the left for the waterfall, **Air Terjun Gitgit** ⓬ (daily daylight hours; fee). The thundering 40-metre (130ft) waterfall is impressive, especially at the peak of the rainy season between January and March. The deep pool at the bottom of the falls is good for swimming, but according to local lore, couples who use the pool together will separate (you have been warned). Like most scenic places in Bali, persistent guides and numerous kiosks selling kitschy souvenirs disturb the atmosphere. For more peace and quiet, 2km (1 mile) further up the hill another path along a river and through forests leads you to a series of multi-tiered waterfalls.

DANAU BRATAN

Beyond the Gitgit waterfalls, the road south continues to twist and turn as it descends into the ancient Gunung Catur crater to the east, which soars to 2,095 metres (6,915ft). In this lovely landscape of vegetable and flower farms and the cooler temperatures of the Bedugal highlands sits serene **Danau Bratan** ⑬ a large lake surrounded by densely forested mountains topped by clouds. The spectacular Handara Golf & Resort is located here.

PURA ULUN DANU BRATAN

Because the lake is an essential water source for surrounding farmlands and rice fields in the southwest and northwest parts of the island, the Balinese worship the goddess of the lake, Dewi Danu, at **Pura Ulun Danu Bratan** ⑭ (daily daylight hours).

Built during the 17th century by a king of Mengwi, this sacred site, dedicated to the lake goddess, is the second most important irrigation temple after Pura Ulun Danu Batur. The graceful 11-tiered *meru* (pagoda) appears to float upon the surface of the water. On the nearby shore are two other temples and a stone stupa with four Buddha statues in niches facing the main compass directions.

CANDIKUNING AND BEDUGUL

On the western side of the lake, the colourful **Candikuning** ⑮ market town is where wild orchids and colourful flowers are sold alongside temperate and tropical food crops grown in the region's fertile soil. The farms here provide a constant supply of flowers for Balinese offerings, along with a wide variety of fruits and vegetables for restaurants.

At the southern shore of the lake is **Bedugul**, which is the name of the small town here as well as the entire mountain resort area. Because of the higher altitude, temperatures in this region are much lower than on the coast, giving it an alpine feel.

BALI BOTANICAL GARDENS

South of the Candikuning market is the lush **Bali Botanical Gardens** ⑯ (tel: 0368-203 3211; http://kebunrayabali. com, daily 8am–6pm, fee). This cool,

The tiny, sweet strawberries for sale at Candikuning market are grown in farms around this high-altitude region.

Naga (serpent) carvings spouting warm water at Air Panas Banjar.

Cloves are pink when picked, turning reddish brown and later almost black when completely dried. Look for them laid out on mats to dry in the area around Munduk.

Hydrangeas are grown for use in offering trays, as here in Munduk.

shady park covers 157.5 hectares (389 acres) and also serves as a research and training station. If time is limited, a road travels under gigantic trees to specific areas hosting plants such as orchids, roses, traditional medicine, bamboos and ferns. Better yet, spend a half day and stroll through the tropical forest walk, where bird-watching is excellent. There is also a guesthouse here for longer stays.

The Botanical Gardens is also home to **Bali Treetop Adventure Park** (tel: 0361-934 0009; daily 8am–6pm), where adults and children can venture from tree to tree through suspended bridges, spider nets, Tarzan jumps, flying swings and zip lines.

DANAU BUYAN AND DANAU TAMBLINGAN

From Danau Bratan, head northeast to **Danau Buyan** ⑰, a quiet lake embraced by hillside coffee plantations. To the west is **Danau Tamblingan** ⑱ sacred to local villagers. The picturesque drive on a narrow, winding mountain road will be alleviated by a toll road which, when completed, will limit traffic to serenity seekers by routing the heavy truck traffic to the new thoroughfare. Between the two lakes is a narrow strip of land with ample vantage points and snack stalls for enjoying views of the lake below.

MUNDUK

Beyond the lakes the road winds its way down 6km (4 miles), west to **Munduk** ⑲, an old mountain settlement with coffee, vanilla and clove plantations started by the Dutch during the late 1890s. The views down to the north coast are spectacular; the air crisp and clear. Resorts, eateries, and accommodations in all price ranges overlook the lakes, making the area an ideal getaway. Munduk Moding Plantation Nature Resort & Spa (tel: 0811-385 059, www.mundukmodingplantation.com) has incredible views and serves coffee grown on-site. From here, you can continue for 26km (16 miles) north to **Seririt** ⑳. Turning right takes you back east to Lovina, while going left along the coastal road West Bali.

Tree ferns flourish in Bali's mountainous areas.

Javanese fishing boats in
Perancak harbour in west Bali.

WEST BALI

Remote west Bali sees few visitors because the attractions are spread so wide. Those who make the trek west will be amply rewarded with dramatic windswept coastal temples, isolated Christian communities, some of Bali's best diving and a massive national park.

Even though the highways heading west are packed with trucks and ferry-riders, both heading for Gilimanuk harbor to cross over into Java, the coastal beaches are relatively uncrowded, making them very attractive to beach-goers. A national park takes up much of this part of the island, while along the southwest coast, black-sand beaches unprotected by offshore reefs are favoured by die-hard surfers and others wishing to escape crowded southern Bali. This is Jembrana, Bali's 'wild west' that was once home to the island's earliest prehistoric inhabitants. Hindu high priests and aristocrats from Java first stepped foot on this part of Bali to spread the faith. Over the centuries, migrants from more populated areas in Bali, Java, Madura, Sulawesi and even distant Malaysia established communities here. This ethnically, culturally and geographically diverse area offers surprises to visitors who make the effort to explore it.

CELUKAN BAWANG

Located 16km (10 miles) west of **Seririt on the north coast**, the small and sheltered **Celukan Bawang ❶** (Onion Cove) harbour has replaced Singaraja as the main port for the north coast. Occasionally, a distinctive *pinisi* (wooden

sailing ship) of the Bugis people from south Sulawesi or a massive cruise ship drops anchor here.

WEST TO PULAKI

Continuing west, the land takes on a drier texture and the agricultural diversity becomes apparent. Near **Grokgak ❷** are the vineyards of Hatten Wines (tel: 0812-3964 5077; www.hattenwines.com), which has a Welcome Centre & Observation Deck (daily 10am–4.30pm, closed Sun and Balinese holidays). The vineyard's 45 hectares are open for tours

Main attractions
Pemuteran
Pulau Menjangan
West Bali National Park
Belimbingsari and
 Palasari
Bunut Bolong

Map on page 182

The unique Bunut Bolong tree near Manggissari village.

Tip

At Pemuteran, endangered sea turtle eggs are rescued and hatched at Reef Seen Diver's Resort (tel: 0812-389 4051, https://reef seenbali.com). The meat and eggs are considered a delicacy by many Balinese, and the program here has gone a long way to educating villagers of the importance of protecting these creatures. For a small donation visitors can sponsor the release of hatchlings into the sea.

and tastings, and there is an Education Centre offering courses.

PULAKI

Another 5km (3 miles) along the road, just past Banyupoh village, in **Pulaki ❸**, is an interesting pair of temples originating from an incident in the 16th century, when the Javanese high priest Danghyang Nirartha came here to escape from the rise of Islam in Java. One day Nirartha's youngest daughter became lost in the forest and was violated by some very bad men, *wong gamang*, from a local village. When the priest found her she was nearly dead; he purified and transformed her into a goddess called Dewi Melanting. Her temple, set against forested hills, is called **Pura Melanting** (daily, daylight hours).

Nirartha cursed those responsible for the crime, making them invisible, and ordered the *wong gamang* to serve his wife whom he deified at **Pura Pulaki** (daily, daylight hours), about 2km (1 mile) to the west. The temple, rebuilt in the 1980s, hugs a ledge cut out of the mountain side that overlooks the ocean and is guarded by a band of frisky monkeys. According to the villagers, the invisible *wong gamang* are said to still roam the island, causing dogs to howl for no apparent reason.

Part of the Pura Pulaki complex is **Pura Pabean** (daily, daylight hours), just opposite and strikingly perched on a hill overlooking the coast. Unusually blending both Chinese and Balinese design elements, this is where fishermen come to pray for safe passage.

PEMUTERAN

A further 3km (2 miles) west of Pulaki is **Pemuteran ❹** with its quiet beaches and great diving and snorkelling at coral reefs offshore. There are a number of medium price-range accommodations here, making it a preferred overnight spot for those who don't wish to pay the big resort fees closer to the national park; however the five-star Matahari Beach Resort & Spa (tel. 362-92312; https://matahari-beach-resort.com) is here. Also in Pemuteran is Reef Seen Divers' Resort (tel: 0812-389 4051, https://reefseenbali.com), which is home

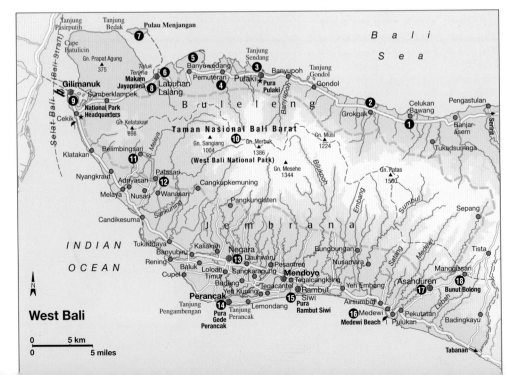

West Bali

0   5 km
0   5 miles

to magnificent reef gardens, thanks to an artificial reef construction system. Reef Seen also organises dive and snorkel trips to national park waters.

BANYUWEDANG

Another 10km (6 miles) west at a bend in the road is **Banyuwedang** ⑤ (Hot Water), which has natural hot springs with medicinal properties, said to heal skin diseases. The springs are a little grubby so a better option is the nearby **Mimpi Resort** (tel. 0362-94497; https:// mimpi.com) where for a modest fee visitors can take a dip in the hot pools that pump in mineral water from the springs at Banyuwedang.

Overlooking Banyuwedang Bay is the eco-friendly Menjangan Dynasty (tel. 0361 335 5000; www.mdr.pphotels. com), the first resort in Bali to introduce 'glamping' (glamorous camping). Their safari-style air-conditioned tented rooms and villas reminiscent of an African adventure guarantee a unique experience. Even if you can't afford the five-star luxury just outside the national park boundaries, do stop in for a meal or snack if for no other reason than to admire the awesome bamboo architecture in the restaurant.

PULAU MENJANGAN

Next along the road is **Labuhan Lalang** ⑥, the jump-off point for Pulau Menjangan. Snorkelling equipment and fishing boats can be rented here for trips to the tiny and uninhabited **Pulau Menjangan** ⑦ (Deer Island). Dive trips are better arranged from Pemuteran. A part of the West Bali National Park and located less than 10km (6 miles) offshore, the island has some of Bali's best diving sites, with diverse marine life, good visibility and pristine coral reefs extending deep into the ocean floor.

The celebrated Javanese high priest Empu Kuturan is said to have arrived here during the 10th century, when a deer led him around Bali. The island's name is a misnomer now as the rare Java deer are rarely spotted.

WEST BALI NATIONAL PARK

Although the headquarters of **Taman Nasional Bali Barat** (West Bali National

⊙ Tip

Thanks to increasing success with breeding the endangered Bali starling, after decades of single digit numbers of individuals in the park there are now over 200 residing in three areas. If trekking to see them in the wild isn't on your agenda, ask if you can visit the breeding centre at Labuhan Lalang.

Temple festival at Pura Pulaki.

The Catholic church in Palasari village.

Harvesting rice from the paddy fields in Negara.

Park) are located south of Gilimanuk at Cekik, the entry for all park activities is at **Labuhan Lalang**. Permits and guides required for hiking in the park can be obtained at the Visitors' Centre (Mon–Thu 7.30am–3.30pm, Fri 7.30am–11am, Sat 7.30am–1pm; fee) in a large parking lot that is also equipped with showers, toilets and snack stands.

The park was originally established by the Dutch in 1941 to protect the endangered *jalak putih*, the small white Bali starling or Rothschild's mynah (*Leucopsar rothschildi*), with brilliant blue patches around its eyes and black-tipped wings. Its 190 sq km (73 sq miles) are mountainous covered with primary monsoon and lowland forest, and its coasts fringed by mangroves and offshore reefs are the last remaining pristine areas on the island.

Treks with knowledgeable guides lasting two to nine hours can be arranged at the Visitors' Centre, and can be tailored to individual interests and physical capabilities. The gentle slopes of **Gunung Prapat Agung** at 375 metres (1,230ft) are criss-crossed with footpaths that make it a favourite for wildlife spotting. With more than 110 species of birds, along with civet cats, several species of deer and monkeys, there's plenty to see.

MAKAM JAYAPRANA

Just 1km (0.5 mile) beyond Labuhan Lalang and located high up a steep hillside with lovely views is **Makam Jayaprana ❽**, the gravesite of the 17th-century local folk hero called Jayaprana. The handsome orphan Jayaprana, who was raised by the lord of Kalianget, near Banjar, had wed the beautiful Layonsari. The lord became jealous and desired Layonsari for himself, so he hatched a ruse to lure Jayaprana to a distant bay and had him murdered. In despair, Layonsari committed suicide rather than submit to the treacherous lord, and was reunited with Jayaprana in heaven. A shrine in the cemetery here has a glass case which contains images of the ill-fated couple. Women

⊘ BULL RACES

The Negara *makepung*, or water-buffalo races, were introduced about a century ago by migrants from Madura, in Java. Wearing colourful banners and crowns, their horns decorated and wooden bells tied around their necks, the bulls race down an erratic 2km (1.25-mile) -long track. It's remarkable to see such docile creatures thunder across the finish line at speeds of up to 60kmph (37mph). The daredevil drivers often ride standing up on a chariot, twisting the bulls' tails to give them extra motivation. The races take place every second Sunday from July to November. Contact the **Jembrana Tourist Office** (tel: 0365-41060) for race dates.

pray here for divine assistance in matters of love.

GILIMANUK

At a T-junction in the main road in **Cekik**, 14km (9 miles) from Labuhan Lalang, turn to the right to **Gilimanuk** ❾. This nondescript town on a small peninsula is marked by a distinctive arch towering above the road, depicting four serpents with their tails entwined. Beyond the commercial stretch is a modern terminal for ferries that shuttle passengers, buses and cars (operating 24 hours daily) between Bali and Java, a distance of only 3km (2 miles) and covered in 30 minutes.

The only attraction worth seeing in Gilimanuk is **Museum Situs Purbakala** (Museum of Prehistoric Man; Mon–Fri 8am–3pm), which displays the excavated prehistoric remains from a small settlement said to be 4,000 years old. In fact some of Bali's earliest evidence of human life has been found in this area, with artefacts like stone adzes and pottery fragments dating back to 1000 BC. Given the narrow strait, it must have been easy enough for people from East Java to make the crossing to Bali. In fact, geologists maintain that Java and Bali were once part of the same land mass.

NATIONAL PARK HEADQUARTERS

Cekik is the location of the headquarters of of **Taman Nasional Bali Barat** ❿ (West Bali National Park; tel: 0365-61060; Mon–Thu 7.30am–3.30pm, Fri 7.30am–11am, Sat 7.30am–1pm). Printed information is limited, but the staff are quite helpful. Obtain the necessary permits for hiking in the park here or at the visitor centre in Labuhan Lalang.

BELIMBINGSARI AND PALASARI

From Cekik, travel 15km (9 miles) to **Melaya** and turn inland to **Belimbingsari** ⓫ village. Home to Bali's largest Protestant community, its impressive church has distinctly Balinese design elements and a *kulkul* (warning drum) instead of a bell signalling the start of

A car and passenger ferry at Gilimanuk Port, bound for Java.

Medewi's black-sand and pebble beach.

service. Sunday services are at 9am (tel: 0365-42192 to check).

Palasari with its 1,500-strong Catholic community is a short drive south. As with Belimbingsari, the early converts settled in remote West Bali under pressure from the Dutch, who were intent on keeping the Balinese-Hindu culture intact. The cathedral, adorned with Balinese touches like *meru* temple roofs, is a stunning piece of architecture in the middle of nowhere. The original structure dates back to 1958, with the present church built in 1991. Friday mass at 5.30pm and Sunday mass at 6.30am are good times to visit but call ahead to check first (tel: 0812-364 6211).

NEGARA AND LOLOAN TIMUR

Part of the road southeast follows the coast before turning inland at Candikesuma to the next port of call at **Negara** ⓭. There is little tourist development along this 30km (19-mile) long road, punctuated by orchards and coconut trees, and the occasional

Surfer at Soka beach.

mosque (Jembrana Regency has a large Muslim migrant population from Java and elsewhere). There is nothing of much interest in Negara even though it is Jembrana's largest town and the main administrative centre.

Just 1km (.5 mile) south of Negara is **Loloan Timur**, a small village populated by Muslim Bugis people from south Sulawesi who settled here many generations ago. A number of their wooden homes retain the unique traditional Buginese style and are elevated on posts.

The Jembrana region's other claims to fame are renowned bull races (see box) and unique *gamelan jegog*, a music ensemble using only bamboo instruments, some of which are gigantic tubes 3 metres (10ft) long and 15 cm (6in) in diameter. *Jegog* music is very fast, rhythmic and precise; the instruments are played in specific sequences and produce some wonderful sounds, while also being visually attractive. Some have likened the resonant sounds to roaring thunder as the music can be heard and even felt from quite a distance away. *Gamelan jegog* accompanies traditional dances like *tari silat* (self-defence dance) and newer ones such as the *tari makepung* (bull racing dance.

Competitions held throughout the region pit neighbouring ensembles in this ethnically diverse region against each other in friendly shows of superiority.

PURA GEDE PERANCAK

From Loloan Timur, follow the road northeast to **Dauhwaru**, then turn right and continue zigzagging all the way to coastal **Yeh Kuning**. From there, go west along the coast to the mouth of **Perancak River**, believed to be the place where 16th-century Javanese high priest Danghyang Nirartha first landed in Bali. While he was resting in the shade of an *ancak* (a banyan species), a local ruler ordered him to pray in the temple there. After the priest did so, it collapsed and was rebuilt by villagers as the small and simple **Pura Gede Perancak** ⓮ (Great Temple of the Ancak Tree).

PURA RAMBUT SIWI

Return to the main road and continue east. At **Yeh Embang**, a side road on the right leads towards a spectacular stretch of black-sand beach where stands **Pura Rambut Siwi** ⓯ (The Lock of Hair Temple; daily daylight hours; donation). Stop at one of several pavilions perched on a cliff overlooking the ocean to the west of this temple and admire the panoramic views.

In the 16th century, Danghyang Nirartha, an esteemed Javanese high priest , is said to have stopped at the village, and put an end to an epidemic that was devastating the population. Before moving on, he presented the people with a gift of his hair, thus explaining the name of the holy site. Nirartha's hair and some of his personal belongings are enshrined within a *meru* (pagoda) in the inner courtyard of the main temple.

MEDEWI

Further east along the main road is **Medewi** ⓰, a rather undistinguished village but with a black-sand and pebble beach; the stretch on the other side of the river mouth is good for surfing. Be aware that the waves can be rough and the undercurrent strong here. Food can be bought from beachside vendors, or restaurants at one of the modest hotels near the beach.

BUNUT BOLONG

Just beyond Medewi at **Pekutatan**, veer left at the Y-junction and begin a steady climb up into the mountains. The narrow, twisting and paved road, just 10km (6 miles) long, passes through rainforest and coffee, cacao

and clove plantations, and the mountain side-hugging **Asahduren** ⓱ village. Stop to have a look at Balinese village life scarcely affected by the demands of tourism.

Heading north, the road passes right through the base of a gigantic *bunut* (a type of banyan) tree in **Manggissari** village. The road used to wend around this grand old tree, but as it continued to grow larger the only choice was to create a tunnel through it. Cutting down the tree would have left its resident spirit without a place to stay. Called **Bunut Bolong** ⓲ (Hole in the Bunut Tree), a small shrine with two tiger figures sits on its right-hand side. This is where drivers sometimes stop to ask for permission to continue on their journey by making offerings to the spirit.

The road continues past isolated mountain villages such as Tista to **Pupuan** in Tabanan Regency (see page 193). Stop here to admire the rice terraces and spectacular views of southwest Bali before continuing either to north Bali or south to Tabanan proper.

Makepung (bull racing) at Perancak.

Rice terraces, Jatiluwih.

Fertile rice terraces at Jatiluwih.

TABANAN REGION

Tabanan is famed for its vast expanses of terraced rice fields. But here there are also historically important towns that are centres for music, dance and religion, as well as Pura Luhur Batukaru, an ancestral temple still maintained by descendants of Bali's royalty.

The fertile plains of Tabanan Regency were once home to the powerful Mengwi kingdom, which emerged around 1700 after the fall of Gelgel. At one time, it controlled Bukit Badung in the south and areas as far away as east Java. Mengwi rule ended in 1891 when it was defeated by its neighbours, and its realm divided between Tabanan and Badung kingdoms. Unlike the kings of Gianyar, Bangli and Karangasem to the east, the Tabanan raja had no agreement with the Dutch, and in 1906, the Dutch took control of his land, which was later distributed among the villages in the area. Rice was the choice crop, and Tabanan today is known as Bali's rice basket.

Despite being deprived of political power by the Dutch, Tabanan's royalty remained leaders among their people. Palaces continued to serve as centres for the arts, and royal families retained their role of presiding over temple ceremonies. In the forests near Gunung Batukaru lies the remote Pura Luhur Batukaru , a royal temple where thousands journey to pay homage.

The central mountains of northern Tabanan rise steeply through some of the more isolated parts of the island, where deer and wild boars roam dense forests. The region's southwest coast still remains fairly undeveloped,

with rough waves pounding quiet stretches of black-sand beaches. The stately Pura Tanah Lot sits on a rocky islet off the coast of Tabanan, but is more easily accessed from tourist centres in South Bali.

TABANAN

Tabanan ❶ town is the administrative capital of Tabanan Regency and is a bustling place with many businesses but few tourist attractions. Near the centre of the city is the so-called **Gedong Mario Theatre**, which is used

◎ Main attractions
Krambitan
Pura Taman Ayun
Sangeh Monkey Forest
Pura Luhur Batukaru
Jatiluwih

Map on page 192

A Krambitan woodcarver.

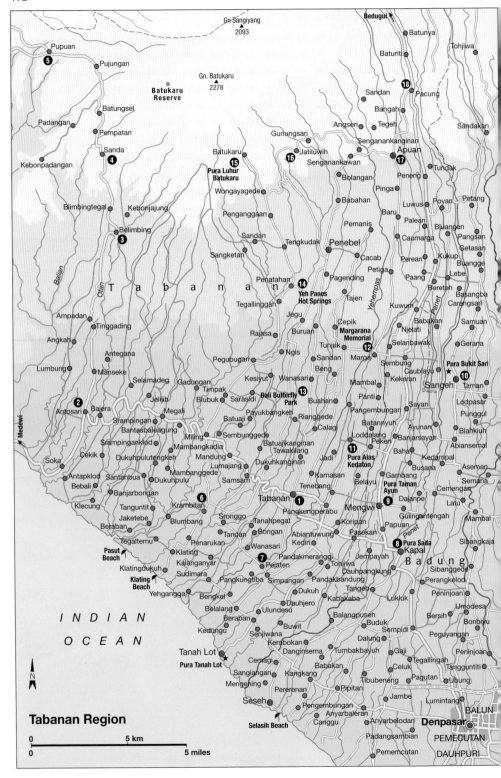

Tabanan Region

Gn Sangiyang
2093

Bedugul

Batunya

Tohjiwa

Pupuan
5

Pujungan

Baturiti

Gn. Batukaru
2278

Sandan

18 Pacung

Sandakan

Batukaru
Reserve

Angseri

Tegeh

Sendananginah

Apuan

Batungsel

Gunungsari

Jatiluwih
16

Sendanankawan

17

Tundak

Padangan

Pempatan

Pura Luhur
Batukaru
15

Bolangan

Peneng

Pinga

Sanda
4

Wongayagede

Babahan

Luwus

Poyan

Petang

Kebonpadangan

Penganggaan

Pemanis

Baru

Palean

Bluangan

Pangsan

Blimbingtegal

Kebonjajung

Sandan

Tengkudak

Cacab

Perean

Caumarga

Kukup

Getasan

Bélimbing
3

Sangketan

Penebel

Pagending

Petiga

Paang

Lebe

Buangge

Bereteh

Basangba

Penatahan

14
Yeh Panes
Hot Springs

Tajen

Kuwum

Babakan

Njelati

Carangsari

Ampadan

Tinggading

Tegallinggah

Jegu

Buruan

Cepik

Margarana
Memorial
12

Selanbawak

Samuan

Angkah

Antegana

Pegubugan

Rajasa

Ngis

Sandan

Tunjuk

Marga

Sembung

Caublayu

Gerana

Pura Bukit Sari

Lumbung

Manseke

Selamadeg

Gadungan

Kesiyut

Wanasari

Beng

Mambal

Kekeran

Sangeh

10
Taman

Antosari
2

Bajera

Jelijih

Timpak

Blubuk

Sarasidi

Bali Butterfly
Park
13

Buahan

Panti

Sayan

Lodpasar

Punggul

Strampingan

Megali

Batuaji

Payukbangkeh

Rianggéde

Calag

Batanyuh

Pangembungan

Ayunan

Blahkiuh

Abiansemal

Bantasbaleagung

Miling

Sembunggede

Loddalang

Peken

Banjarsayan

Baha

Soka

Cekik

Srampinganklod

Dukuhpulutengkeh

Mambangkadia

Mandung

Batuajikanginan

Tawakilang

Jadi

Pura Alas
Kedaton
11

Belayu

Gambang

Busana

Kedampal

Aseman

Semana

Antapklod

Santanbua

Dukuhpulu

Lumajang

Dukuhkanginan

Kamasan

Tenebang

Gulingantengah

Cemengan

Latu

Bebali

Banjarbongan

Mambanggede

Samsam

Pura Taman
Ayun
9

Dalanpe

Mambal

Klecung

Tanguntit

Krambitan
6

Tabanan
1

Mengwi

Papuan

Penet

Jaketebe

Blumbang

Stronggo

Pangkungperabu

Koripan

Pasekan

Pura Sada
8
Kapal

Sibangkaja

Beraban

Tegaltemu

Tandan

Bongan

Abiantuwung

Kediri

Jempayah

Dauhpangkung

Tangeb

Badung

Sibanggede

Pasut
Beach

Penarukan

Wanasari
7

Pandakmeranggi

Tohjiwa

Pejaten

Pandakbandung

Dukuh

Lukluk

Peninjoan

Perangkelod

Klating

Kalanganyar

Simpangan

Klatingdukuh

Sudimara

Pangkungtiba

Dauhjero

Kabakaba

Umodesa

Bersih

Bonbiyu

Klating
Beach

Yehganggal

Bengkel

Belalang

Ulundesu

Balangpuseh

Buduk

Sempidi

Peguyangan

Kedungu

Beraban

Buwit

Dalung

Gaji

Peninjoan

Tanah Lot

Pura Tanah Lot

Cemagi

Senjiwana

Kerobokan

Danginsema

Tumbakbayuh

Tegallingah

Tangguntiti

Sangiangan

Kangkang

Babakan

Celuk

Tibubeneng

Pagutan

Ubung

Mengehing

Pipitan

Jambe

Lumintang

Seseh

Pererenan

Pengembungan

BALUN

Selasih Beach

Canggu

Anyarbaleran

Anyarbelodan

Denpasar

PEMECUTAN

Padangsambian

DAUHPURI

Pememcutan

INDIAN
OCEAN

N

0   5 km

0   5 miles

for irregular performances of music and dance. Not much more than an unkempt community hall, it was built in 1974 to honour the region's late, great male dancer I Ketut Marya, better known simply as Mario. Born at the end of the 19th century, Mario was already dancing at the age of six. During the early 1920s, he developed and perfected the spectacular solo dances *kebyar duduk* and *kebyar trompong* (see page 71), which originated in north Bali during the 1910s. Mario's grace and movement enraptured European audiences who saw him dance on a tour of Europe during the 1930s.

At the eastern end of Tabanan town is the often overlooked **Museum Subak** (tel: 0361-810 315; Mon–Sat 8am–4.30pm, Fri 8am–12.30 pm), dedicated to rice cultivation, the mainstay of Tabanan's economy. Although rice is such an important part of Balinese life, visitors rarely come to see the museum's well documented displays of agricultural tools that trace the history and process of rice from paddy field to kitchen. Ask to see the adjacent traditional Balinese house with a *lumbug* (rice storehouse).

SCENIC DRIVE TO PUPUAN

Armed with information about rice growing in Tabanan, head west along the curving road wending its way to **Antosari** ❷. From here and at vantage points north at villages such as **Belimbing** ❸ and **Sanda** ❹ are spectacular rice terraces carved from hillsides on either side of the road as far as the eye can see. Continuing north leads to **Pujungan** where a track on the right leads to a scenic waterfall. From this point onwards clove and coffee plantations are interspersed with rice fields until the road reaches **Pupuan** ❺.

On Pupuan's main road, take a few moments to stop by **Vihara Dharma Giri** (tel: 0362-71029; donation). On the second level of a lovely three-tiered garden is a 10 metre (33ft)-long Buddha statue in a reclining position known as the "Sleeping Buddha". The centre offers meditation classes several times a year.

Museum Subak has well-documented displays about rice cultivation in Bali.

Tending rice on the terraces at Belimbing.

Detail of Boma image at Pura Sada.

The monkey forest at Sangeh.

From Pupuan, there are two options. Heading north for 12km (7.5 miles) will lead to Mayong and all the way to the coast at Seririt. Continuing southwest, the twisting road descends via Tista, Manggissari and Asahduren villages to Pekutatan in west Bali.

KRAMBITAN

Some 3km (2 miles) southwest of Tabanan town is **Krambitan** ➏, where a branch of the Tabanan royal family owns the atmospheric 17th-century **Puri Anyar** (New Palace) and **Puri Agung** (Great Palace), both with beautiful architecture and ambience of the past. The latter, where Tabanan royalty still live today, doubles as a guesthouse and restaurant (tel: 0851-0042 6060. Krambitan village has a unique style of traditional *wayang* (puppet figure) painting that depicts episodes from epics, myths and romantic tales. The men also maintain large *tektekan* ensembles, playing giant wooden cattle bells and rhythmically striking bamboo tubes to create exciting music.

PEJATEN

Southeast of Krambitan, a road zigzags through rice fields to **Pejaten** ➐, where traditional pottery is a home industry. Terracotta roof tiles, decorative wall plaques, whimsical figures and tableware are often glazed and painted with colourful accents. Stop by **Tanteri Ceramics** (tel: 0361-831 948; www.tantericeramicbali.com; daily 8am–4.30pm) to see a good selection of products. The range of vases, bowls, teapots, soap dishes and candle holders in greenish glaze are embellished with frogs, dragonflies and leaves.

PURA SADA

Southeast of Tabanan, the main road leads 10km (6 miles) to **Kapal** (Boat), where the roadsides are lined with temple shrines, guardian statues, and other temple paraphernalia. Much more important is **Pura Sada** ➑ (daily daylight hours), an ancestral shrine honouring the deified spirit Ratu Sakti Jayengrat (Powerful World Conquering Lord), whose identity still remains uncertain.

The original foundations may date to the 12th century, but the temple was rebuilt by one of the early Mengwi kings during the 17th century and is the oldest of the kingdom's state shrines. It was destroyed in the great earthquake of 1917 and was restored in 1949. A large brick and stone *prasada* (tower) with 11 tiers dominates the inner courtyard, giving the temple its name.

PURA TAMAN AYUN

Travel north 4km (2.5 miles) to **Mengwi**, turning right at the crossroads to **Pura Taman Ayun** ❾, built in the 18th century by a Mengwi king as a royal family temple. The surrounding moat gives the impression of a garden sanctuary with soaring *meru* (pagodas) resembling the masts of a majestic ship in the middle of a pond. Only worshippers are allowed inside, so you must admire this architectural masterpiece from behind the low temple walls.

This temple is a place to worship the gods of other sacred sites, with individual shrines to the Batukaru, Agung and Batur mountain deities, as well as to the resident god of the Pura Sada temple. Important Mengwi kings are also venerated here. Note the small and beautifully carved doors of the shrines.

SANGEH

From Pura Taman Ayun, travel east to Latu and then head north uphill to **Blahkiuh** and the sacred **Sangeh monkey forest** (daily daylight hours; fee). According to the Indian *Ramayana* epic, the monkey general Hanoman broke off a Himalayan mountain peak laden with magical plants to revive the fallen heroes of Rama's forces. When this feat was accomplished, Hanoman returned the peak but part of it fell to earth at Sangeh along with some of his monkey soldiers. Today, the forest is home to mischievous monkeys, so take the same precautions as you would at Ubud's Monkey Forest (see page 136). Towering 40-metre (130ft) tall *palahlar* (*Dipterocarpus trinervis*) trees, said to be 300 years old, make up this forest and are incorrectly assumed to be nutmeg trees. The place is a protected sanctuary and no one is permitted to chop down any of the trees or harm the monkeys.

In the heart of the forest lies **Pura Bukit Sari** ❿, a moss-covered 17th-century holy site originally built as a meditation temple and then converted to an agricultural temple. In the central courtyard, a large statue of the mythological Garuda bird symbolises freedom from suffering.

PURA ALAS KEDATON

Alternatively, to get to a more accessible monkey forest, head north out of Mengwi for some 5km (3 miles) and turn left at the junction to **Belayu**, where there is an amazing 35 ha (86 acre) flower farm. Continue past Belayu to **Pura Alas Kedaton** ⓫ (daily daylight hours). Besides the usual souvenir stalls, many fruit bats and

◎ Tip

While in Tabanan area, spend a few languid days at Puri Taman Sari (tel: 0361-894 5397, https://puri tmansari.com) near Marga. This lovely home of a descendant of the Mengwi royal family is open to guests who wish to experience authentic life in a Balinese village.

Sacrificial offerings at Pura Sada.

Yeh Panes' hot springs are said to have healing properties. After soaking in the hot pool, cool off in the adjacent fresh-water swimming pool.

Pura Luhur Batukaru, Tabanan.

mischievous monkeys – again, take heed – inhabit the surrounding trees.

MARGARANA MEMORIAL

Return to the crossroads at Belayu, turn left uphill and travel 6km (4 miles) to **Marga**, the site of the important **Margarana Memorial** ⓬ (daily 8am–5pm). In 1946, the commander of Indonesian nationalist troops in Bali, Lt Col. I Gusti Ngurah Rai, and his company of 94 guerrilla fighters were surrounded and outnumbered by Dutch forces in Marga. As an added measure, the Dutch also bombarded them from the air. Ngurah Rai and his men refused to surrender. Instead, they attacked the Dutch positions and died to the last man in a suicidal assault reminiscent of the royal *puputan* (finishing off) 40 years earlier in Badung, also in defiance of the Dutch.

The Margarana Memorial was built to honour these valiant soldiers. It is a five-sided pillar 17 metres (55ft) tall, inscribed with a courageous letter written by Ngurah Rai stating his refusal to surrender until freedom

was won. Nearby are 94 stone markers, each bearing the name and home village of a fallen hero. The anniversary of the massacre is remembered in a solemn ceremony every 20 November; Bali's airport and a university in Denpasar are named in honour of Ngurah Rai.

BALI BUTTERFLY PARK

From Marga, return to the main road and go west to **Tunjuk**, then head downhill to **Wanasari**. Just down the main road is the **Bali Butterfly Park** ⓭ (tel: 0361-894 0595; daily 8am–5pm). Around 15 species of butterflies flutter in an enclosed area; they are more active on warm, dry days, but you won't see them if it's raining.

YEH PANES

Head north uphill for another 9km (6 miles) to get to **Penatahan**, where hot water surges from a river bank at **Yeh Panes** ⓮. The Balinese believe that such an unusual natural phenomenon is inhabited by spirits, so a small temple was built at the site.

During World War II, occupying Japanese forces made the first additions to the place when they tried to create a Japanese-style outdoor bathing place here. The hot springs are now a part of the **Yeh Panes Hot Springs Resort** (tel: 0361-262 356 or 484 052; daily 9am–9pm), where for a fee non-guests can take a relaxing soak in its waters – there are private and semi-private pools here.

PURA LUHUR BATUKARU

Continue north up the road 10km (6 miles) via **Wongayagede** to one of Bali's most venerated temples, the **Pura Luhur Batukaru ⑮** (Temple of the Stone Coconut Shell; daily daylight hours), on the slopes of Gunung Batukaru The modest structures are devoid of ornate carving and gilding, blending in well with the surrounding forests. Although the 1991 renovations have detracted from the temple's mystique, it is still a quiet and beautiful place for reflection.

The main temple in the complex is dedicated to the god of **Gunung Batukaru**, second highest mountain on the island, at 2,278 metres (7,475ft). It's so important that every temple in southwest Bali has a shrine dedicated to this exalted deity. As the ancestral temple of the Mengwi and Tabanan royal families, there are also shrines for their deified ancestors. In the inner courtyard, the seven-tiered *meru* (pagoda) is dedicated to the ruler who established the Mengwi kingdom around the end of the 17th century; a three-tiered one is dedicated to the 18th-century founder of Tabanan. Descendants of both dynasties still maintain the temple today.

JATILUWIH

Back down the road 3km (2 miles) in Wongayagede is a T-junction. Turn left and follow the twisting road uphill to **Jatiluwih** mountain village ⑯, since 2008 a Unesco World Heritage Site for its preservation of traditional Balinese farming techniques. True to its name, which means extraordinary or truly marvellous, this scenic point at 850 metres (2,700ft) above sea level offers one of the most impressive panoramic views imaginable, with rice terraces stretching all the way to southern Bali. *Padi Bali* (indigenous Balinese rice) with long graceful stalks is grown here, and during harvest time women bear heavy bundles of the ripe yellow grains home on their heads while men carry yet more on each end of bamboo shoulder poles.

APUAN AND PACUNG

The road twists and turns further east to **Apuan ⑰**. This small mountain village is the spiritual home of sacred Barong masks from throughout Tabanan. From a T-junction in Apuan head 5km (3 miles) uphill where the road joins the main route at **Pacung ⑱**. Stop to admire the views of beautiful rice terraces from this vantage point. Taking the road north leads to the Bedugul area (see page 177).

(see page 177)

> ### ⊙ Tip
> Gunung Batukaru with its three ancient craters and primary rainforests is known to have the greatest biological diversity in Bali. Local guides will lead visitors on treks to the summit. Sarinbuana Eco-Lodge (tel: 0813-3902-8839, www.baliecolodge.com), a leader in sustainability, offers treks, bird-watching, cultural workshops and yoga at its resort located on the slopes of the mountain.

Zooming past Jatiluwih's rice terraces.

Snorkelling off Gili Meno, Gili Islands.

Sunset, Gili Twanangan.

LOMBOK

Lombok charms visitors with its unspoilt natural beauty of pristine white-sand beaches, forests and mountains as well as its largely untouched culture. Tourism impacts lightly on the traditional lifestyle.

Kuta Beach, Lombok.

Lying to the east of Bali and accessible by a 25-minute flight or two-hour fast boat ride from that better known island, Lombok is a haven for those seeking the unblemished beauty of the old Bali; however, the landscapes and cultures here are unique to Lombok.

At roughly 5,300 sq km (2,380 sq miles), Lombok is slightly smaller than Bali, and has a wide range of natural attractions and outdoor activities to suit more adventurous travellers.

Formerly one of the main tourist areas, west coast Senggigi's glory is fading, replaced by more serene Manggis to its north, while the three Gili islands off the northwest coast still attract the young at heart. On the south coast is Lombok's Kuta, bearing no resemblance to Bali's beaches. Once the domain of surfers, Lombok's southern beaches are in the throes of rapid development with high-end resorts and villas being added to the backpacker scene. Off the southwest coast, another set of islands, also called Gilis, attract solace-seeking snorkellers and divers, while climbers flock to summit Gunung Rinjani during the dry season.

The beaches surrounding Lombok are pristine, with clean waters bordered by long stretches of sand. The west of the island is especially green, with a series of beautiful bays skirting the entire coastline. The southern coast is even more stunning: long stretches of beaches and cliffs facing a vast ocean that provides some of the best surfing in Indonesia. Dominating north Lombok is a mountain range, crowned by the magnificent volcano, Gunung Rinjani, surrounded by forests embellished with waterfalls. To the south, agriculture is the mainstay. Many fields are still tilled using water buffalo and antiquated equipment, and the villages there are timeless.

An old woman making yarn with a spindle wheel at a traditional Sasak village.

For those seeking authentic cultural experiences, the ancient traditions of the local Sasak people are largely undisturbed by outside influences. The Sasak still live in traditional villages, farm, fish and produce handicrafts. Colourful ceremonies, dance and music are an authentic part of local life. Lombok pottery is exported all over the world, while old weaving techniques are still handed down through the generations.

Lombok may not have the spit and polish of Bali, but it does have the tropical paradise atmosphere that the larger island once had.

Sasak fisherman repairing his boat on the west coast.

WEST LOMBOK

West Lombok has a tourism infrastructure that almost rivals South Bali – but thankfully it doesn't overwhelm. The serenity of Mangsit invites some serious chilling out, but the more active can also explore old temples, markets and the unique Sasak culture further south.

Denpasar

The Sasak, a Malay race inhabiting Lombok for at least 2,000 years, probably settled on the island's coastal areas as long as 4,000 years ago. For much of the last 600 years, Lombok was a feudal state with many small kingdoms, some of which followed animistic beliefs, while others practised a combination of animism with Hinduism or Buddhism. Over the centuries, Java influenced Lombok in varying degrees, eventually conquering it in the 14th century and incorporating it into the Hindu Majapahit Empire. Several small kingdoms on Lombok were once ruled by Javanese nobles who had been exiled to Lombok; in fact Sasak aristocracy today still claims Javanese ancestry. Java introduced both Hinduism and Islam to Lombok, but its religious and political influence waned by the 17th century. Islam gradually spread through eastern and central Lombok, while the west coast, being closer to Bali, was predominantly Hindu.

From the mid-17th century onwards, the Hindu Balinese Karangasem kingdom colonised Lombok, ruling the island until 1894. Balinese influence always centred in the west, where Balinese still constitute at least 10 percent of the population today. The Balinese king, Anak Agung Ngurah Gede Karangasem, gained extensive influence over western Lombok during the mid-1800s and

oversaw development of the arts and the construction of an impressive number of temples. He also restricted the land rights of the Sasak aristocracy on Lombok, introduced an inflexible taxation system, and demanded forced labour of Sasak peasantry. Revolts erupted several times in the 19th century, with Islam the rallying cry among the Sasak.

Sasak leaders approached the Dutch for help in overthrowing Balinese rule in the early 1890s. The Dutch, mistakenly believing that Lombok was rich in tin, assisted and the Sasak War broke

◎ Main attractions
Mayura Water Palace
Banyumulek
Gunung Pengsong
Taman Narmada
Pura Suranadi
Pura Batu Bolong

◉ Map on page 204

Malimbu fishing beach, along the coastal road between Senggigi and Bangsal.

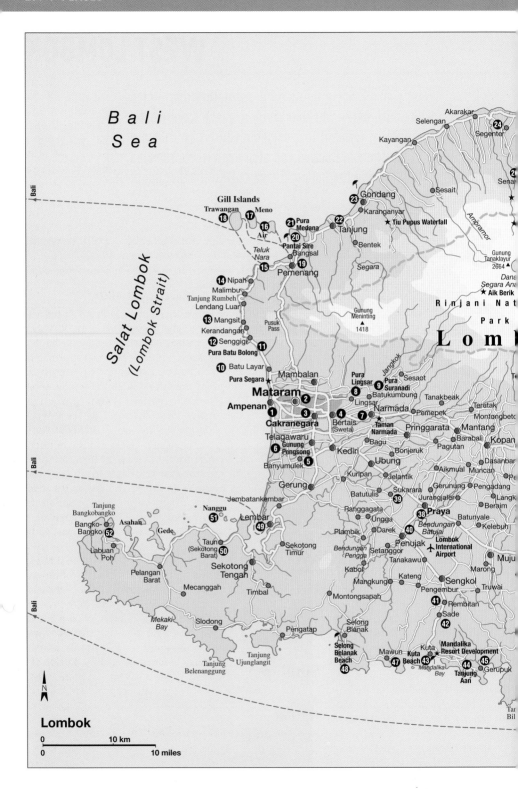

B a l i
S e a

Akarakar
Selengan
Kayangan
Segenter 24

Sesait
Senal

Gill Islands
Trawangan Meno
18   17 16 21 **Pura Medana** 22 Gondang 23
Air
20 **Pantai Sire**
Teluk Nara 15 Bangsal
19 **Pemenang**

Karanganyar
★ Tiu Pupus Waterfall
Tanjung
Bentek

Ambramor

Gunung
Tanaklayur
2664 ▲

Segara

Dana
Segara Ana
★ Aik Berik

14 Nipah
Malimbu
Tanjung Rumbeh
Lendang Luar
13 Mangsit
Kerandangan
12 Senggigi 11
Pura Batu Bolong

Gunung
Meninting
▲
1418

Pusuk
Pass

R i n j a n i   N a t

P a r k

L o m l

10 Batu Layar
Pura Segara ★

Mambalan

Pura
Lingsar Pura Sesaot
9 Suranadi
8   Batukumbung Tanakbeak
Lingsar

Jangkok

Terutak
Montongbet

Mataram 2
Ampenan 1 3
Cakranegara 4 7
Bertais
(Sweta)

Narmada
Pemepek

Taman Narmada Pringgarata Mantang
Barabali Kopan
Pagutan

Telagawaru
6 **Gunung Pengsong**
5
Banyumulek

Bagu
Bonjeruk
Kediri **Ubung**
Kuripan Jelantik

Dasanan
Aikmual Muncan
Pe

Gerung
Jembatankembar

Batutulis
Sukarara Gerunong Pengadang
39 Jurangjaler Langk
Beraim

Tanjung
Bangkobangko
Bangko- **Nanggu**
Bangko 52 Asahan 51 **Lembar**
Gede 49

Ranggagata
Ungga
38 **Praya** Batunyale
Plambik Darek 40 Bendungan Kelebuh
Batujai
**Lombok
International
Airport**

Taun
(Sekotong
Barat) 50
**Sekotong
Tengah**
Mecanggah
Timbal

Bendungan
Pengga Setanggor
Kabol Tanakawu
Mangkung Kateng
Montongsapah Pengembur

Penujak

Muju
Marong
Sengkol Truwai
41 Rembitan
Sade
42

Pelangan
Barat
Mekaki
Bay Slodong
Pengatap

Selong
Blanak

Tanjung Tanjung
Belenanggung Ujunglangit

Selong
Belanak
Beach
48

Mawun **Kuta**
47 Kuta
Beach 43

**Mandalika
Resort Development**

*Mandalika
Bay*

44 Gerupuk
**Tanjung
Aan**
45

Tar
Bil

▲
N
↑

Lombok

0   10 km
0   10 miles

*Salat Lombok
(Lombok Strait)*

Bali
Bali
Bali

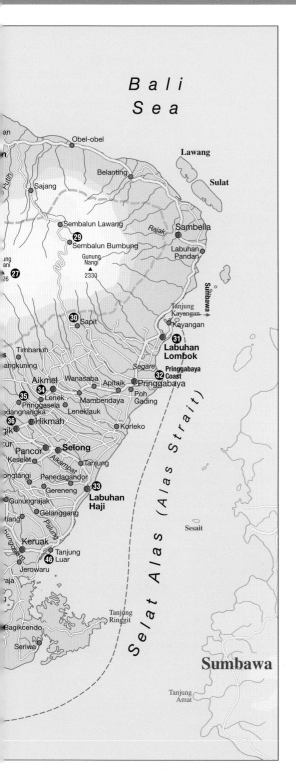

out in 1894. The Balinese were eventually defeated, and a number of temples and palaces on Lombok were destroyed. Many of the final confrontations ended in *puputan*, the mass suicides of Balinese palace nobles, their families and followers.

With the defeat of the Balinese, the Sasak leaders believed they had the right to rule. Instead, the Dutch took over the island, banishing the king and his family and offering only minor government positions to Sasak and Balinese leaders. Colonialism intensified land use and taxation until the Japanese took control of the island in 1942. When the Japanese left in 1945, the Dutch returned briefly but were repelled by nationalist guerrillas. Lombok has remained independent ever since.

RELIGION IN LOMBOK

There are two main groups among the Sasak: Wektu Lima and Wektu Telu. The Wektu Lima are orthodox Sunni Muslims, while the Wektu Telu are nominal Muslims who combine a belief in Allah and some Islamic observances with a mosaic of animism, ancestor worship, Hinduism and Buddhism. The Wektu Lima have adopted the Islamic identity of Muslims throughout Indonesia, while the Wektu Telu are generally uninterested in the world at large, focusing instead on their strong ties to ancestral lands.

While the Wektu Lima Muslims observe Islamic religious practices, especially fasting during the month of Ramadan, the Wektu Telu do not. Other religions, particularly Hinduism and Buddhism, peacefully co-exist alongside the local Muslim population, and there are a variety of mosques, churches and temples to visit on the island.

Today, Lombok retains many traits and customs similar to those of Java and Bali, and the Sasak language has many words from Javanese and Balinese (although Bahasa Indonesia is spoken outside of the home). However, the Sasak culture is distinct from that of Java and Bali, with many traditions and beliefs specific only to Lombok.

WEST LOMBOK TOWNS

The west coast of Lombok has been the most developed area of the island with small

⊙ Tip

Lombok has a reputation for producing excellent pearls. Sellers on the streets and beaches will offer pearls at what seem to be very low prices. These are genuine pearls, although usually of low quality, so be sure to bargain hard. Better yet, shop at a reputable pearl dealer. Lia Pearl in Ampenan (0819-1791 8919) buys their pearls from a farm on Lombok's northwest coast and purchases come with a guarantee.

towns, relatively good roads, shops, restaurants and hotels, however, that is changing with construction in the south.

Mangsit, just five minutes north of Senggigi, is the west coast's most popular resort area and is located about one hour north of the Lombok International Airport. The west coast of Lombok faces Bali across the Lombok Strait and affords wonderful sunsets with the sacred volcano, Gunung Agung on Bali, silhouetted against the orange-tinted evening sky.

The west is also lush, with mountains inland and the wide Lombok Strait forming a series of picturesque bays and beaches along the western and northwestern coastline. West Lombok, being closest to Bali, has a long history of Hindu settlement. Traces of the old empires are still very much visible in its large Balinese-Hindu population, and its many Balinese-style temples and ceremonies.

AMPENAN

The three main cities in western Lombok – Ampenan, Mataram and Cakranegara – blend together to create what is, for Lombok, an urban sprawl. **Ampenan ❶** is the old port town and some Dutch colonial architecture is still visible in the buildings there. This area becomes a boisterous market at night, filled with *warung* (food stalls) and *kaki lima* (food carts) hawking cheap and tasty food.

There are occasional performances of the *gandrung* dance or the shadow puppet play known as *wayang Sasak* on special holidays. With its numerous shops, cheap hotels, dusty roads, plentiful *cidomo* (horse-drawn carts), gold and pearl shops, Ampenan is a colourful town to explore on foot.

MATARAM

Mataram ❷ is the main administrative centre for Lombok and Sumbawa, which comprises **Nusa Tenggara Barat (NTB)** province, and has government offices, banks, mosques, the main post office and Mataram University.

Mataram's **Museum Negeri Nusa Tenggara Barat** (West Nusa Tenggara State Museum) (tel: 0370-632

Two Sasak children ride in a tumbrel (two-wheeled cart), pulled by a pony, in Lombok.

159; Tue–Thur, Sat–Sun 8am–3pm, Fri 8–11am) houses historical and cultural artefacts from Lombok and Sumbawa, and it occasionally hosts special exhibits. Displays cover geology, history and culture.

Another interesting stop is the cultural centre, **Taman Budaya Provinsi NTB** (tel: 0370-622 428) on Jalan Majapahit, where there are regular performances of traditional music and dance.

CAKRANEGARA AND BERTAIS

Just to the east of Mataram town is **Cakranegara** ❸, Lombok's main shopping area. It is also home to many Chinese and Balinese, who make up over 50 percent of the town's population. Many of Lombok's weaving and basketry industries are located near Cakra, as it is called locally. Turn left at the main traffic lights and look for the market on the right near the bridge; the baskets made here are sold in Bali at many times what you pay in Lombok.

Further east, near the bus terminal, is **Bertais** ❹, the next large town east of Cakra. Also sometimes called **Sweta**, it has a huge daily market which sells everything that is made or produced on the island, from foodstuffs to clothing, exotic birds, handicrafts and more. As always, take precautions with your belongings in crowded areas.

PURA MERU

There are several interesting sights in Cakranegara, foremost of which is **Pura Meru** (daily 8am–5pm; donation) at Jalan Selaparang. Built in 1720 by Balinese prince Anak Agung Made Karang, this is the largest temple on Lombok. Its three main *meru* (pagoda) represent the Hindu trinity – Siwa (Shiva), Wisnu (Vishnu) and Brahma.

On Lombok, this is the most important temple for the Balinese, and its annual Pujawali festival celebrating the temple's birthday, held over five days during the September or October full moon, is the biggest Balinese-Hindu celebration. The outer courtyard hall has drums that call the devout to ceremonies and festivals. Two buildings with raised offering platforms are found in the central courtyard, while the interior enclosure has 33 shrines and the three multi-tiered *meru*.

PURA MAYURA

Just across the street from Pura Meru stands **Pura Mayura** (daily 8am–5pm; donation), built in 1744 as the court temple of the last Balinese kingdom in Lombok, Karangasem. Part of the **Taman Mayura** (Mayura Park), a large artificial lake here holds *a bale kambang* (floating pavilion) once used as Karangasem's justice hall. Today, the palace gardens are a playground for children and grazing livestock. The temple sits behind the lake.

BANYUMULEK AND GUNUNG PENGSONG

About 7km (4 miles) south of Cakranegara is **Banyumulek** ❺ village, a major centre for the production of the

The daily market at Bertais (Sweta), east of Cakranegara, is a hive of activity, with traders from the surrounding villages converging on this small town.

Pura Meru, built by a long-ago Balinese prince.

The Pura Mayura water gardens.

View of the pool at Taman Narmada.

distinctive terracotta pottery that Lombok is so famous for. In the mornings, visitors can watch the women potters at work. The eye-catching pots, plates, saucers, bowls, lamps, planters and goblets are decorated, etched and engraved in unique traditional and contemporary designs with paints, textiles and other finishes.

Just 3km (2 miles) west of Banyumulek village is **Gunung Pengsong** ⑥, where a holy shrine (daily 8am–5pm) sits on a hilltop and has lovely vistas of rice fields, the coast and Gunung Rinjani. Populated by aggressive monkeys, this is the hill the Balinese aimed for in the mythical account of their initial arrival in west Lombok.

NARMADA

Continuing some 10km (6 miles) east of Cakranegara is **Narmada** ⑦. The structures and pool at **Taman Narmada** (Narmada Park; daily 9am–4pm; fee) were reportedly built in 1727 as a replica of Gunung Rinjani and Danau Segara Anak (see page 220), the crater lake within Gunung Rinjani's

caldera. When the ruling king, Anak Agung Ngurah Gede Karangasem, became too old to make the long and mandatory trek to Segara Anak, he built Taman Narmada – comprising a large lake surrounded by terraced gardens, pools and a temple, **Pura Kalasa** – allowing him to perform his rituals. The annual pilgrimage to Segara Anak, where pilgrims threw gold pieces into the lake as offerings, still exists to this day, and the festival at Taman Narmada coincides with this pilgrimage during the full moon of either October or November.

The gardens at Pura Narmada are splendid, and on special occasions, *gandrung, gendang belek* and other traditional dances are performed here. The two swimming pools at Narmada, where you can splash around (separate admission charge), are very popular with local children.

PURA LINGSAR

Northwest of Narmada is **Pura Lingsar** ⑧ (daily 8am–5pm), with two shrines, one Hindu and the other for

Muslim Wektu Telu followers. This is the temple where people of various religions – Hindus, Buddhists, Christians and Muslims – come together to pray for prosperity, rain, fertility and health. The temple is associated with irrigation and rice, and the annual festival here features a ritualised mock battle.

Built around 1714, Pura Lingsar was originally based on the prevailing animist beliefs of the time, and some of the original animist statues still remain today. While the main courtyard symbolically unites the deities of Bali and Lombok, the second courtyard, called Kemaliq, is used by the Wektu Telu and contains sacred pools and unique altars of rocks, reminiscent of ancient megalithic worship. These rocks, brought down from the top of Gunung Rinjani and dressed in ceremonial cloths, are believed to contain the spirits of the ancestors of the land.

Pura Lingsar has a spring-fed pool which contains large freshwater holy eels. Visitors are welcome to accompany a temple priest who will feed the eels hard-boiled eggs, purchased at nearby stands.

PURA SURANADI

Located a few kilometres northeast of Narmada in **Suranadi** is **Pura Suranadi** ❾ (daily 8am–5pm), a complex of three temples. Pura Suranadi is among the oldest and holiest of the Balinese temples in Lombok, founded by the 16th-century Javanese high priest, Danghyang Nirartha. Underground streams bubble up into restored baths used for ritual bathing; this is also where locals obtain the holy water for cremation ceremonies.

Huge sacred eels live in the pools and streams here and, as at Pura Lingsar, can sometimes be lured out with an offering of hardboiled eggs, purchased from a nearby stall. The eels are considered holy (to see a sacred

eel is deemed lucky) and it is taboo to eat them or to contaminate the waters.

Beyond Suranadi, on the main road before the temple, is **Suranadi Nature Park** (daily 8am–5pm; charge). Stroll through this small botanical forest with labelled specimens and observe birds, monkeys and deer.

WEST COAST

The main road starts at Ampenan and winds its way up the entire west coast, around the north of the island and down the east coast, making orientation and travelling around easy. Heading north from Ampenan is **Pura Segara**, a Balinese sea temple. The Chinese cemetery on the main road has interesting sea-facing graves painted in bright colours with Chinese decorations.

Batu Layar ❿, on the hill a few kilometres before Senggigi, has an important ancestral makam *cemetery* where Muslims come to picnic and to pray for health and success. There are many such *makam* all over Lombok (the graves of key religious leaders generally become shrines).

Capes for ritual dancers.

Temple architecture.

Nearby **Pura Batu Bolong**  (daily 8am–5pm) meaning "hollow rock" is an interesting Hindu temple on a cliff facing Bali across the Lombok Strait. Built on a large rock outcrop with a hole at the base, from which the temple takes its name, it is said that beautiful virgins were once sacrificed to the sea from the seat-like rock at the outermost point. Colourful Hindu ceremonies are held here every month at the dark and full moons, and also at Balinese-Hindu festival times. This is a great place to watch the sunset, with fantastic vistas across to Gunung Agung on Bali.

SENGGIGI

About 10km (6 miles) north of Ampenan is **Senggigi**  formerly one of the main tourist centres on Lombok, but one that has now lost its lustre. Its renowned restaurants, bars and nightclubs are – for the most part – a shadow of their former selves. Nowhere near as large or as busy as its Bali counterparts, Senggigi still has deluxe resorts as well as budget accommodation, along with

Looking out over Malimbu beach.

other tourist facilities – tour agencies, supermarkets, moneychangers and a post office.

Senggigi beach is the large bay that forms the area's centre, with the main road running parallel and slightly inland, and large resorts occupying the space between. The beach provides picturesque views of Bali's Gunung Agung.

Just off the spit of land at the south end of the beach is **Senggigi Point**, a good spot for snorkelling and, in the right conditions, some decent surf breaks.

NORTH OF SENGGIGI

Tourism development now runs north along the coastal road for about 10km (6 miles), with hotels and restaurants along the beautiful beaches that line the entire west coast. About 2km (1 mile) north is **Kerandangan**, with a popular beach nearby and some nice hotels and villas in a pretty valley.

Further north, **Mangsit**  has replaced Senggigi as west Lombok's star with its serene atmosphere and boutique-style hotels positioned along beautiful bays. Mangsit is a good base for exploring the rest of the island, with day trips to places of interest within a few hours' drive. The pace here is laid back, with activities centred around total relaxation.

Deserted white-sand beaches continue all the way north along the coastal road. **Malimbu**  and **Nipah** are two pretty bays that are good for snorkelling. A few *warung* (eateries) dot Nipah's shoreline. **Teluk Nara**  is on a large bay about 25km (15 miles) north of Senggigi. There is a small private port and all the main dive operators have boats here to transfer guests to the **Gili Islands** (see page 213) as an alternative to the public harbour at nearby **Bangsal Harbour**, the main jumping-off point (see page 217). Also located at Teluk Nara is Autore Pearl Farm & Showroom (tel. 0813-3992 0020; daily 9am–5pm), which offers tours to see how the gems are cultivated.

Sunset at Senggigi beach.

Gili Trawangan beach.

THE GILI ISLANDS

Tropical island aficionados declare these islands perfect for snorkelling and diving, or just plain lolling about. If picture-perfect, white-sand beaches lapped by aquamarine waters harbouring colourful coral reefs and fish are not sufficient draws, head for Gili Trawangan, the "party island".

The three best known Gili islands lie just off Lombok's northwest coast. For years they have attracted visitors from around the world for their pristine waters, great diving and snorkelling, and for their funky, laid back charm, with no cars, motorbikes or dogs to disturb the peace. The word "Gili" means "small island", in fact, there are many Gili islands surrounding the mainland, and so the three most famous have come to be known as the 'Gilis' by travellers. Connoisseurs of equatorial settings have long considered the Gilis to be on par with the appeal of Thailand's south coast island havens and the coral atolls of Maldives.

Over the years, each of the Gilis has developed a unique personality. Although previously the domain of backpackers and more intrepid travellers, word has got around and the Gili islands now attract a diverse range of both upmarket and budget visitors, from serious diving enthusiasts to families and couples of all ages. The Gilis are small, flat coral islands with sparse vegetation and rainfall, and it can seem much hotter here than on the mainland. There is no fresh water on the Gilis, so be prepared for salt-water showers in budget accommodations. Water is drawn from wells or shipped from the mainland, hence the need to conserve the islands' limited resources. Drink

only bottled water, eat well-cooked food, and, if staying in budget hotels, choose places with mosquito nets. There have been several fatal cases of methanol poisoning in Indonesia, contracted from home-made alcohol laced with unhealthy substances; the best advice is to drink only brand-name spirits or wine, or stick to beer. The only form of transport, apart from bicycles and walking, are the delightful *cidomo* (horse-drawn carts).

A good number of reputable and internationally accredited dive

Main attractions

Gili Air
Gili Meno
Gili Trawangan

Map on page 204

A perfect view of the beach on Gili Trawangan.

⊙ Fact

Although the Gilis are generally laid-back, it's important to remember that the local people are primarily Muslim. Nude and topless sunbathing is offensive to the islanders. Please respect local customs and keep your clothes on.

operators based in Lombok have dive shops on the Gili islands. While much of the coral in the shallow waters is in various stages of regrowth, at greater depths and at the specific dive locations around the three islands, the pristine waters are home to an abundant variety of corals, aquatic life and thousands of species of tropical fish.

The Gilis are easily reached from the mainland by boats from Bangsal Harbour, or through Lombok-based tour and dive operators.

GILI AIR

Gili Air ⑯ is the island closest to the mainland. It has the largest local population of the three and combines the charm of a tropical island with easy access to the people and culture that has made Lombok so special.

Accommodations, eateries and a few bars encircle island. On the east coast, facing Lombok and the towering Gunung Rinjani, there are spectacular sunrises; sunsets over Gunung Agung on Bali are visible from the south and western coasts of Gili Air. The best

beaches are also found on the east side, with clear turquoise waters and soft white sand.

Diving facilities abound and there is good snorkelling directly from the shore, particularly from the east and northeast beaches. **Air Wall**, off the east coast, is a popular dive site, with soft corals that gleam yellow and orange in the sunlight, and harbour scorpion fish and thousands of glassfish. In the deeper waters are white-tip reef sharks and schools of larger fish species.

Manta Dive (tel: 0878-6555 6914; https://manta.dive.com) is a training facility certified by both PADI and SSI that offers courses in several languages. Their experienced instructors can take you to the area's best dive spots.

There is a good range of accommodation on Gili Air, from simple guesthouses to more expensive hotels with all the attendant creature comforts. Dining opportunities range from good-quality restaurants to simple beach *warung (food stalls)* and, while the bars aren't as loud as on Gili Trawangan, there are still opportunities to have fun.

Fire dancing on Gili Trawangan.

GILI MENO

Gili Meno ⓱ is the middle and smallest island of the three, with the lowest population. The pace here is slower than on its sister islands. Small hotels and basic beach side huts provide accommodation for those seeking less crowded beaches, clean waters and quiet walks under the star-filled skies.

The landscape is flat, with coconut groves inland and a small lake in the west from which the locals harvest meagre supplies of salt. **Meno Wall**, off the west coast, **Meno Bounty** off the southwest side and **Mirkos** in the east are popular dive sites around Gili Meno. Hawksbill and green turtles call the waters around Gili Meno home and are a common sight, particularly on the northwest corner, while the reefs just offshore feature outcrops of brilliant blue coral.

Accommodation, beachside bars and *warung (food stalls)* are found throughout the island and provide plenty of opportunities for viewing spectacular sunrises and sunsets over the volcanoes.

GILI TRAWANGAN

Gili Trawangan ⓲ is furthest from the mainland and the largest, most famous island of the three with a reputation as 'the party island' – thanks to the wild parties held at its bars and restaurants. The scene here has evolved rapidly, whereas Gili Meno and Gili Air have developed at a slower pace. Famililarly known as Gili T, Trawangan still maintains its timeless tropical paradise charm, but now has a wider range of facilities to cater to a broader spectrum of travellers.

Backpackers flock here to enjoy the gorgeous white-sand beaches, cheap accommodation, and (naturally) the parties held at different locations every night, while more up-market travellers stay at the better resorts and boutique villas. There is good snorkelling just off the shore with waters that teem with a still abundant variety of tropical fish

species. Strong currents are sometimes a bother, especially in the strait with neighbouring Gili Meno. Further out are vast gardens of coral, regarded as one of the best dive spots in Lombok, particularly **Shark Point** to the north of the island.

The small hill in the south of the island is a great lookout from which to enjoy the spectacular sunsets across the ocean to Bali; or, the brilliant sunrise over Gunung Rinjani on Lombok. At the far southern end of the hill are remnants of old World War II Japanese gun emplacements and crumbling bunkers, but the hand-dug tunnels have been blocked up.

There is accommodation throughout the island, but most of the action takes place in the southeast in the area called "Sentral" where boats dock. Hotels on the north coast offer peaceful alternatives. Gili Trawangan has the best tourism infrastructure of the Gilis, including shops, tour agencies, moneychangers, ATMs, a non-emergency 24-hour medical clinics and internet cafés.

The waters around Gili Meno are home to hawksbill (pictured) and green turtles.

Snorkelling off Gili Meno.

Mount Rinjani volcano rising
high above the clouds.

NORTH AND EAST LOMBOK

Trekking in the Mt Rinjani National Park, a Unesco Global Geopark, brings you to awesome forests and waterfalls. Summit the volcano, if you dare, or head east to a part of Lombok that few travellers bother to visit.

North Lombok is reached by two main roads. The coastal road that runs from Ampenan all the way up the west coast to the north provides stunning views of the many beautiful bays and beaches that line this coast, as well as vistas over the Gili Islands and Bali to the west. Alternatively, the **Pusuk Pass**, a winding mountain road, starts in Gunungsari, just a bit north of Mataram, and runs through the mountains inland, terminating at Pemenang in the north. The drive up the pass provides wonderful views of valleys and gorges, with rivers running through the tropical forests and small villages scattered among the trees. Families of grey monkeys live in the jungle and sometimes hang out beside the road. Beyond Pemenang, the northern coastal road winds past stunning seascapes and sparsely populated villages. Heading inland from Anyar leads to the lofty Gunung Rinjani, the main attraction in this area.

PEMENANG AND BANGSAL

Pemenang ⑲ is the crossroads where the coastal road (Jalan Raya) meets the Pusuk Pass road and continues north around the island. The road to the west runs only about 1km (.5 mile) to **Bangsal Harbour**, which is the main point of departure for public boats to the beautiful Gili Islands. The road is blocked roughly halfway down at a parking

Hiking up to the volcano.

area, and you must continue on foot about another 400 metres to the beach. *Cidomo* (horse cart) drivers will entice you to pay high prices for the ride to the beach, but it isn't that far. The harbour area is rife with persistent touts who hang around trying to force travellers to charter boats and buy goods before going to the islands. All the supplies found on the mainland can be purchased on the Gili Islands, so ignore the overpriced mosquito repellent and water bottles sold here. Don't let anyone touch your bag and if you do use

Main attractions

Pantai Sire
Tanjung Market
Senaru
Tiu Kelep Waterfall
Gunung Rinjani
Sembalun Bumbung and
  Sembalun Lawang

Map on page 204

a porter, negotiate a price beforehand of around Rp 10,000 per bag. Tickets for the public boats out to the islands can be purchased from the large white building directly to the left on the beach, and boat charters can also be organised from here, with fixed prices clearly displayed inside the building.

PANTAI SIRE AND TANJUNG MEDANA

Further north, a small signposted road branches off from the main road to **Pantai Sire ⑳**, a beautiful, long, whiter-than-white sand beach. This is also the site for the Sire Beach Golf Club,, an 18-hole course with magnificent views from the manicured greens. A scattering of luxurious holiday villas rest beside the beach, already the location of the funky-fantastic, antique-chic Hotel Tugu Lombok.

On the tip of the next peninsula north at **Tanjung Medana** is a small temple, **Pura Medana ㉑** (daily 8am–5pm), with wonderful sunset views and a peaceful atmosphere. On the road out to the temple is the lovely Medana Resort and, at the very end, the luxurious Oberoi Lombok, in a fantastic beach-side location.

TANJUNG AND GONDANG

About 4km (2 miles) north of Pura Medana is **Tanjung ㉒**. Muslims, Hindus and Buddhists live here and, as a result, a wide variety of ceremonies originate from this area. Tanjung has an interesting daily market and on Sundays a cattle market where cows, goats and horses from all over the island are bought and sold.

Up the coast is **Gondang ㉓**, a small town near a good beach. **Tiu Pupus Waterfall** is a 20-minute walk beyond the end of a rocky road. The spring-fed falls are spectacular during the rainy season (November–April), and flow into a deep pool where you can swim. Sadly, **Kerurak** traditional Sasak village was devastated in the 2018 earthquake. Another 30-minute trek leads to the **Kerta Gangga Waterfalls**, with three beautiful falls set in the jungle.

SEGENTER

Travel about 20km (13 miles) from Gondang and head inland at **Sukadana**

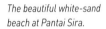
The beautiful white-sand beach at Pantai Sira.

to find dusty **Segenter** Sasak village ㉔, which provides a glimpse into the harsh reality of life on the island's dry side. The people in this small northern interior village eke out a living growing corn and beans, yet they welcome visitors with a smile and proudly share their simple life with tours.

BAYAN

Back on the coastal road, turning right at **Anyar** leads to **Bayan** ㉕, a village that maintains old dance and poetic traditions, as well as *kemidi rudat*, a theatre based on the fables, *The Thousand and One Nights*. The village is also the site of the phenomenal Alip festival held once every three years. Bayan is the home of the Wetu Telu religion, which combines the practices of Islam with Hinduism, Buddhism and animist beliefs. The adherents of Wetu Telu (meaning 'three times') pray three times a day instead of five, fast only three days during Ramadan and recognise only three of the five pillars of Islam.

The most important Wetu Telu celebration is the Prophet Muhammad's birthday in October or November. One of the island's oldest and most important Wetu Telu mosques is in Bayan and is decorated with mythical creatures.

SENARU

The inland road from Bayan leads to of **Senaru** ㉖, one of four gateways to Mt. Rinjani National Park (officially Taman Nasional Gunung Rinjani; hotline: 0819-1722 2228), a nature reserve of 41,000 hectares (101,313 acres) inside park boundaries, plus another 66,000 hectares (163,010 acres) of protected forest outside that surrounds Gunung Rinjani volcano. It was named an Unesco Global Geopark in September 2018. The whole area is a picturesque haven, featuring magnificent waterfalls, lush jungle treks, traditional villages, and plantations of tobacco and cashew nuts, tended alongside verdant rice terraces. Flora and fauna of the Wallacea transitional zone are apparent in the surrounding jungles.

The **Sendang Gile Waterfall** at Senaru is spectacular. The water cascades in a steep vertical drop down the hillside

Trekking Gunung Rinjani requires sturdy hiking boots.

The Gili Islands can be reached easily from north Lombok – the main departure point is at Bangsal Harbour.

⊙ Tip

There are many hadji (Muslims who have been to Mecca) in both Sembalun Lawang and Sembalun Bumbung, but the latter has retained the older traditions, such as *tandang mendat*, a men's martial dance, and a unique version of *wayang wong* theatre.

into a rocky stream below. It's best to hire a local guide for the gentle 30-minute trek through the jungle to the awesome Tiu Kelep Waterfall, dominated by a projectile jet of pure white energy. The 2018 earthquakes damaged some of the pathways and the youth-giving pool at the base is no longer there. Despite tricky footing due to scattered debris in lieu of a path, this trek is still worth it.

CLIMBING MT RINJANI

In addition to long-established starting points for climbing, Senaru and Sembalun Lawang (see below), there are two more recent entry points for trekking at Lombok's celebrated volcano, **Gunung Rinjani ㉗**. The Sembalun route to the summit is slightly shorter than the Senaru path, but there is more accommodation at Sembalu. The new routes begin at **Aik Berik** to the south and **Timbanuh** to the east. Aik Berik has two stunning waterfalls, Benang Kelambu and Benang Stokel, at the beginning of the ascent; however, from Aik Berik there is no access to the crater. The route from Timbanuh is the steepest of the four options.

Rinjani soars some 3,726 metres (12,224ft) above sea level and is the second highest volcano in Indonesia, attracting thousands of trekkers and climbers annually. The huge crater near the top contains a beautiful crescent-shaped lake, **Danau Segara Anak ㉘** (Child of the Sea Lake). A smaller volcanic cone, **Gunung Baru Jari**, juts out from one side of the crater. There are a number of caves, small waterfalls and hot springs scattered around the volcano, most important of which is **Air Kalak** on the northeast of the crater, where the volcanically heated waters are said to cure illnesses, such as skin diseases and high blood pressure. Note that this pool is sacred to the Sasak people, who bring their sacred items here to cleanse them. Visitors are welcome to soak in the warm waters, but only if the proper respect is shown.

The climb to the summit requires an overnight stay on the mountain, and only guides licensed by the Rinjani authorities are allowed to operate here. At all four entry points a park entry permit is required and a fee must be paid, which is posted on Rinjani's online ticketing site, www.erijani.id. You can pre-pay the fee at that site, and trekking packages using authorised guides can be booked through the park's official website, https://rinjaninationalpark.com. Reputable organisations offering hiking programs are **Rinjani Trekking Center** (https://rinjanitrekingcenter.com), an association of licensed guides with headquarters at Sembalun; **Rinjani Trek Organisation**, a guides' association based at Senaru, and **Rinjani Women's Guide Association** (www.rinjaniwomen adventure.com), also based in Senaru.

The park is often closed in the heart of the rainy season, January–March, and can be closed if volcanic activity occurs. Check current conditions upon arrival. Also note that it gets very cold at night; jackets and gloves are advised. Most trekkers stop at the crater rim. It's another 1,000 metres

Thundering Sendang Gile Waterfalls.

(3,280ft) to the summit, requiring a high level of fitness.

SEMBALUN BUMBUNG AND SEMBALUN LAWANG

Branching off the main coastal road from Bayan, a smaller road runs inland through the mountains with wonderful scenery of dense forests opening up to valley vistas and towering mountain ranges. **Sembalun Bumbung** ㉙ is located in a high, cool valley on Rinjani's slopes, along with a neighbouring village, **Sembalun Lawang**. Both are surrounded by verdant fields and valleys planted with garlic, fruit and vegetables, which thrive in the cooler climate. The traditional weaving interests of the village were abandoned many years ago at a time when cultivating garlic proved to be a more attractive source of income. Since then, weaving has experienced a revival as many Sasak women return to their heritage.

The road through the mountains is steep and rough in places, and eventually ends in **Sapit** ㉚, a pleasant mountain village to the southeast.

EAST LOMBOK

Continuing on the main road around the island, the route passes coastal scenery on the left and mountain vistas on the right, eventually traversing the north coast and descending to the east. In comparison to the west coast, this part of Lombok receives few visitors, and many of the villages in eastern Lombok are strongly Islamic. It is imperative that modest dress and behaviour are adhered to in this area.

The coastline is extremely beautiful, with many pristine beaches and wonderful views across the water to neighbouring Sumbawa. **Labuhan Lombok** ㉛, also sometimes called Tanjung Kayangan, is the eastern port, with regular ferries departing for Sumbawa and the islands to the east. At **Pringgabaya** ㉜, stop by the side of the road to see a forest of giant *Ficus albipila* trees, locally called *pohon lian*. Towering some 50 metres (164ft) in height, villagers say the trees pre-date Dutch colonization. There's a beautiful beach at **Labuhan Haji**.

Camping while hiking Gunung Rinjani.

Craftsman at work in Penujak pottery village.

CENTRAL AND SOUTH LOMBOK

Isolated villages in the cooler central zone produce handicrafts such as songket cloth, ceramics and baskets. As you head south, there is magnificent coastal scenery, including splendid beaches better than any you will find in neighbouring Bali.

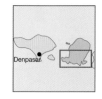

Central Lombok, located on the southern slopes of Gunung Rinjani (see page 220), is cooler and more verdant than the south, receiving much rainfall in the wet season and protected by forests and jungle throughout the year. Traditional villages dot the slopes, their livelihoods centred on handicrafts such as pottery, textiles, woven grass and bamboo crafts, and woodworking. Continuing south, away from the mountains, the landscape becomes much drier and fields of tobacco, corn, cassava and peanuts become the norm. On reaching the south coast, the landscape opens up to reveal a long coastline with some of the most sublime beaches and views in Indonesia.

AROUND LENEK

Heading from the east coast on the main road from Labuhan Lombok is **Lenek** ㉞. This whole area has many small villages whose people still practise *adat* (traditional) Sasak customs. Well known as a source of Sasak music and dance, Lenek excels at *tari pepakon*, a medicinal trance dance. A local cultural patron of the arts has established an organisation to reinvigorate the performing arts. To the west is **Pringgasela** ㉟, a village steeped in tradition and a major centre for songket weaving. Sadly, tourism interest

has encouraged Lombok authorities to 'upgrade' some popular traditional villages by including such amenities as modern housing. Pringgasela was one of those chosen for a makeover.

Southeast of Lenek is **Bonjeruk**, known for its *wayang* (shadow play) puppet craftsmanship. It is now a *desa wisata* (tourist village), thanks to the local government. Past Bonjeruk is **Masbagik** ㊱, best known as a centre of pottery and ceramic crafts. It remains a good place to see this traditional art form put into practice.

> **Main attractions**
> Loyok
> Sukarara
> Penujak
> Rembitan and Sade
> Kuta
> Tanjung Aan
> Tanjung Luar
> Sekotong
> Gili Nanggu

> **Map on page 204**

Lombok's Kuta Beach.

Traditional thatched lumbung (rice barns) at Rembitan village.

Songket weaving at Sukarara village.

LOYOK AND TETEBATU

Following the main road another few kilometres further west, a road leads north to **Loyok**, a small dusty village where families make traditional woven products using rattan, grasses and bamboo. The baskets, boxes, mats and other weavings are of good quality. Visit the shops and the family compounds out at the back, where often several generations of the same family weave.

Continuing north is **Tetebatu** ⑳, on the southern slopes of Gunung Rinjani. This is a cool mountain retreat with beautiful rice terraces, forests and bright green fields of tobacco. It is wet and misty during the rainy season, and cool and lush during the dry. To the north of Tetebatu, about an hour's trekking through a monkey-filled forest, is the **Jeruk Manis** waterfall. It's best to take a local guide with you on this trek.

PRAYA, SUKARARA & PENUJAK

About half-an-hour's drive southeast of Cakranegara, **Praya** ⑳ is Lombok's second largest city and is more or less a link between central Lombok's traditional villages and the beaches to the south. Its Saturday morning market is always lively.

Some 5km (3 miles) to the west of Praya is **Sukarara** ⑳, where hand-woven *songket* fabric is made. Weavers work outside many of the shops, using antiquated back strap looms to produce works of art. Some of the larger pieces can take several months of painstaking work to weave, and collectors from around the world visit this village to purchase the blankets, sarongs and cloth.

South of Praya is **Penujak** ⑳, one of Lombok's main pottery making centres. Shops and workshops line the main road, and local children will run out to greet you and guide you into the shops when you arrive. Please refrain from giving them sweets or pens, which originally encouraged their begging. Penujak pottery uses mainly animal motifs, including frogs and geckos, as decoration.

REMBITAN AND SADE

Travelling down to the south coast, you pass small farming villages and a drier, flatter landscape then in the north. You'll reach **Rembitan** ㊶ village first, on the right, and then **Sade** ㊷, on the left along the main road just before Kuta. These are traditional Sasak villages sandwiched between the main road and the rice fields. Rembitan is a popular tourist stop with clusters of thatched *lumbung* (rice barns). Unfortunately, both have received facelifts from the government; however, Sade remains a more authentic hilltop village with the oldest mosque in Lombok, **Mesjid Kuno**. This ancient, thatched-roof house of worship can only be entered by Muslims. Both villages are interesting examples of traditional Sasak architecture and communal living. Residents, who act as guides for a small fee, encourage walks through both villages.

KUTA AND MANDALIKA

After decades of revelling in relative isolation due to poor infrastructure, southern Lombok is in the throes of enormous change. The new airport and an expansive highway now connect it to the capital city, and an enormous Nusa Dua, Bali-type resort development is going ahead at full throttle. **Kuta** ㊸, and the surrounding region have some of the best surfing spots in Southeast Asia. It is here that the gentle waters of Lombok meet the currents of the Indian Ocean, forming great surf breaks and fantastic vistas of cliffs, headlands and beaches carved out of the rugged southern coastline.

Kuta, about 45km (28 miles) south of Mataram, remains the domain of surfers for the present with plenty of budget accommodation and shaded *warung* (food stalls) lining the beach. Water activity gear can be rented here. Abutting Kuta's shoreline is **Mandalika** beach, the site of the annual Bau Nyale Festival. This unusual event attracts thousands of people every year (see box).

North of Kuta and Mandalika on the same inlet, the new resort

Spice tray in a Lombok market.

⊙ BAU NYALE FESTIVAL

The Bau Nyale festival commemorates the legend of the beautiful Putri (Princess) Mandalika, who was much sought after as a bride by every king in Lombok. According to local lore, the princess was so torn between the suitors that she threw herself into the sea, crying out "Kuta" ("Wait for me here") in the local Sasak language. When she disappeared into the waves below, hundreds of *nyale* – sea worms – floated to the surface.

Thus, every February or March, when the conditions are right, the *nyale* worms return to the site. People come from all over Lombok to collect the ugly sea worms, which are fried and eaten (the worms are said to be an aphrodisiac). A *dukun* (shaman) wades into the sea to observe the spawning *nyale* and predict the impending rice harvest based on the number of worms that appear.

Bau Nyale is the only time of the year when young people are permitted to strut and flirt openly. When night falls, the youngsters compete with each other by singing pantun, an improvised poetry of rhyming couplets, and watch men fighting the *peresean* mock battle.

Freshly caught fish at Tanjung Luar.

In a peresean, two men, armed with rattan sticks and shields made of cowhide, duel with each other.

development is called **Kuta Mandalika**, and five-star resorts and spas are under construction with up-market boutiques and cafes already open for business.

TANJUNG AAN AND GEREPUK

East of Kuta are a series of beautiful, remote beaches. **Tanjung Aan** ⓙ has spectacular scenery off the peninsula, with a few vendor shacks and sandy-bottom, calm waters that are good for swimming. Another 3km (2 miles) east is **Gerupuk** ⓚ located on the spit of land that juts out into the ocean, with stunning views of the sea and the surrounding islands and bays. Gerupuk is a top-notch surf location and is ideal for windsurfing or bodysurfing.

SOUTHEAST COAST

If further exploration is warranted, head north from Kuta to Sengkol, then east through Majur to the southeast coast at **Tanjung Luar** ⓛ, site of a vibrant fish market. This area is inhabited by Bugis fishermen from Sulawesi, and the beach is lined with Bugis-style

stilted houses in the same strong colours as their fishing boats. Few tourists make it to this remote area, so the people are friendly, with the added bonus that there are no hawkers here.

Continuing around the bay to the south is **Jerowaru**, where there is an amazing pink beach whose colour is even more vibrant than the famed Pantai Merah at Komodo. The snorkelling here is excellent.

MAWUN AND SELONG BELANAK

Returning to the south coast, about a 30 minute drive to the west of Kuta over a bumpy road, the beach at **Mawun** ⓜ rings a perfect half-moon bay, popular for swimming and picnicking. There are good right- and left-hand barrels for surfing when the swell is large enough. This deserted beach, flanked by massive headlands, has very few trees, thus accentuating the spectacular scenery and sound of crashing waves.

Further west, a picturesque little fishing village and a few *warung* (food

stalls) serving snacks and beer lies on the fringe of **Selong Belanak** 48 beach. Colourful fishing outriggers rock in the gentle waves at the bay's east end and buffaloes are herded along the beach daily. White, sugary sand skirts the gorgeous bay, but what makes this place so stunning is the scale of the surrounding landscape – which is of continental proportions. On the cliffs overlooking the bay between Mawun and Selong Belong Belanak there are villas and restaurants.

SOUTHWEST PENINSULA

The roads from Selong Belanak to the southwest peninsula coast are in very poor condition, making it best to return to Praya and turning west from there.

Lembar 49, about an hour south of Mataram, is the centre for Lombok's shipping transport and the harbour for boats arriving from Bali and the west. South of Lembar, the road south winds first around the wide natural harbour and through small villages set in valleys inhabited by fisher folk who use *bagans* (floating platforms) in shallow waters.

Finally, the road opens out into the marvelous scenery at **Sekotong**. The large calm bay just before **Taun** 50 (Sekotong Barat) is one of the most beautiful on Lombok. Investors are snapping up real estate in this area, with at least one major resort development occupying the hillside overlooking the sea. This is a good base for day trips to the first trio of islands: **Gili Nanggu** 51 with its soft white sand and sparkling clear waters, **Gili Sudat**, the isle closest to the mainland, and **Gili Tangkong**. Gili Nanggu has a small basic hotel and the island is perfect as a castaway escape, with a good reef for snorkelling off the beach. There is a signposted parking area at Sekotong Barat where small boats can be chartered to explore these lovely islands.

Winding down the coast, the road hugs the bays and beaches that make up the magical southwest, with views of the many small islands sitting just offshore and the outline of Bali's Nusa Penida on the horizon. Boats can be chartered at **Pelangan** to explore the numerous islands off the coast, including the huge **Gili Gede**, the most developed of the southwest Gilis. Gili Gede's accommodation choices make it a very good base for exploring this group of islands, all of which are excellent for snorkelling and diving

The road southwards deteriorates dramatically, although it is still passable in the dry season. Winding through tiny villages, it continues to the south-westernmost point of Lombok – a sheer cliff framing **Bangko Bangko** 52 beach. Also known as Desert Point, it juts into the sea, forming a junction with the Indian Ocean and creating incredible surf breaks that attract serious surfers from around the world. It regularly rates as one of the top five surf destinations in Southeast Asia. Wild and desolate, the limestone cliffs here have been carved by the tides, and the surrounding scenery is dramatically beautiful.

⊙ Fact

Ko-ko-mo Gili Gede Resort (tel. 0819-0732 5135; www.kokomogiligede. com) is on the upper end of the spectrum for the Gilis. It's an all-villa resort with tennis court, putting green, spa and private fast boat service. Who could ask for more?

Kuta Beach, Lombok.

Women carrying offerings.

BALI AND LOMBOK

TRAVEL TIPS

TRANSPORT: BALI

Getting There **230**
    By Air.................................... **230**
    By Minivan or Car **230**
    By Bus.................................. **230**
    By Ferry................................ **231**
Getting Around **231**
    From the Airport **231**
    Orientation **231**
    Public Transport **232**
    Private Transport................. **233**
    On Foot................................ **233**

TRANSPORT: LOMBOK

Getting There **234**
    By Air.................................... **234**
    By Sea **234**
Getting Around **234**
    From the Airport **234**
    Orientation **234**
    Transport **235**

A – Z

Addresses **236**
Admission Charges................... **236**
Age Restrictions....................... **236**
Budgeting for your Trip............. **236**
Business Travellers **236**
Children.................................... **237**
Climate..................................... **237**
Clothing.................................... **237**
Consulates **238**
Crime & Security **238**
Customs Regulations................ **238**
Economy.................................... **238**
Electricity **238**
Emergency Numbers................. **238**
Etiquette................................... **238**
Health & Medical Care............. **239**
Internet **240**

Left Luggage **241**
LGBTQ Travellers **241**
Lost Property **241**
Maps... **241**
Media.. **241**
Money.. **241**
Opening Hours **242**
Packing & Shipping................... **242**
Postal Services **242**
Public Holidays **242**
Public Toilets............................ **243**
Religious Services..................... **243**
Smoking **243**
Taxes & Tipping......................... **243**
Telephones **243**
Time Zone **244**
Tourist Offices **244**
Travellers with
    Disabilities **244**
Visas & Passports **244**
Websites.................................... **244**
Weights & Measures................. **244**
Women Travellers **244**

LANGUAGE

Bahasa Indonesia...................... **245**
    Useful phrases...................... **245**
    Forms of Address **245**
    Directions & Transport **245**
    Food & Drink......................... **246**
    Shopping **246**
    Signs **246**
    Days of the week................... **246**
    Numbers................................ **246**
Glossary **246**

FURTHER READING

History & Culture **248**
Fiction **248**
Art/Music/Dance....................... **248**
General...................................... **248**

TRANSPORT: BALI

By Air

Ngurah Rai International Airport in Bali (sometimes referred to by the city, name, Denpasar) is served by direct flights from cities in Europe, US, Australia and Asia. In addition, there are daily flights from several key Indonesian cities such as Jakarta, Yogyakarta and Surabaya. Some international airlines fly only to Jakarta's Soekarno-Hatta International Airport, from where domestic flights to Bali (flight time: 80 minutes) are frequent while others fly in and out of Jakarta's Halim Airport.

Foreign airlines serving Bali include: AirAsia, Air India, Air New Zealand (seasonal), Cathay Pacific, Cebu Pacific, China Airlines, Emirates, EVA Air, Hong Kong Airlines, Japan Airlines, Jetstar Airways, KLM, Korean Air, Malaysia Airlines, Malindo Air, Philippine Airlines, Qantas, Qatar Airways, Rossiya Airlines, Royal Brunei Airlines, Scoot, Shanghai Airlines, Silk Air, Singapore Airlines, Thai Airways, Turkish Airlines, Vietjet Air, Virgin Australia and Xiamen Air.

Indonesian airlines serving Bali include: Batik Air, Citilink, Garuda Indonesia, Indonesia Air Asia, Lion Air, NAM Air, Sriwijaya Air and Wings Air.

The international terminal, which was inaugurated in 2013, has a Balinese architectural theme and has separate departure and arrival halls. The refurbished domestic terminal reopened in 2014. The departures area has 62 check-in counters that are equipped with electronic scales and luggage conveyors. Ten of the international gates have aerobridges and automated aircraft parking systems. The international terminal also has prayer rooms, showers and a massage service.

Various lounge areas are provided, some including children's play areas and movie lounges, broadcasting movies, news, variety and entertainment and sport channels.

The contact details for **Ngurah Rai International Airport** are: tel: 0361-935 1011.

If leaving Bali by air on a domestic airline, you are advised to reconfirm your reservation. Some local airlines tend to overbook. Reconfirmation is usually not required for international airlines.

Check in two hours before flight time. The **international departure tax**, as well as the **domestic tax**, are both included in the price of the ticket.

Flying from UK and US

From the UK (and European cities three airlines fly into Bali with one stop. Garuda Indonesia stops in Jakarta and along with several other carriers flies direct to Bali. British Airways stops in Doha and Qantas operates non-stops from Doha to Bali. Malaysia Airlines has non-stops to Kuala Lumpur and provides service to Bali, along with Air Asia.

From the US, connections can be made by using international carriers such as Japan Airlines, which flies from the US to Tokyo and, as with all international airlines, connects to Bali via codeshare partners. Also convenient is Singapore Airlines, which flies out of Los Angeles, San Francisco and New York to Singapore. Qatar Airways also connects to New York and to Washington DC via Doha. It is also possible to fly from the US to Asian cities like Kuala Lumpur, Bangkok and Hong Kong, and then connect to Bali.

By Minivan or Car

In Java, you can hire an air-conditioned minivan with driver for about US$250 per day, plus fuel, food and accommodation. This costs about the same as flying, but you get to see more if you plan stopovers and side-trips. If you have an international drivers' license, you can rent a car in Java and drive to Bali yourself, but the cost will be about the same as hiring both a driver and car, and there is the added hassle of navigating unfamiliar roads and returning the vehicle.

By Bus

Budget travellers who plan to take the public *bis malam* (overnight bus) from Java to Bali should be wary of drivers who speed on dark roads (some have been known to fall asleep at the wheel). In addition, professional thieves operate on

⊘ Official Taxi Rates

The official fixed taxi rates from the airport to key destinations are currently in the region of:

Amanusa/Mulia/Tanjung Benoa Rp175,000
Ayana Resort Rp150,000
Batubulan Rp175,000
Candidasa Rp425,000
Canggu Rp225,000
Denpasar I Rp125,000
Denpasar II Rp135,000
Denpasar III Rp150,000
Gatsu/Ubung Bus Station Rp165,000
Gatsu Timur Tohpati Rp175,000
Jimbaran I/Intercontinental Rp100,000
Jimbaran II/Jl Uluwatu II/Four Seasons Rp125,000
Kedonganan Rp85,000
Kuta I Rp70,000
Kuta II Rp80,000
Legian Rp95,000
Nikko Bali Rp185,000
Nusa Dua Rp150,000
Oberoi/Kerobokan Rp150,000
Padangbai Rp400,000
Pecatu/Uluwatu Rp225,000
Sanur Rp150,000
Seminyak/Pantai Double Six Rp110,000
Tanah Lot Rp300,000
Tuban Rp55,000
Ubud Centre Rp300,000
Umalas/Br Semer/Kuwum Rp135,000
Ungusan/Uluwatu Rp200,000

the counter outside the arrival hall. Pay the cashier at the desk and you will receive a coupon to hand to your designated taxi driver.

There are no other forms of public transport from the airport apart from airport taxis and hotel pick-up services, except for the touts who freely operate near the cashier.

The fixed airport rates are about 50 percent more expensive than metered taxi rates. If you are on a tight budget and are prepared to haul your luggage outside the airport gates, you will be able to flag down a taxi and pay the metered fare. Otherwise, you could try your luck negotiating with the touts.

Orientation

Roads in Bali are heavily used, not only for traffic but also as a parade ground for escorting deities to the sea and cremation processions. Side roads are not regularly maintained and are speckled with potholes or sometimes partly blocked by piles of gravel dumped at the sides. Traffic jams in the tourism-dense south can be horrific, caused by ceremonial processions, by rush-hour congestion, floods, a truck stuck in a storm drain, or a gaggle of geese – the reasons for gridlocks are manifold.

Congestion on Jalan Legian and Jalan Seminyak, however, has been somewhat eased by the opening of the Sunset Road, which bypasses Kuta, Legian and Seminyak. Likewise, the toll road to Tanjung Benoa and Nusa Dua has also helped to alleviate traffic problems, as has the Sunrise Road highway along the east coast, which gives access to the ruggedly beautiful beaches and traditional fishing villages of this area.

Although it is possible to get around Bali in a couple of days, this is not a good idea; if based in the south, it's far better to explore the area you are in rather than make long treks across the island. Half-day outings are best accomplished by starting early, which leaves the rest of the day for relaxing on the beach or in a restaurant, taking a stroll through a nearby village or market, and then attending an evening festival or performance.

The main tourist hub is the southern triangle formed by the frenetically busy **Kuta/Legian/Seminyak** stretch, with quieter **Jimbaran** on the west and the slightly more sedate

some buses, stealing your belongings while you are sleeping. In isolated areas, road gangs are known to hold up buses and rob the passengers, perhaps even working in cahoots with the drivers.

Air-conditioned express buses to Denpasar from Jakarta (with a ferry connecting the two islands) take 24 hours, from Surabaya 14 hours, and from Yogyakarta 15–16 hours. Restaurant and toilet stops are made along the way. Be sure to specify that you want an air-conditioned bus; some "executive class" companies offer non-smoking buses without on-board video entertainment, which is very loud. There are numerous operators and fares vary considerably, depending on the level of comfort you require.

From Jakarta to Bali, expect to pay around Rp470,000 from Yogyakarta Rp290,000 and from Surabaya Rp 250,000. Executive class services will bus you direct from major cities in Java, and some include drop-off services at your hotel in Bali.

Other buses travel daily from the Lombok to Sumbawa, Bali and Java. The cost from Lombok to Bali is Rp 175,000 (including the ferry crossing), or over Rp 500,000 via fast boat. There are also connections direct to the Gili Islands.

By Ferry

From Java: Ferries make the 45-minute trip between Gilimanuk in West Bali and Ketapang in East Java. The fares are around Rp6,000 per person, Rp159,000 per car and Rp35,000 per motorbike; you won't have to pay for

a person if you pay for a motorcycle: 2 people + 1 motorcycle = Rp5,000. Note: the cost of the ferry ride is included in the service offered by most of the bus services.

From Lombok: From Lembar, Lombok, public ferries take 4 hours (in good weather) to reach Padangbai in East Bali. Their safety records are not stellar. The ticket costs around Rp46,000.

It's best to travel between the islands safely via fast boat. **BlueWater Express** (www.bluewater-express.com), daily from Padang Bai to Gili Trawangan around Rp870,000 one way. BlueWater also departs from Serangan, Bali and from Gili Air and Teluk Kode (mainland), Lombok. Tickets can be booked online.

GETTING AROUND

From the Airport

From the airport, depending on the traffic, which can be bad, it takes approximately 15 minutes to reach Tuban and Kuta, 20–25 minutes to Legian, 30 minutes to Seminyak, 40 minutes to Kerobokan, 45–50 minutes to Canggu, 25 minutes to Sanur, 20 minutes to Nusa Dua, 10 minutes to Jimbaran, 75 minutes to Ubud, and 3 hours to Lovina.

If you have not made prior arrangements with your hotel to pick you up, there is a reliable taxi service from the airport that you can use; fixed rates to various destinations are clearly posted on a board at

Nusa Dua/Tanjung Benoa and **Sanur** areas on the east. If you're a beach lover, enjoy dining out at a different restaurant every night and like lively nightlife, then stay in these areas.

Those who prefer something quieter but still close to the beach, should head for **Candidasa** or **Padang Bai** and **Amed** on the east coast, **Lovina** in the north or **Pemuteran** in the northwest. Be aware, however, that outside of the south the beaches are pebbly rather than sandy. There are white-sand beaches at Padang Bai and the Nusas.

Those bent on seeing cultural attractions should base themselves in the **Ubud** area, where nearby villages in the Gianyar regency provide the opportunity to see arts and crafts, music and dance performances, as well as numerous ancient temples. **Denpasar** has little of interest, apart from the markets and the museum. If you like mountain scenery and cooler climes, consider spending some time in the **Bedugul** area near the lovely **Danau Bratan**, or to the east, **Danau Batur** at the foot of **Gunung Batur**.

Public Transport

Minivans

The ubiquitous and horrible bemo (minivans) that plied the Kuta area route have happily been replaced by a modern minivan service called Kura-Kura Bus (tel. 0812-3833 5742; http://kura2bus.com). With five lines operating to the popular tourist destinations, including Ubud, prices are fixed and one-, three- and seven-day passes are available at Rp100,000, Rp150,000 and Rp250,000 respectively. Single-trip tickets for most destinations go for Rp20,000. An excellent website in English explains how to make purchases online or at several locations frequented by tourists. They also have an app that shows the locations of buses, traffic conditions and other useful information. Kura-Kura buses operate 9am–8pm daily, except Nyepi day.

Buses

In Denpasar, **Mengwi** is the main bus terminal for transportation on the overland to Java journey. Ubung: bemo service northwest and central Bali (e.g. Tanah Lot as well as Bedugal and Tabanan Regencies). Go to Tegal terminal for southern areas, including Sanur and Nusa Dua. And Trans Sarbagita

air-conditioned buses ply the routes between Jimbrana and Tabanan Regencies at the Trans Sarbbagita terminal. At Batubulan, south of Ubud, you can find buses heading for most of Gianyar and eastern Bali.

Tourist Shuttle Services

Perama Tour (tel: 0361-751 875; www.peramatour.com) operate daily shuttle services from Kuta, and the airport to Ubud, Sanur, Lovina, Candidasa, Padangbai, Amed, Tulamben and Tirtagangga, as well as boat crossings to Senggigi, the Gili islands and Mataram, Lombok. Additional routes are to Nusa Lembongan, Bedugal, Kintamani, and onward to Mt. Bromo, Java. Although they cost a bit more than public buses or *bemo*, they are faster and more comfortable. The fares from both Kuta and the airport to various other points in Bali are approximately as follows:
Kuta–Sanur Rp35,000
Kuta–Ubud Rp50,000
Kuta–Lovina Rp125,000
Kuta–Padang Bai Rp75,000
Kuta–Candidasa Rp75,000
Kuta–Bedugul: Rp75,000
Kuta–Kintamani (minimum 2 people) Rp150,000
Padang Bai–Amed (minimum 2 people) Rp100,000

Taxis

Taxis are air-conditioned and charge metered fares. The only fixed rates are from the airport to the major hotels. When entering the taxi, be sure the driver turns the meter on. If he doesn't, find another cab.

Few taxis outside of the Kuta-Legian-Seminyak area cruise the streets for passengers, so call one of the numbers below (or ask your hotel concierge to call for you). The best company is **Bali Taxi** (Bluebird Group), with light blue cabs and a reputation for providing reliable, safe and honest service. Make sure it's a Bali Taxi that you're getting into, as there are other blue taxis that are unscrupulous. The meters run at approximately Rp7,000 per kilometre with a flag rate of Rp7,500. If you call and book a taxi by phone, the minimum charge is Rp30,000. Most drivers speak some English, especially Bali Taxi drivers.
Bali Taxi: tel: 0361-701 111
Komotra: tel: 0361-249249 249 249

There are no taxis originating in Ubud. The only ones you will see are those that have brought passengers from other tourist areas and are hoping for a fare back. You can arrange private transport with your hotel or negotiate a fare with one of the many young men offering transport on the street.

⊘ Beaches of South Bali

People who have seen the blinding white-sand beaches and clear aquamarine waters of Thailand are invariably disappointed by south Bali's beaches. Because of the island's volcanic origins, most of the beaches here are either grey or black sand, and often pebbly.

Nusa Dua is among the few stretches of white sand beach in the south. It is nicer and wider along the southern stretch where the Grand Hyatt and Ayodya are located, and a bit narrow and a little less pleasant past the little spit of sand where the Melia Bali is located to the north, all the way up to the Nusa Dua Hotel. North of Nusa Dua is **Tanjung Benoa**, which has white sand but is disappointingly calm (for those who like some surf) due to a ring of coral reefs in the distance.

The beach at **Sanur** has more of a golden hue and is only swimmable

at high tide; at low tide the water recedes to your waist (or sometimes knees) and is littered with coral and rocks.

The broad stretch of grey sands along **Kuta, Legian** and **Seminyak** sees gorgeous mango-streaked sunsets when the conditions are right. They are great for beach walks and for frolicking in the surf, boogie boarding, and if you venture far enough out, for surfing – albeit a bit rough for children and with a strong undertow at times. The sand bed is relatively flat and firm, and free of rocks and other debris. Much of the same also applies to the beach at **Jimbaran**.

South of Jimbaran are the stunning white-sand beaches of **Uluwatu, Suluban, Padang Padang, Impossibles, Bingin, Dreamland** and **Balangan**. They produce fabulous breaks for surfers but are not safe for swimmers.

Motorcycle Taxis

Young men operate motorcycle taxis known as *ojek*, and wait at designated places for customers. This is very convenient for locations not serviced by public transport. Agree on the price beforehand, and make sure you wear the helmet the driver provides, as it's required by law. The drivers do tend to weave in and out of heavy traffic but are usually very experienced. Fares are negotiable, usually just a few thousand rupiah for a short journey and no more than about half what you would pay for a taxi. Alternatively download the app from either GoJek or Grab, and order an ojek by phone.

Private Transport

Vehicle with Driver

Chartering a car or minivan with driver can be done by the half-day or full-day. Rates are cheaper if negotiated on the street rather than from your hotel (look out for young men who call out 'transport-transpor!' and move their hands as if driving a car). If chosing this option, do check out the vehicle before closing the deal.

Rates vary according to the kind of vehicle, its condition, actual travel time, and total number of hours hired. This amount should include fuel. Full-day rates generally range from about Rp500,000–700,000, half day from Rp250,000–400,000. Alternatively you can rent a car yourself and pay about Rp150,000 extra per day for the services of an English-speaking driver.

It is courteous to give your driver money for a meal if you stop for lunch or dinner, or you may even invite him to eat with you (although some drivers may feel shy about doing this). If you are pleased with the driver, a tip of Rp50,000 per trip is appropriate. You will usually get a better rate if you arrange to use the same driver for all the trips during your stay.

If you're not comfortable chartering a vehicle off the street, ask a tour agency or your hotel (which can also arrange for a guide) to get you a vehicle and driver. Rates will be substantially higher though.

Kuta Transport (tel: 0821-4405 5763; www.kutatransport.com) is recommended. Another option is to hire a car and driver from a reputable travel agency, such as Viatour (tel: 0855-339 8830; www.viatour.com).

Private Car Hire

Driving in Bali can be dangerous. Generally, drivers do not drive defensively, roads are narrow and poorly maintained, and dogs and chickens dart into the road. Street lighting at night is limited. If you collide with anything, you are responsible for all costs. It's safer to hire a driver while you relax and enjoy the sights.

Self-drive cars are available, for which you must have an International Driving Permit. If you do not have one, you must go to the Denpasar police station to obtain a temporary tourist permit, for which you will need your passport, driving license from your home country, and three passport-sized photos. If renting from an individual, it's advisable to pay the extra cost to get full insurance coverage. Petrol is not included. You can book a car through your hotel or from any of the companies listed below. They will deliver the car to you and pick it up at the end of the rental period. Always test-drive the car and check that it is in good working order before paying. Note: Driving is on the left side of the road with the steering wheel on the right.

Prices (per day) range between US$29-50 depending on the size of the vehicle. These rates should include collision insurance, unlimited mileage and pick-up service.

Recommended rental agencies:

Jimbaran

Golden Bird Bali: Jalan Bypass Nusa Dua 4, Jimbaran, tel: 0361-701 791; www.bluebirdgroup.com.

TRAC Astra: Jalan Bypass Ngurah Rai, Jimbaran, tel: 0361-703 333.

Canggu Eco Beach

Bima Sakti Car Rental: tel: 0361-748 9036; www.bimasakticarrental.com. Has automatic transmission cars.

Denpasar

Bali Car Hire: Jalan Tunjung Sari No. 69, Denpasar, tel: 0361-411 499 or 0812-287 1684; www.balicarhire.com.

Motorcycle Hire

Motorcycles are a convenient and inexpensive way to get around the island, but there are risks due to heavy traffic and poor roads. Helmets are required by law but the cheap ones provided by rental agencies offer little protection. Bring your own or buy a good one from a local shop, especially one with a face shield for

protection from sun, rain, bugs and dust. Drive slowly and defensively, as more and more people are injured or killed every year in accidents.

The cost of motorbike hire varies according to the model, condition of the machine, length of rental, and time of year. Expect to pay around Rp80,000 per day. Petrol is not included. Buy full insurance so that you are not responsible for any damage. Be sure to test drive it to check that everything is in working order, especially brakes and lights.

You must have an International Driving Permit valid for motorcycles, or else go to the Denpasar Police Office to obtain a temporary tourist permit, valid for three months on Bali only. Bring your passport, driving licence from your home country, and three passport-sized photos.

Motorbike and scooter rentals can be found in most tourist areas, but there is also western-managed Bali Bike Rental (tel: 0821-4741 6202; www.balibikerrental.com). Or for a real thrill, Harley Davidson tandem tours are offered at Bali BigBike Rental (https://harley-davidson-bali.weebly.com).

Bicycles

Mountain bikes are available for rent everywhere, but before you pay for one, make sure the wheels are properly aligned, the brakes work well, and that there is a working light. Because of the hazardous main roads, stick to the quieter country roads for maximum enjoyment. When you are pedalling, you don't feel the heat, just a cool breeze. The sweat begins when you stop, so be sure to carry a bottle of water and to drink frequently to replenish fluids.

Wear a helmet for extra safety, and try not to ride at night because roads are very poorly lit, or not lit at all. Hire prices vary from about Rp20,000 to Rp60,000 per day, depending on the type and quality of the bike.

TRANSPORT: LOMBOK

GETTING THERE

By Air

Lombok International Airport, (Bandara Udara Internasional Zainuddin Abdul Madjid Lombok, airport code LOP) is Lombok's only airport and is located in Praya; tel: 0370-615 7000. If you need a visa on arrival (and qualify for one), you can get it at the airport. Other facilities include hotel reservations desk, cafés, moneychangers, ATMs and internet access.

The airport is primarily served by domestic flights from other parts of Indonesia. **International flights include Air Asia**, which operates direct flights between Lombok and Kuala Lumpur in Malaysia and from Perth stopping over at Kuala Lumpur. SilkAir has direct flights from Singapore. All other international connections are available via Jakarta and Bali.

Domestically, **Garuda Indonesia** has direct flights between Lombok and Bima, Jakarta Soekarna-Hatta, Makassar, Semarang, Sumbawa Besar and Surabaya. **AirAsia** domestic flights into Lombok fly from Bali, Jakarta Soekarna-Hatta and Yogyakarta. **Batik Air** flies from Jakarta-Halim to Lombok, as does **Citilink**. Citilink also connects with Surabaya. **Lion Air** has daily flights from Bali, Bandung, Banjarmasin, Jakarta Soekarna-Hatta, Makassar and Yogyakarta. NAM Air connects Lombok with Bali and Bima. **Wings Air** has daily flights to Lombok from Bali, Bima, Labuhanbajo and Sumbawa Besar.

By Sea

The picturesque sea crossing by public ferry from Bali to Lombok is well worth the inconvenience of travelling to and from the ports but is risky. Public ferries depart every

⊘ Key Airline Offices

International Carriers:
AirAsia: tel: 021-29270999; www.airasia.com
SilkAir: tel: 0370-628 254; www.singaporeair.com
Indonesian Carriers:
Batik Air: tel: 0370-662 7444; www.batikair.com
Citilink: tel: 0370-615 7047; www.citilink.co.id
Garuda Indonesia: tel: (call centre) 0804-1807 807; www.garuda-indonesia.com
Lion Air: tel: 0804-177 8899; www.lionair.co.id
NAM Air: tel: 0370-615 7201; www.flynamair.com
Wings/Lion Air: tel: 0804-177 8899 or 021-6379 8000; www.lionair.co.id

hour, weather permitting, for the trip between Padang Bai **Harbour** (Bali) and **Lembar Harbour** (Lombok), about 20km (12 miles) south of Mataram; the crossing takes about four hours in calm seas. (Note that they don't have stellar safety records). A one-way ticket costs Rp46,000. Padang Bai Harbour is about two hours' drive from Kuta and South Bali, depending on whether you travel by car or public transport. Try to get an early start, or, better yet, stay at Padang Bai or at Candidasa, just 20 minutes away, the day before departure.

Lembar Harbour is about one hour south of Senggigi in Lombok. Arrange your own transport to the harbour and buy tickets direct from the desk, or use a reputable tour company which can provide a complete transfer package.

The most reliable tour agent is **Perama** Tour, which offers a complete transfer package that includes pick-up from destinations throughout Bali and Lombok, bus transfer to the

local harbour, ferry ticket and transfer from the harbour to your destination on either island. Contact Perama in **Lombok**, tel: 0370-635 928 or **Bali**, tel: 0361-751 875; www.peramatour.com.

Fast Boats

In addition, there are several daily fast boat services from Bali to Lombok. **BlueWater Express** (www.bluewater-express.com) is highly recommended, daily from Padangbai to Gili Trawangan around Rp870,000 one way. BlueWater also departs from Serangan Island, Bali and from Gili Air and Teluk Kode (mainland), Lombok. Tickets can be booked online.

GETTING AROUND

From the Airport

Lombok International Airport is 28km (17 miles) from Kuta and 50km (31 miles) from Senggigi.

If your hotel offers free pick-up, look for someone holding a sign-board with your name on it outside the baggage claim area. If you have not booked your transfers in advance with your hotel or travel agent, you can use one of the **airport taxis** that operate from the arrival hall. Be sure to purchase a prepaid voucher from the taxi desk; fixed prices to all locations on Lombok are displayed on a sign on the wall.

A shuttle service is also available via DAMRI air-conditioned buses. Buy your ticket outside the arrival area, about Rp25,000 to Mataram, Rp35,000 to Senggigi and Rp30,000 to Selong in southern Lombok. Buses run 7am–10pm daily.

Orientation

Lombok is an excellent escape from the tourist crowds of Bali, and many people combine a visit to both islands to make the most of their holidays. A week each on Bali and Lombok is a good introduction to both islands. Located about 35km (22 miles) east of Bali, Lombok is only slightly smaller in size than its neighbour. The main roads are generally in good condition and traffic is less congested than on Bali, making travel easier and safer for self-driving, motorbike riding and cycling tours.

The Indonesian word for road is 'Jalan' abbreviated to 'Jl.' in street addresses. Names change without warning, but are essentially the same main roads, locally called 'Jalan Raya' (main road). Many of the roads in Lombok are named Jalan Raya and then appended by the area that the main road passes through (e.g. Jalan Raya Senggigi).

Ampenan, Mataram and **Cakranegara** in West Lombok have merged into an urban sprawl, making it no longer obvious where one ends and the next begins. A main road links the cities, starting with Jalan Pabean in Ampenan, then becoming Jalan Yos Sudarso, then changing to Jalan Langko and Jalan Pejanggik in Mataram, before later becoming Jalan Selaparang at Cakranegara. Basically this is one major road that runs across the island from west to east, dividing into one-way streets heading west or east at the cities, and then reuniting to traverse across the island.

Another main road links Ampenan to **Senggigi** and continues north, eventually circumventing the island and ending in East Lombok, where it links to the main west–east road. Connected to this west–east road in the middle of the island is another major road that runs south to the airport and central Lombok hub **Praya**, continuing on to the south coast and ending at **Kuta**.

Transport

Taxis

Light blue Bluebird Taxis are easy to find and cheap. Drivers normally switch on their meters when you board and are not open to bartering. Metered taxis can be booked in advance directly from the hotel desks and taxi stands in Senggigi, or flagged down along the streets. Taxies can also be chartered for the day from:

Bluebird Taxi
Jalan Koperasi 102, Ampenan
Tel: 0370-635 968
Express Taksi
Jalan Diponegoro No.10, Cakranegara
Tel: 0370-661 0023

Public Bemo and Bus

Bemo (minivans and buses) service all towns on the island but it's time consuming to rely on them. Mandalika Terminal, the central terminal, is at the crossroads at Sweta, east of Cakranegara; there is another terminal at Sengkol in the south. A signboard displays the official fares to all destinations. Bemo connect to other locations, but you usually have to change buses at each terminal.

Small *bemo* ply the routes between Senggigi and Ampenan,

and the main road up the west coast from Senggigi; use these for transport to Mangsit and areas north of Senggigi.

Perama Tour (tel: 0370-635 928; www.peramatour.com) operates tourist shuttle buses that connect the airport, Mataram, Senggigi, Bangsal, Kuta, Tetebatu and Lendang Nangku.

Motorcycle Rental

It is easy to rent motorcycles in Ampenan, Mataram and Senggigi. Ask at your hotel or at any motorcycle shop on the main streets. Inquire at your rental agency in Bali if you can take your motorcycle to Lombok (only if you have an international drivers' license), but rental cars definitely cannot leave Bali.

Vehicle Rental

Privately operated cars and *bemo* are available for charter in the cities and Senggigi. You can charter a *bemo* to go anywhere on the island, but they are slow and uncomfortable. A better option is renting an air-conditioned car the day or hour. Prices start from US$20 a day without driver or US$50 with a driver (best option). If your hotel can't arrange for a car and driver, contact one of the following, both of which also rent motorbikes and arrange tours.

Car Rental Lombok
Jalan Raya Senggigi Km. 8, tel: 0812-372 7633
www.carrentallombok.com
Lombok Car Rental
Jl. Raya Senggigi Km. 8, tel: 0821-446 4413
www.lombokcarrental.com

Passenger boat in the Gili Islands.

A - Z

A

Addresses

Street names in Bali and Lombok are confusing because many have been renamed due to historical or political figures falling in and out of fashion. In many cases, streets are still referred to by their old names but the signposts will always show the new names.

Furthermore, in tourist areas it is not uncommon for a street to have a nickname (eg Double Six Street for Jalan Arjuna and Jalan Oberoi for Jalan Kayu Aya) taken from a long-established restaurant, nightclub or hotel that perhaps dominates the street.

House numbers cause even greater confusion. Although in some areas buildings have been renumbered by the government, it is rare to find a street where the buildings display consecutive numbers. To make things worse, duplicated numbers within the same street are commonplace (some people just think of their lucky number and use it for their house address). It is not unusual to find private houses and businesses with numbers such as 100x, 100xx and 1000x. In these cases, Google Maps might be your best option.

Admission Charges

Generally there is a small admission charge for entering government-run tourist sites. This is generally less than Rp 20,000 per adult and half-price for children. Don't be surprised if there is a higher cost for foreigners. The ticket offices will issue tickets, but if you are travelling in a car, you will also be charged a car park fee. Some of the major temples charge

entrance fees, but the majority will allow you to enter free of charge. In this case, you will be asked to give a donation towards the upkeep of the temple. Unless you have brought your own sarong and sash, you will be expected to rent one for around Rp5,000.

Age Restrictions

In Indonesia the age of consent for heterosexual sexual activity is 16. The age of consent for homosexuals is 18. The legal age for drinking is 18. There is no enforced law against drinking and driving, but do NOT drink and drive, as the accident statistics are very high.

B

Budgeting for your Trip

Since the late 1990s Bali has become a lot more up-market with chic new bars and restaurants, exclusive villas, luxury hotels, designer boutiques and opulent spas. Lombok is generally cheaper for food and accommodation. However, what remains special about both islands is the availability of choice; there really is something for everyone. Backpackers and surfers (who, after all, started the influx of tourism in the 1970s and 1980s) have not been forgotten.

Accommodation in Bali and Lombok can cost anything between US$5 and US$5,000 per night. Likewise, when it comes to eating out, the islands cater for every taste, from street-food served out of boxes balanced on bicycles, to chic, fine-dining restaurants.

Anything imported is expensive; this is probably most noticeable in

terms of food and alcoholic drinks. A bottle of local beer, for example, generally costs about half of its imported counterpart. Bar prices in the more up-market hotels are high, and tax and service are included in better restaurants and cafes.

While imported spirits and fine wines from around the world are available, the selection is often limited and prices are excessive due to the application of high customs and excise tax.

Taxis are relatively cheap; the transport that the locals use is even cheaper but not particularly comfortable. If you live frugally you can survive on as little as US$25–30 per day for both meals and lodging, but if you intend to live it up by eating out at good restaurants then be prepared to spend $50 for a 3-course meal alone.

To help you with budgeting for your trip, the list below provides some average costs:
A small beer Rp25,000, glass of house wine Rp70,000 (local) or Rp120,000 (imported)
A main course at a budget restaurant Rp25,000; at a moderate restaurant Rp90,000; at an expensive restaurant Rp150,000–250,000
A cheap hotel US$10–50 per night; moderate hotel US$60–200; luxury hotel US$200–1,000
A taxi journey to or from the main airport Rp35,000–335,000
A single bus ticket costs from Rp10,000.

Business Travellers

Most people come to Bali and Lombok to relax. However, all of the large hotels, especially the 5-star resorts in the Nusa Dua, Bali area, have the expertise and facilities to coordinate professional meetings, seminars, receptions, private dinners and functions. Comprehensive

Prayers and an offering at Pura Ulun Danu Batur.

business and conference facilities include fully equipped business centres, meeting rooms, board-rooms and auditoriums. Most villas and hotels provide Wi-fi access, though connection speeds vary according to locations.

C

Children

Children are universally loved in Bali and Lombok, welcomed everywhere and given a great deal of attention. Bali especially is a paradise for kids, offering a whole host of activities. Babysitters are available at major hotels, and many hotels offer children's activities, child care facilities and children's clubs. The owners of even the smallest of homestays will be happy to look after your children for a few hours. Some of the large department stores and malls in Bali have amusement centres packed with video games.

Disposable nappies (diapers) are expensive in Bali and Lombok, and not always available, so bring your own. Baby food and soybean formula are available at the supermarkets, but at exorbitant prices. Remember to bring sunhats and sunscreen to protect delicate skin from the strong sun.

Climate

Temperatures in Bali vary between 21–32°C (70–90°F), with an average annual temperature of 27°C (80°F). Higher elevations can get cooler, especially during the dry season which, lasts from May to September (August is the coolest month). The hot rainy season, with accompanying high humidity levels, lasts from November to March; January is the wettest month with intermittent thunderstorms. April and October are transitional months with intermittent rain and sun. Humidity is around 75 percent year-round.

Lombok has a similar weather pattern to Bali, but tends to be drier and less humid.

Clothing

Bring casual clothing of light-weight natural fabrics, which offer the best comfort in the heat and humidity. Bali has a thriving garment industry and clothes are readily available everywhere.

Sandals or footwear that can be slipped off easily are a good idea, especially if planning to visit homes – shoes are always removed before going into a house. Suits and ties are rarely worn. For formal occasions, men wear shirts made from local batik fabric. You'll need a light jacket or sweater if you're planning to visit mountain spots, where temperatures are considerably lower.

When visiting villages and temples (especially in more remote areas) as well as government offices, wear modest clothing and avoid showing too much skin: a T-shirt and a skirt or trousers are fine.

Temple Attire

Anyone visiting a temple must tie a sash (umpal) around the waist. Many temples require exposed legs to be covered with a sarong, especially if a ceremony is taking place. Men may also be required to wear a head-cloth (udeng) and short overskirt (saput) at important temple festivals. Temple visitors (especially women) with bare shoulders or exposed midriffs may be denied entrance, so be sure to dress appropriately. Some large temples have sashes and sarongs that can be borrowed in return for a small donation (usually Rp5,000), but if you intend to visit many holy

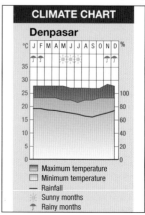

CLIMATE CHART

Denpasar

- Maximum temperature
- Minimum temperature
- Rainfall
- Sunny months
- Rainy months

places it makes more sense to pur-chase your own.

Consulates

Many countries have consulates in Bali. There are no consulates in Lombok. The major ones are:
Australia: Jalan Tantular 32, Renon, Denpasar, tel: 0361-241 118; email: bali.congen@dfat.gov.au; www.bali.indone-sia.embassy.gov.au.
Consular hours: Mon–Fri 8am–noon and 12.30–4pm. Visa hours: Mon–Fri 8.30am–noon.
Canada: Enquiries are handled by the Australian consulate.
United Kingdom: Jalan Tantular No 32, Renon, Denpasar, tel: 021-2356 5200; email: use contact form on website: www.gov.uk/contact-con-sulate-bali. Consular hours: Mon, Wed and Fri 8.30am–noon.
United States: Jalan Hayam Wuruk 310, Denpasar, tel: 0361-233 605; email: CABali@state.gov; https://id.usembassy.gov. Office hours: Mon–Fri 9am–noon and 1–3.30pm. Does not process visas.

Crime & Security

As with most countries, be vigilant at all times and minimise risks by avoiding large gatherings and crowded places where possible, and check your country's travel advice if you are concerned.

While personal safety is not a general problem in Bali and Lombok, as with anywhere else in the world, be attentive with your belongings and observe the follow-ing common-sense precautions:

Be careful with bags, wallets and backpacks in crowded places. Don't count money in the open. Pickpockets, car break-ins and bag snatching seem to be the most common complaints.

On public transport, you may be flanked by two friendly, usually English-speaking young men; one will engage you in conversation as a distraction while the other picks your pocket. Or they might ask you to change a large note to see how much money you're carrying before deciding if it's worth going any further. Don't fall asleep on public transport either, as you may wake up without your valuables.

Don't walk alone along Kuta beach at night. Tourist Police who patrol the main road from Tuban

to Seminyak speak some English and are helpful. Sanur and Nusa Dua beaches are fairly quiet, and its hotels are patrolled. In **Lombok** don't travel alone to the more iso-lated villages in the east.

All narcotics are illegal in Indonesia, and it has very strict drug laws. Their use, sale or purchase is punishable by death. Don't keep or carry packages for people you don't know.

Customs Regulations

In addition to your embarkation card, a customs declaration form must be completed before arrival in Bali and Lombok.

Indonesian regulations prohibit the entry of weapons, narcotics and pornography. Animals, fish, plants and their associated products, and exposed films and videos may be checked or even confiscated. Photographic equipment, laptop computers, mobile phones and other electronics can be brought in pro-vided they are taken out on departure.

A maximum of 1 litre of alcohol, 200 cigarettes or 25 cigars or 100 grams of tobacco may be brought into the country.

Bank notes in any currency exceeding Rp100 million are prohibited.

Upon departure, limited quan-tities of duty-free purchases and souvenirs are exempt from taxes, but the export of antiques over 50 years old is not permitted. Ivory, tortoiseshell and crocodile skin products cannot be taken out.

E

Economy

While agriculture, especially rice farming, is the main economic activ-ity for most Balinese, tourism is the largest source of income per capita. This includes those employed in related industries, such as arts, crafts and souvenirs. Textiles and garments are also a major industry. Bali's fishing industry and seaweed farming provide other important export products. On Lombok, rice, soybeans, coffee, tobacco, cinna-mon, cacao, cloves, vanilla, coconuts and bananas are the major economic factor, with tourism number two.

Electricity

Indonesia (including Bali and Lombok) uses the 220-volt system, 50 cycles. The round, two-pronged plug is common; adapters are readily available but it's probably easier to bring one from home. Power failures are common, as are scheduled power cuts, but most hotels and restaurants have back-up generators.

Emergency Numbers

Bali has an **Emergency Response Centre**: just dial 112 from a local phone to be in touch with the mod-ern communications centre that co-ordinates all emergency services on the island, including police and medical emergencies.
Ambulance: tel: 118
Fire Brigade: tel: 113
Immigration: tel: 0361-9350 1038
Tourist Police: tel: 0361-754 599

Lombok
Ambulance: tel: 118
Fire Brigade: tel: 113
Regional Police Office: tel: 110
Lombok Police: tel. 0370-693 110
Immigration: tel: 0370-632 520

Etiquette

The people of Bali and Lombok are remarkably friendly and courte-ous. They are also conservative, as tradition is the backbone of their culture, Hindusim in the case of the Balinese, and Islam in the case of most Lombokians. Keep the following etiquette guidelines in mind:

Don't venture beyond the beach or poolside area in a swimsuit. What appears to be a quaint beach side alley may lead to the court-yard of a house or temple. Nude bathing is not only considered improper, it is illegal.

Using the left hand to give or to receive something is taboo (the left hand is for personal hygiene purposes and therefore consid-ered unclean), as is pointing with the left hand. Never touch any-one, even a child, on the head; a person's head is considered to be the most sacred part of the body. Crooking a finger to call someone is impolite. Beckon to the person by waving the fingers together with the palm facing down instead.

Aggressive gestures and postures, such as standing with your hands on your hips when talking, are considered to be insulting. Avoid pointing with the index finger as this gesture may be taken as a physical challenge.

It is offensive to point with your toes (as when indicating an item displayed on the ground in the market) or sit with the soles of your feet pointing at other people – the feet are considered to be the lowliest part of the body. When passing in front of an older person or high-ranking person, especially if they are sitting down, bend your body slightly.

Don't make an offer for something unless you intend to buy it. When bargaining remember that Rp3,000 can make a great difference to the day's meal for local people, although to you it is nothing.

Don't display large sums of money. In a place where the average annual income is under US$1,500, all tourists are considered wealthy. The locals have a strong sense of pride.

Unless there is a set admission fee, it is common to give a small donation (Rp5,000) when visiting a temple. This is used to help with maintenance.

Apart from being properly attired when visiting temples, menstruating women and anyone with a bleeding wound must not enter temples. This is due to a sanction against blood on holy ground.

At temple festivals, photography without flash is fine but never stand in front of a seated priest, as one's head should not be higher than that of a holy person. It is rude and even sacrilegious to climb on temple walls to get a better view. You should not remain standing when people are praying, so move to the back and wait quietly until the blessing is finished. If Balinese kneel in veneration as a procession goes by, do the same or move out of the way. These events are sacred rituals, not meant for the benefit of tourist cameras, and due respect should be observed.

In mosques, remove shoes before entering, and then only if invited. There are separate areas for males and females. It is impolite to photograph someone who is praying, particularly from the front.

H

Health & Medical Care

International health certificates of vaccination against yellow fever are required only from travellers coming from infected areas. It is recommended that you ensure vaccinations are up to date for the following: Hepatitis A, Typhoid, Tetanus, Polio and Measles. Check the following websites for health updates:

World Health Organisation
www.who.int/ith/
Tropical Medical Bureau
www.tmb.ie

Malaria: Malaria is not a significant problem in Bali, but, dengue fever is. Dengue-carrying mosquitoes are distinguished by their black-and-white banded legs; they generally bite in the daytime. Protect yourself with long sleeves and trousers or use insect repellent. If you are sleeping in the open air or a non-air-conditioned room, use a mosquito net, ideally one impregnated with permethrin, which kills insects on fabrics. Malaria can be a problem in some parts of Lombok, particularly during the rainy season, although tourist areas are not high risk.

Minor Ailments: Treat any cut or abrasion immediately with antiseptic or antibiotic cream as it can easily become infected in the humid climate. Antihistamine cream for relief of itches, antibiotic cream for cuts, ointment for fungal skin infections, insect repellent, and aspirin or other pain relievers are available at local *apotik* (pharmacies).

STDs: Sexually transmitted diseases are on the rise; Indonesia has one of the fastest growing HIV infection rates in the world, and Bali is one of the provinces with the highest increase in HIV prevalence. Prostitutes are not subject to health checks, and the "Kuta Cowboys" or local gigolos have multiple partners from all over the world. Condoms – Indonesian and imported brands – are available at *apotik*.

Stomach upsets: If you come down with a severe case of "Bali Belly", taking Lomotil and Imodium will stop the symptoms, not cure the infection. Drink strong, hot tea and avoid spicy food. Charcoal tablets

will help alleviate the cramping. If you get a fever along with diarrhoea and cramps, see a doctor who will prescribe antibiotics. Mineral replacement salts for dehydration are available at local *apotik*.

General precautions: Bottled water is widely available. Brushing your teeth with untreated water is usually safe (but don't swallow the water).

Ice in eateries is generally safe as it is manufactured at licensed factories, but it is sometimes dumped right in front of the restaurant on the dirty pavement and not properly washed. If in doubt, drink only chilled drinks in cans or bottles.

Fruit should be peeled before eating, and avoid eating raw vegetables except at better restaurants geared towards tourists. Go easy on spicy food if you're not used to it. It is best not to take chances with street-food vendors, but if you are dead set on trying street food, stick to those that don't serve meat unless your system is already well adjusted.

Hospitals & Clinics

Both Bali and Lombok have made giant leaps toward providing good medical care for those who can afford it, including tourists. Since the expertise of international-standard hospitals and clinics focuses on common illnesses and injuries, it is still a good idea to make sure you have adequate medical insurance that includes evacuation (e.g. to Singapore or Bangkok) in case of a life-threatening emergency.

For minor problems, most villages have a government public health clinic called *puskesmas*, used by local people and very inexpensive. For major problems, go to one of hospitals or clinics below, which are geared towards the needs of tourists, which will direct you to a specialist if need be. All have 24-hour service. All major hotels also have on-call doctors.

Many hospitals and clinics charge different rates for Indonesians and foreigners. Be sure to check the list of fees for services so that you don't get a nasty shock when presented with the bill.

Bali
BIMC (https://bimcbali.com) has three locations:

BIMC Hospital Kuta: Jalan By Pass Ngurah Rai 100X, Kuta; tel: 0361-3003 911.

BIMC Siloam Hospital Nusa Dua: Kawasan ITDC Blok D, Nusa Dua, tel: 0361-3000 911.

BIMC Ubud Medical Centre: Jl. Raya Sanginang No. 21, Ubud; tel: 0361-209 1030.

SOS Medika Klinik Bali: Jalan By Pass Ngurah Rai No. 505X, Kuta, tel: 0361-720 100; www.sos-bali.com.

Lombok

Blue Island Medical Clinic (helpline: 081-9997 07705 and 081-8052 37373; www.blueislandclinic.com) is affiliated with BIMC (Bali) and Siloam (Indonesia's largest medical group). It provides services for all three northwest Gili islands via its clinic at Hotel Villa Ombak, Gili Trawangan, and to Mataram and Kuta through its clinic on Jl. Raya Senggigi, Senggigi.

Pharmacies (Apotik)

If you are using prescription drugs bring a sufficient supply and a copy of the prescription, if possible. Pharmacies can often provide refills, but the dosage may not be quite the same as your doctor has prescribed. Alternatively, they may be able to recommend another brand by locating your product in a directory of pharmaceuticals available in Indonesia that all apotik (pharmacies) have on hand. Also, while travelling you should keep your vital medication with you or in your carry-on – in case your luggage is lost. *Apotik* are widespread in towns and tourist areas. They often sell medicines which you would need a prescription to buy back home.

In the southern beaches area, Bali, and in Lombok, look for Apotik K24, which usually has a doctor on site during certain hours and is open 24/7. Kimia Farma is an Indonesian chain of pharmacies usually found in stand-alone locations with several branches on both islands, while Century Health Care and Singapore-based Guardian have multiple outlets in shopping malls. Outside tourist areas, ask at your hotel for a reputable *apotik*.

Internet

Free Wi-fi is widely available at airports, most accommodations, shopping malls and in many cafes. Internet speed can depend on how many users there are online at the same time you are. The best way to get internet on your mobile phone is to buy a prepaid SIM card on arrival. (See page XXX.)

Temple festival.

L

Left Luggage

There is a 24-hour facility for storing luggage near the entrance of the international terminal of Bali's Ngurah Rai Airport. There is no luggage storage facility at Lombok International Airport.

LGBTQ Travellers

Male homosexuality is tolerated to a certain degree in traditional Balinese society, but those involved are eventually expected to marry and have children. Flagrant displays of romance, both gay and straight, are considered distasteful in Bali and especially so in predominately Muslim Lombok.

The tourist industry has helped to establish Bali as a gay-friendly destination; gay travellers will encounter few problems on the island, especially in the tourist areas of the south. Homosexual behaviour in Indonesia is not illegal, and gay and lesbian couples are unlikely to have any difficulties when booking a hotel room and will be welcomed at bars and restaurants.

A few bars and nightclubs in Seminyak cater to the gay community. The gay scene in **Lombok** is generally much less obtrusive. Part of the reason is the conservative Muslim culture.

Lost Property

If your baggage goes astray, file a claim before leaving the airport. In theory, they will bring your luggage to your hotel when it has arrived. If you have left behind items in one of the blue **Bali Taxi** vehicles, contact Customer Care tel: 0361-701 621 or Bluebird Lombok Customer Care tel: 0370-645 000.

M

Maps

Free maps of the island are available at many of the travel agencies. Most bookstores also stock maps of Bali. Useful map publications are **Insight Guides Flexi Map Bali** (www.insight-guides.com) and Google Maps.

Media

Newspapers

Newspapers such as the *International Herald Tribune*, the *Bali Times*, *Asian Wall Street Journal* and local English-language daily the *Bali Times* are sold at major hotels, Periplus bookstores in Bali and Lombok, and some magazine kiosks in Sanur, Kuta, Denpasar and Ubud.

The *Bali Advertiser*, filled with articles and advertisements, is available free at hotels and restaurants. In Lombok, you will find the *Lombok Times*, *The Lombok Guide*, a free tourism-oriented newspaper.

Magazines

In Bali, several free local tourism-oriented magazines with restaurant and nightlife reviews and articles on local culture and lifestyles – like *Bali Now*, *Hello Bali* and *The Beat* – are available free at some hotels and shops. Others such as *The Yak*, *The Bud*, (delete comma) *KuBan*, *Exotic* and *FRV Travel* Bali are available for sale in bookstores.

Bookshops

Periplus (www.periplus.com) stores are Indonesia's only English-language bookshops, and there are many locations in Bali and at the airport in Lombok. Most large hotels and department stores have a limited supply, usually tourist publications, coffee-table books, novels, and English-language newspapers.

Located near the main post office in Ubud, one of the best bookshops in Bali is **Ganesha**, which specialises in books about Indonesia. It also has a music section and a corner devoted to second-hand books. They also stock bilingual (Indonesian/English) children's books.
Ganesha Bookshop
Jalan Raya Ubud
Tel: 0361-970 320
www.ganeshabooksbali.com

Radio & Television

There are a plethora of radio stations in Bali and a few in Lombok, including the government station Radio Republik Indonesia or RRI (100.9 FM), but none of them feature English language programming. The government's television station TVRI has 'Bali Vision', a locally produced English news broadcast that's not very exciting. Apart from online streaming, your

best bet for good old fashioned TV and radio is satellite TV, found in better accommodations and some cafes and bars, which air Star TV, HBO, CNN, BBC and a few foreign language channels.

Money

The Indonesian monetary unit is the rupiah, abbreviated to Rp. Coins are in Rp100, 200, 500 and 1,000 denominations. Paper currency is printed in Rp1,000, 2,000, 5,000, 10,000, 20,000, 50,000 and 100,000 notes. Be aware that there are several versions of the same denomination in circulation. At time of press US$1 was roughly equivalent to Rp14,000, but this figure fluctuates frequently.

Change for higher value notes (Rp 50,000 and above) is often unavailable in smaller shops, stalls or from taxis, so hang on to coins or paper currency of Rp20,000 and below, especially when travelling in outlying areas.

Changing Money

Foreign currency is best exchanged at authorised money changers. There are counters at the airport offering a fairly competitive rate, and it's a good idea to get enough rupiah there to get you started on your journey.

Bring only new and crisp paper currency (US dollar bills are the most widely accepted) as many places will not accept old and faded ones. Also, smaller US dollar denominations and traveller's cheques usually get a slightly poorer exchange rate. Note that rates are often lower away from the Kuta Bay beaches.

You will see signboards throughout tourist areas posting exchange rates. If the rates seem to be too good to be true, then they probably are. Be vigilant when dealing with money changers – they are renowned for their quick fingers and rigged calculators, particularly in the Kuta Bay area. Verify the exchange calculation using your own calculator and count your change before you leave the window. Be sure to ask for a printed or handwritten receipt as there are many unofficial (and illegal) money changers around. Ask if there is a "no commission" policy, otherwise you will get less than what is offered.

Never exchange money in shops, the exception being Ubud where almost everyone gives the correct rate and there are few rip-offs. It is possible to change money in up-market hotels but hotels generally quote rates far below the official exchange rate.

Rupiah may be converted back into foreign currency at the airport when leaving the country, or you can spend your remaining notes at the shops there.

Recommended moneychangers in Bali are:

Central Kuta, Jalan Raya Kuta No. 168; tel: 0361-762 970, open 8am–9.30pm, the largest, with many outlets.

Dirgahayu Valuta Prima, Jalan Raya Kuta No 168, tel: 0361-762 970, open 8am–9.30pm, with several branches.

BMC (Bali Maspintjinra), Jalan Raya Kerobokan No. 50/87, tel: 0361-737 070, open 8am–9pm.

In Lombok there are BMC branches at Jalan Raya Senggigi No. 88, tel: 0370-692 247, open 8am–10pm and at the airport, tel: 0370-615 8442, open 8am–7pm.

Credit Cards

Many large shops accept major credit cards, but an additional 3–5 percent will be added to your bill. Generally, places outside the major hotels and big restaurants accept American Express because of its higher commission charges.

Cash Advances

You can find at least one ATM machine in almost every Indonesian city or town. In cities and tourist areas they are everywhere, especially in shopping centers and at bank branches. Look on the ATM for the logo that matches your card. Notes are dispensed in rupiah in either 50,000 or 100,000 denominations, which is usually posted on the machine.

O

Opening Hours

Government offices in Bali are open Mon–Thu 8am–3pm, Fri –Sat 8am–noon, closed (delete extra space) Sun. Indonesians like to get their work done in the morning before the heat of the day, so it's best to get there before noon. Banking hours are from Mon–Fri 9am–3pm. Retail shops, especially in tourist areas, are open daily from 9am–9pm, but many are closed on Sun. Shopping malls are generally open 10am–10pm.

In Lombok, business and government offices are open from Mon–Fri 9am–4pm. With a predominantly Muslim population, some offices will close between 11.30am and 2pm on Fridays for prayers at the mosque, while others remain open but have limited staff. Some banks and business offices are open on Saturday until noon. Otherwise, shops, restaurants and bars have similar operating hours to those on Bali.

P

Packing & Shipping

Packages weighing between 2kg (4.5lbs) and 30kg (66lbs) can be sent through the regular post. For larger items, find a reliable shipper who does packing, and can handle export documentation and insurance. For fragile items, you may want to oversee the packing yourself. Shippers will even pick things up from the shop or come to your hotel. Be aware of restrictions or extra expenses (like customs duties) you may encounter in your home country.

Air cargo is charged by the kilo (minimum 45kg/99lbs) and can be expensive. Sea cargo is much cheaper because it is charged by volume, but takes two to three months to reach its destination. Some reliable shippers in Bali are:

Limajari Cargo, Jalan Raya Kerobokan No. 100X; tel: 0361-730 024; https://limajaricargo.com;

Jetfast Cargo, Jalan By Pass Ngurah Rai No. 542; tel: 0823-4937 1244; www.jetfastbalicargo.com;

In Lombok:

Freight Express Indonesia, Jalan Saleh Sungkar No. 100X, Ampenan, tel: 0270-649 154; http://freightexpressindo.com.

Postal Services

In Bali, post offices (Kantor Pos) are open Mon–Sat 7am–2pm. The main post office in Denpasar is at Jalan Raya Puputan, Renon, tel: 0361-223 565, and there are many branches throughout the island.

Overseas letters to Western Europe and America take, on average, 10–18 days to arrive. In larger post offices, the parcels section is usually in a separate part of the building. For customs purposes, the staff will ask what's inside the package.

In Lombok, post offices open at varying times. The main post office is at Jalan Sriwijaya 37, Mataram, tel: 0370-632 645 and is open Mon–Sat 7.30am–6pm, Sun 7.30am–12.30pm. The Senggigi post office is located at Jalan Raya Senggigi tel: 0370-693 711 and is open Mon–Thur 7.30am–3pm, Fri 7.30–11.30am, Sat 7.30am–1.00pm.

Courier Services

DHL: www.dhl.co.id; Jalan Teuku Umar No. 174A, Denpasar, tel: 0361-966 9169; Jalan Raya Kerobokan No. 147, Kuta, tel: 0361-966 9171; Jalan Raya Ubud No. 16, Ubud, tel: 0361-972 195.

Federal Express: www.fedex.com; Jalan Bypass Ngurah Rai Mumbul, Nusa Dua, tel. 0361-960 4228.

TNT: www.tnt.com; Jalan Bypass Ngurah Rai, Mumbul, Nusa Dua, tel: 0361-960 4228.

Public Holidays

National holidays in Indonesia observe important Muslim, Christian, Hindu and Buddhist holy days, which are determined by various lunar calendars and change every year. The only fixed dates for public holidays are:

New Year's Day: 1 January
Labour Day: 1 May
Pancasila Day: 1 June
Independence Day: 17 August
Christmas: 25 December

Changing public holidays are:

Imlek or Chinese New Year occurs in late January or early February, with most celebrations happening in cities with large Chinese communities.

Nyepi: Hindu Day of Silence in March or April. Note that in Bali no electricity is used, except in hotels, the airport is closed, and no one is allowed on the streets.

Isra Mi'raj: Ascension of Muhammad in March or April.

Waisak: celebrating Buddha's birth, enlightenment and death, falls on the full moon in May.

Ascension of Jesus: May or June.
Idul Fitri, marking the end of the fasting month of Ramadan, is the most important Muslim celebration, in May or June. It is a 5-day public holiday; in Bali it is celebrated only by Muslims but in Lombok it is a grand occasion for its majority Muslim population.
Idul Adha: Muslim day of sacrifice, usually in July or August.
Hijriyah: Islamic New Year, in July or August.
Ma'ulud: Prophet Muhammad's birthday, October or November.

Other Balinese public, but not national, holidays are **Siwalatri** (Night of Shiva), **Galungan**, **Kuningan** and **Saraswati**.

Public Toilets

There are few public toilets in Bali and Lombok, and those that exist are generally dirty and unpleasant. Better maintained public toilets can occasionally be found at the site of tourist attractions, where you will be expected pay a small fee – Rp1,000 or 2,000 – that pays the cleaners. Alternatively, if you're prepared to pay for a drink, you will be able to use the toilet in a restaurant or *warung* (café). Expect to find squat toilets in the simple *warungs*, *warung*, and take tissues with you.

Religious Services

In **Lombok**, the **Gereja Catholic Santo Antonius** (Jalan Majapahit No.10, Mataram, tel: 0370-634397), has mass on Sun at 7.30am and 6pm. The GKT (Gereja Kristus Tahun) Gloria (Jalan Subak II Cakra Barat No.15, Cakranegara; tel: 0370-627 066) has Protestant Sunday services at 7am and 10am.

In **Bali**, services are as follows:

Catholic
St. Fransiscus Xaverius Catholic Church Jalan Kartika Plaza No.107, Kuta, tel. 0815-5869 3301. Mass Sunday at 6pm. Bible study every Tuesday at 6pm in the meeting hall.
Gereja Katolik Canggu, Jalan Raya Babakan No. 54, Canggu; tel. 0361-844 5456. Masses: Mon–Thu 5.30am, Fri 6.30 pm, Sat 5.30 am, Sun 7am.

Interdenominational
Several interdenominational churches have services in English for Indonesians and expats, see www.isbchurch.com for a list.
International Service Bali (ISB), The Trans Resort Seminyak, Jalan Sunset, Seminyak; tel: 0812-3901 8301, www.isbchurch.com. Services Sat 5.45pm, Sun 11am.
Kuta International Christian Church, Jalan Patimura No. 25, Legian, tel: 0817-9765 673; wwwkutainternationalchristianchurch.org. Sun 11am; Fri prayer meeting 7pm.

Smoking

Indonesian law limits smoking to designated areas only. Any outlet serving food or drink can only allow smoking in separate rooms with their own ventilation systems.

Taxes & Tipping

Most hotels and restaurants in Bali and Lombok add a 10 percent government tax to your bill, with many high-end places charging an additional 10 percent for service, for a total of 21 percent. Tips of about 10 percent for attentive service are appreciated in places without service charges. In *warung* (foodstalls) away from tourist areas, tipping is not expected.

If you hired a car and liked the driver, a tip of 10–15 percent is appreciated. Always carry small banknotes with you, as taxi drivers are often short of change, or so they claim. Rounding up the fare to the nearest Rp 5,000 is standard.

A sign in Bali airport advises that porters should be tipped Rp20,000 each for regular-sized suitcases; more for larger bags. It follows that hotel porters in high-end resorts should be tipped similarly.

Telephones

Most mobile phones work in Indonesia as long as they are operating on the GSM network. You can purchase a prepaid SIM card on arrival. Reception quality is generally good.

There is a mind-boggling array of providers and prepaid cards, and deciding which one to buy can be a struggle. The first question is if you will be staying in one location or if you will be travelling to other islands. If staying put, a *lokal* package is sufficient and is cheaper. If travelling to more than one island, look for a 'flash' package that covers all of Indonesia. In addition to knowing how many gigabytes you need for calling, texting and internet, also look for the number of days the package covers.

There are two major providers in Indonesia and a slew of smaller ones. Telkomsel is usually fastest but more expensive, whereas XL can be less confusing to set up and the range covered is smaller. Both have 4G networks. Telkomsel (customer care: 0807-181 1811; www.telkomsel.com) has a package called simPATI Tourist Wonderful Indonesia that includes 300 sms text messages, 30 minutes of international talk time and 10 GB internet quota for Rp100,000. Add-ons are available. The basic starter package for XL (call center: 0817-012 3442; www.xl.co.id) is Super Ngobrol Baru and offers free calls and sms, internet Rp50/mb, with additional charges for international and video calls.

There are small kiosks throughout Indonesia selling the same SIM cards at fluctuating prices. You can save a few rupiah by shopping around or you can take the easy way out by paying a bit more and taking care of business in Bali at one of the kiosks outside the airport building when you exit. The advantage of doing this could be significant. A 2018 regulation requires all foreigners to register phone numbers, and at an official Telkomsel or XL kiosk they can do that on the spot, whereas a small kiosk might even tell you there's no need to register and later you discover your new number has been blocked due to lack of registration. In Lombok, ask at your accommodation which card to buy and where to purchase it.

Telephone Area Codes
Indonesia's **country code** (IDD) is 62. When calling Bali or Lombok from overseas, dial 62, the area code (without the zero) and the phone number. Indonesia has more than

one telecommunications company, and each has its own international operator connection number, coverage areas and prices. Government-owned Telkom has the widest range: 007 or 0107; private company Indosat has the second widest: 001 or 008; and Bakrie has the smallest: 009. To make an international call from anywhere in Indonesia, first dial one of the international operator numbers, followed by country and area codes and the phone number.

When calling from within the same region in Bali from a land line, no area code is needed but if you are calling a hotel in another regency, e.g. in Lovina (North Bali) from Kuta (South Bali), dial the area code (with the zero) plus the phone number.

The following are Bali area codes:
Denpasar, Kuta, Sanur, Nusa Dua, **Ubud, Gianyar, Tabanan**: 0361
Buleleng Regency (Singaraja, Lovina): 0362
Karangasem Regency, (**Amlapura**, **Candidasa, Buitan, Amed**): 0363
Jembrana Regency (Negara): 0365
Bangli and Klungkung Regencies: 0366
Part of Tabanan Regency (**Bedugul**, **Bratan**): 0368
The area code for most places in **Lombok** is 0370; east Lombok uses area code 0376.

Time Zone

Bali and Lombok follow Central Indonesian Standard Time, eight hours ahead of Greenwich Mean Time. It is one hour ahead of Java, and in the same time zone as Singapore.

Tourist Offices

Don't expect the highest standards of efficiency from Bali's tourist offices. The quality of service varies enormously and may not be as efficient as one would expect. It really depends on the ability of the person answering the phone when you call. Only the ones worth contacting are listed here:
Bali Tourist Information Centre: Jalan Bunisari 7, Kuta, tel: 0361-754 092.
Tourist Information Center: Jalan Raya Ubud (opposite the palace), tel: 0361-973 285.
Lovina Government Tourist Information Service, Jl. Seririt-Singaraja, Singaraja, tel: 0819-3635 2377.

In **Lombok**, there are two poorly managed tourism offices with a limited amount of printed information available. Better information is available at the tourist agencies in Senggigi and on the Gili Islands.
West Nusa Tenggara Tourist Office: LOP Service Road, Tanak Awu, Pujut, tel: 0878-8250 8888.

Travellers with Disabilities

The Balinese believe that all physical and mental disabilities are punishments for improper behaviour in past lives. That said, people with physical disabilities are also viewed with compassion.

Generally, there is very little consciousness in Indonesia about the special needs of people with disabilities. Due to rough pavements, high kerbs, an abundance of steps and a lack of ramps, it is difficult to move around in a wheelchair. However, you will never have problems finding people who are more than willing to help you. A number of luxury hotels in Bali and a few in Lombok are wheelchair-accessible.

V

Visas & Passports

The following information is accurate at time of press, but things may change at any time. Visitors from 62 countries, including the UK, US, Australia New Zealand, Canada and most European countries are eligible to enter Indonesia without a visa for up to 30 days. Your passport must be valid for at least six months from arrival date, have at least one blank visa page and a ticket for exiting the country.

Those who overstay their 30 days by a few days (less than a week) are charged Rp1million per day by immigration at the port of departure.

The only way to stay longer than your visa allows is to leave Indonesia and come back in again, the nearest place being Singapore. Alternatively, apply for a 60-day visa at an Indonesian embassy or consulate before arriving in Indonesia.

Extending business and social-cultural visas involves lots of paperwork at the **immigration office** in Bali, near Ngurah Rai International Airport (tel: 0361-935 1038), at Jalan Panjaitan in

Denpasar (tel: 0361-227 828), both are open Mon–Fri 8am–4pm, and in Singaraja, Jl. Seririt-Singaraja, (tel: 0811-499 343). In **Lombok**, the immigration office is at Jalan Udayana No.2 (tel: 632 520) in Mataram.
Other entry formalities: Be sure to complete a white, disembarkation-embarkation document, half of which must be retained and then presented upon departure. Do not lose this card or you will face a lot of problems when leaving.

W

Websites

The following websites provide useful information on **Bali**:
www.balidiscovery.com – Comprehensive site promoting hotels, tourist activities and Bali news.
www.theyakmag.com – Luxury lifestyle magazine that lets you in on what's hot and what's not.
http://bali-indonesia.com – Although this is a Bangkok-based booking site, it has more good information in one place than any other web.
For Lombok, the most complete compilation of current information is www.thelombokguide.com.
The Lombok Times is Lombok's only English-language newspaper (no website).

Weights & Measures

Indonesia uses the metric system. Temperatures are measured in degrees Celsius.

Women Travellers

Bali is generally safer for women than some other parts of the world, but it is important to respect local customs. A female travelling alone in Bali will probably be hit on at least a few times a day, especially at Kuta beach, by local men. This may be annoying but it is not aggressive behaviour. For solo women it is advisable to avoid unlit alleys and the beach at night, and it's best to travel by taxi at night and sit in the back.

Women travelling alone on Lombok are generally no more at risk than in any other area, as long as they dress and behave modestly and take basic safety precautions.

LANGUAGE

BAHASA INDONESIA

English is widely spoken in all tourist areas of Bali, and many local guides are also trained in Japanese and the major European languages.

Although more than 350 languages and dialects are spoken in the archipelago, the Indonesian language and national tongue, known as Bahasa Indonesia, is spoken everywhere and easy to learn. Derived from Old Malay, which was for centuries the trading language of the Indies, it was first embraced in 1928 by the nationalist movement as the "language of national unity", a political tool to bring the diverse religious and ethnic groups of the archipelago together. Bahasa Indonesia is also the official language used in commerce, schools and in the media.

Bahasa Indonesia is a non-tonal language and is written in the Roman alphabet. It is among the easiest of all spoken languages to learn as there are no tenses, plurals or genders, and often just one word can convey the meaning of a whole sentence.

There are a few basic rules of grammar in Bahasa Indonesia. To indicate the past, prefix the verb with *sudah* (already) or *belum* (not yet); for the future, prefix the verb with *akan* (will). The word *pergi*, for example, is used to say that you are going, you went, and you have gone. The word *makan* is used to say that you are eating, you ate, and you have eaten. *Saya sudah makan* means 'I already ate'; *saya belum makan* means *'I've not yet eaten'*; *saya akan pergi* means 'I will go'. To make a noun plural, the word is usually just repeated, e.g. *anak* (child), *anak anak* (children).

Spelling is phonetic with a few twists: The letter 'c' is pronounced 'ch' (e.g. Candidasa, Canggu); the letter 'g' is always hard (e.g. gamelan, Garuda); 'y' is pronounced 'j' (e.g. Yogyakarta); the letter 'c' is sometimes spelled 'tj'

(e.g. Tjampuhan instead of Campuhan); the letter 'j' can also be spelled 'dj' (e.g. Djakarta instead of Jakarta); and there is no letter 'v': November, for example, is spelt Nopember.

Adjectives always follow the noun: *rumah* (house) with *besar* (big) means 'big house'. Word order is usually subject-verb-object: *saya* (I) *mau* (want) *minum* (to drink) *air* (water) *dingin* (cold), means 'I want to drink cold water'. The personal pronoun goes after the noun: *rumah saya* is 'my house' The easiest way to make a question is to simply add a question mark and use a rising intonation, ie *Mau minum?* ('Want to drink?').

Indonesians always show respect when addressing others, especially their elders. The custom is to address an older man as *bapak* or *pak* (father) and an older woman as *ibu* or *bu* (mother).

Both Bali and Lombok have their own indigenous languages, Bahasa Bali or in Lombok, Bahasa Sasak, as well as other dialects, which are more difficult to learn. However Bahasa Indonesia is used outside homes on both islands.

Useful phrases

thank you terima kasih
good morning selamat pagi
good day selamat siang
good afternoon selamat sore
good evening/night selamat malam
goodbye (to person going) selamat jalan
goodbye (to person staying) selamat tinggal
I'm sorry ma'af
welcome selamat datang
please come in silahkan masuk
please sit down silahkan duduk
what is your name? siapa nama Anda?
my name is... nama saya...
where do you come from? asal dari mana?

I come from... saya datang dari...
how are you? apa kabar?
I am fine kabar baik
nice to meet you senang berkenalan dengan Anda
see you later sampai jumpa lagi
please (requesting) tolong
please (offering) silakan
you're welcome kembali or sama-sama
I do not understand saya tidak mengerti
I do not speak Indonesian saya tidak bicara Bahasa Indonesia
what is this? apa ini?
excuse me permisi/ma'af
please help me minta tolonglah

Forms of Address

I saya
you (singular) Anda/kamu (informal)
he, she, it dia
we kami (excluding the listener)
we kita (including the listener)
you (plural) Anda
Mr Bapak, Pak
Mrs Ibu, Bu
Miss Nona

Directions & Transport

left *kiri*
right *kanan*
straight *terus*
near *dekat*
far *jauh*
from *dari*
to *ke*
inside of *didalam*
outside of *diluar*
here *disini*
there *disana*
in front of *didepan*
at the back *dibelakang*
next to *disebelah*
car *mobil*
bus *bis*
train *keretapi*
bicycle *sepeda*

motorcycle *sepeda motor*
where do you want to go? *mau kemana?*
where is? *di mana?*
I want to go to... *saya mau ke...*
stop here *berhenti disini, stop disini*
railway station *stasiun keretapi*
petrol station *pomp bensin*
bank *bank*
post office *kantor pos*
immigration office *kantor imigrasi*
tourist office *kantor pariwisata*
embassy *kedutaan besar*

Food & Drink

restaurant *restoran; resto*
food *makanan*
drink *minuman*
breakfast *makan pagi*
lunch *makan siang*
dinner *makan malam*
boiled water *air putih*
iced water *air es*
tea *teh*
coffee *kopi*
milk *susu*
rice *nasi*
noodles *mie, bihun, bakmie*
fish *ikan*
prawns *udang*
chicken *ayam*
beef *daging sapi*
pork *babi*
vegetables *sayur*
fruit *buah*
egg *telur*
sugar *gula*
salt *garam*
black pepper *merica, lada*
chilli pepper *cabe*
cup *cangkir*
plate *piring*
glass *gelas*
spoon *sendok*
knife *pisau*
fork *garpu*

Shopping

shop *toko*
money *uang*
change (of money) *uang kembali*
money changer *penukaran uang*
to buy *membeli*
price *harga*
expensive *mahal*
cheap *murah*
fixed price *harga pas*
how much? *berapa?*

Signs

open *buka, dibuka*
closed *tutup, ditutup*

entrance *masuk*
exit *keluar*
don't touch *jangan pegang*
no smoking *jangan merokok; dilarang merokok*
push *dorong*
pull *tarik*
gate *gerbang*
ticket window *loket*
ticket *tiket*
information *informasi*
city *kota*
market *pasar*

Days of the week

Monday Hari Senin
Tuesday Hari Selasa
Wednesday Hari Rabu
Thursday Hari Kamis
Friday Hari Juma'at
Saturday Hari Sabtu
Sunday Hari Minggu

Numbers

Zero *nol*
Half *setengah*
Approximately *kira-kira*
1 *satu*
2 *dua*
3 *tiga*
4 *empat*
5 *lima*
6 *enam*
7 *tujuh*
8 *delapan*
9 *sembilan*
10 *sepuluh*
11 *sebelas*
12 *dua belas*
13 *tiga belas*
21 *dua puluh satu*
30 *tiga puluh*
100 *seratus*
150 *seratus limapuluh*
200 *dua ratus*
1000 *seribu*
2000 *dua ribu*
10,000 *sepuluh ribu*
100,000 *seratus ribu*
1,000,000 *sejuta*
Note: the teens are *"belas"*, the tens are *"puluh"*, the hundreds are *"ratus"*, thousands are *"ribu"*, and the millions are *"juta"*.

A

adat *customary law*
alang-alang (or *lalang*) tall grass used for thatching in roofs
aling-aling a short wall designed to deflect troublesome spirits
Anak Agung title given to someone of the princely caste
arak strong spirit from sugar palm

B

babi guling spit-roast suckling pig
bale open-air pavilion with roof, also called wantilan
bale banjar village meeting place
balian traditional faith healer; shaman
banjar small hamlet that is part of a larger village; the basic social and political unit in Bali
banten religious offerings
Bali Aga aboriginal pre-Hindu inhabitants of Bali
Barong mythical beast representing good; danced by two men inside an ornate costume
bebek betutu duck cooked in banana leaves
bemo public minibus
Brahmana the priestly caste; highest of the four castes
brem a sweet rice wine
bukit a hill or hilly area

C

candi bentar split entrance gateway to a temple
Cokorda title of prince or king

D

dalang puppet master
danau lake
desa village
dewa generic name for god
dewi generic name for goddess
Dewi Sri Goddess of Rice
dokar two-wheeled pony cart

E – G

endek Balinese *ikat* cloth
gado gado steamed vegetables served with peanut sauce
Galungan key Balinese festival celebrated every 210 days
gamelan percussion orchestra
gang small lane or alley
garuda mythical bird, the vehicle of the god Wisnu (Vishnu)
geringsing rare double *ikat* cloth woven in Tenganan
gunung mountain
Gusti title given to members of the *wesia* caste

H–I

homestay small family-run guesthouse; also called *losmen*
Ida Ayu/Ida Bagus title used by the male/female members of the Brahmana caste
ikat traditional hand-woven textile made with yarns that are tie-dyed to create a pattern prior to weaving

J

jalan street, road; to walk
jukung outrigger sailing boat

K

kain cloth; also sarong
kantor office
keris dagger with a wavy blade
kulkul hollow wooden drum to summon villagers

L

legong Balinese dance; also the name given to the dancer
leyak a witch or sorcerer
lingga a Hindu phallic symbol
lontar a species of palm; also refers to a palm-leaf manuscript
losmen see *homestay*
lumbung a traditional rice barn

M

Mahabharata Hindu epic
Melasti purification ceremony
meru holy Hindu mountain; also a temple's pagoda-style roof

N

naga dragon, water serpent
nusa (used in names) island
Nyepi Balinese New Year, usually occurring in March or April

O

odalan temple anniversary festival
ogoh-ogoh huge papier-maché monsters
ojek motorcycle taxi

P

padi rice in the husk, when growing in the field
pantai beach
paras sandstone used in building temples and for stone carving
pasar market
pedanda bramana high priest
pemangku temple lay priest
puputan Balinese fight to death or ritual suicide
pura temple
pura dalem temple of the dead

purnama full moon
puri palace

R

Ramayana Hindu epic
Rangda the widow-witch representing evil
rumah sakit hospital

S

satria princely class, second in ranking to *brahmana*
sawah irrigated rice field
subak irrigation society
sudra lowest of the four Balinese castes; also called *jaba*

T

taman garden
tirta holy water
topeng mask
tuak palm wine

U & W

udeng Balinese man's head-covering
wantilan open pavilion used as a hall in a village or temple
warung simple café where food and drinks are served
wesia the third and lowest of the aristocratic class

A few words will help at the night market in Ubud.

FURTHER READING

HISTORY & CULTURE

A Short History of Bali, by Robert Pringle. The history of Bali from before the Bronze Age to the presidency of Megawati Sukarnoputri and the tragedy of the Kuta bombings in 2002.

Bali: A Paradise Created, by Adrian Vickers. Bali, the "last Paradise", seen through Western eyes. Fresh insights on the history and culture of a traditional island faced with a massive invasion of paradise-seekers.

Bali: Sekala & Niskala Volume I – Essays on Religion, Ritual, and Art, by Fred B. Eiseman. An exploration of Balinese religion, ritual and performing arts.

Bali Sekala and Niskala Volume II – Essays on Society, Tradition and Craft, by Fred B. Eiseman. Covers the geography, social organisation, language, folklore and material culture of Bali.

FICTION

A Little Bit One O'clock, by William Ingram. A beautifully written novel exploring the web of relationships within a Balinese family.

Midnight Shadows, by Garrett Kam. Historical novel with the Communist coup of 1965 as the setting. It looks at the reasons behind the terrible violence that engulfed the island by interweaving actual events and history with mythology, dreams and rituals.

A Tale from Bali, by Vicki Baum. First published in 1937, this wonderful and classic tale of love and death in Bali is set against the backdrop of turmoil faced by the Balinese in their struggle against the Dutch colonialists.

Under the Volcano, by Cameron Forbes. Written in a compelling style and traversing a vast array of subjects relevant to Bali today, this book will open your eyes to Bali's history and the current challenges communities here face.

ART/MUSIC/DANCE

A House in Bali, by Colin McPhee. First published in 1947 and one of the most enchanting books ever written about Bali, this book tells the story of how, in 1929, a young Canadian-born musician chanced upon rare gramophone recordings of Balinese *gamelan* music that were to change his life forever.

Offerings, the Ritual Art of Bali, by Francine Brinkgreve and David Stuart-Fox. This beautifully illustrated book provides a rare glimpse into the pageantry, ritual and devotion that accompany the creation of offerings in Bali.

Dance and Drama in Bali, by Beryl de Zoete and Walter Spies. This important

⊘ Send us your thoughts

We do our best to ensure the information in our books is as accurate and up-to-date as possible. The books are updated on a regular basis using local contacts, who painstakingly add, amend and correct as required. However, some details (such as telephone numbers and opening times) are liable to change, and we are ultimately reliant on our readers to put us in the picture.

We welcome your feedback, especially your experience of using the book "on the road". Maybe you came across a great bar or new attraction we missed.

We will acknowledge all contributions, and we'll offer an Insight Guide to the best letters received.

Please write to us at:
Insight Guides
PO Box 7910
London SE1 1WE

Or email us at:
hello@insightguides.com

ethnographical book documents the history of Balinese dance and drama. Spies lived in Bali for 12 years from 1927 and was an accomplished painter, musician and dance expert. De Zoete was trained in European dance.

Balinese Paintings (second edition), by A.A.M. Djelantik. A concise but well-documented guide to traditional Balinese paintings, including that of Ubud's Pitamaha painters and the Young Artists of Batuan and Penestanan.

GENERAL

Fragrant Rice: My Continuing Love Affair with Bali, by Janet de Neefe. The memoir of an Australian restaurateur who married a Balinese man and raised four children here, this is another easy-read introduction to the culture of the island — with recipes.

The Island of Bali, by Miguel Covarrubias. First published in 1937, this book is still regarded by many as the most authoritative text on Bali and its culture and people.

Our Hotel in Bali, by Louise G. Koke. A re-issue of the 1987 publication that documents how a young American couple, Bob Koke and Louise Garret, came to build Bali's first hotel in 1936, the Kuta Beach Hotel.

Bali Today – Real Balinese Stories, by Jean Couteau. Couteau is well known for his humorous stories in the Indonesian press about Bali and the Balinese way of life. His observations are witty, ingenious and hilariously funny.

Eat, Pray, Love, by Elizabeth Gilbert. Traces the author's journey through Italy, India and Bali on a quest to discover worldly pleasure, spiritual devotion, and what she really wants out of life. The story was made into a Hollywood movie starring Julia Roberts and partly filmed on location in Bali.

Bali Daze – Freefall off the Tourist Trail, by Cat Wheeler. A Canadian writer moves to the country town of Ubud in Bali and learns to deal with randy ducks, rampant vegetation, roasted spiders, a haunted river bank and all the quirks and delights of living in a Balinese community.

Secrets of Bali, by Jonathan Copeland with Ni Wayan Murni. From Balinese gods to Balinese gamelan, difficult subjects are simply explained in this beautifully written and illustrated work.

CREDITS

123RF 158, 166B, 217, 221
Alamy 9TR, 11B, 66, 129B, 191
Archives of the Royal Tropical Institute, Amsterdam 40, 41, 42, 43
AWL Images 1, 16/17, 18/19, 20, 32/33, 60, 82, 91, 98/99, 100
Begin Ende Voortgargh Vande Oost-Indische Compagnie 39L, 39R
Bigstock 226B
Corbis 206
Corrie Wingate/Apa Publications 6MR, 6BL, 6BR, 7ML, 7TL, 8B, 10T, 10B, 22, 23, 24, 25L, 25R, 26, 27, 28, 29, 30, 31R, 31R, 50, 52R, 52L, 53, 56, 58/59T, 61, 62, 63, 64, 65, 69L, 69R, 70, 72, 73, 74, 75, 76, 77, 79, 81BL, 83, 84, 88, 90, 101T, 101B, 104, 105, 107B, 107T, 108B, 108T, 109, 110T, 110B, 111, 112B, 113, 114T, 114B, 115T, 115B, 116, 117, 119T, 119B, 120, 121T, 121B, 122/123T, 122BL, 123ML, 124, 125, 127B, 127T, 128, 131T, 131B, 132, 133, 134B, 135T, 135B, 136, 137B, 138, 139, 141T, 141B, 144T, 145T, 145B, 146T, 146B, 147, 148, 149B,

150, 152, 153, 155, 156, 157B, 159, 160T, 160B, 162, 163B, 163T, 164B, 165B, 166T, 167B, 167T, 168BR, 168BL, 168ML, 168/169T, 169BL, 171, 174B, 175B, 176T, 176B, 177B, 177T, 178B, 180, 181, 183, 184B, 186T, 186B, 190, 193B, 194B, 196B, 197, 198/199, 200, 201T, 203, 212, 213, 214, 215B, 222, 223, 224T, 224B, 225, 227, 228, 230, 234, 236, 237, 240, 244/245
Design Pics Inc/REX/Shutterstock 211
Dreamstime 7TR, 7MR, 55, 68, 170, 187, 220
Francis Dorai/Apa Publications 37, 129T, 165T, 169BR, 172T, 174T, 175T, 178T, 193T, 226T
Getty Images 7BL, 14/15, 45, 48/49, 67, 85, 86, 94/95, 96/97, 179
Ida Bagus Nyoman Rai 44
iStock 4, 6ML, 7BR, 9BL, 21T, 21B, 57, 59TR, 71, 202, 209T, 219B, 235, 247, 248
Jack Hollingsworth/Apa Publications

58/59B, 112T, 123BR, 130B, 142T, 144B, 157T, 207T, 207B, 208T, 208B, 209B
John Anderson/Apa Publications 51
Martin Westlake/Apa Publications 38, 58BL, 59ML, 59BR, 80BR, 80BL, 122BR, 130T, 134T, 137T, 151T, 164T, 172B, 173, 194T, 196T, 218, 219T
Otto Stadler/imageBROKER/REX/Shutterstock 140
Patrick Frilet/Shutterstock 8T
Prime Plaza Hotels & Resorts 92
Private Archives 78
Public domain 34
Robert Harding Picture Library 216
Shutterstock 9TL, 11T, 12/13, 35, 46, 47, 80/81T, 81BR, 81TR, 87, 89, 93, 123TR, 123MR, 142B, 143T, 143B, 149T, 151B, 161, 184T, 185, 195, 201B, 210
Starwood Hotels & Resorts 215T
Tirta Ayu Hotel & Restaurant 169TR
University of Leiden, Amsterdam 36
ZUMA/Rex Features 54

Front cover: Ulun Danu Beratan Temple *Shutterstock*
Back cover: Malimbu beach *Shutterstock*
Front flap: (from top) Fire dance performance *iStock*; Pura Beji Sangsit

carving *Shutterstock*; Ubud Market stall *Shutterstock*; Sasak weaver *Shutterstock*
Back flap: Lombok coastline *Shutterstock*

INSIGHT GUIDE CREDITS

Distribution
UK, Ireland and Europe
Apa Publications (UK) Ltd;
sales@insightguides.com
United States and Canada
Ingram Publisher Services;
ips@ingramcontent.com
Australia and New Zealand
Woodslane; info@woodslane.com.au
Southeast Asia
Apa Publications (SN) Pte;
singaporeoffice@insightguides.com
Worldwide
Apa Publications (UK) Ltd;
sales@insightguides.com
Special Sales, Content Licensing and CoPublishing
Insight Guides can be purchased in bulk quantities at discounted prices. We can create special editions, personalised jackets and corporate imprints tailored to your needs.
sales@insightguides.com
www.insightguides.biz

Printed in China by RR Donnelley

All Rights Reserved
© 2020 Apa Digital (CH) AG and
Apa Publications (UK) Ltd

First Edition 1970
Twenty-First Edition 2020

No part of this book may be reproduced, stored in a retrieval system or transmitted in any form or means electronic, mechanical, photocopying, recording or otherwise, without prior written permission from Apa Publications.

Every effort has been made to provide accurate information in this publication, but changes are inevitable. The publisher cannot be responsible for any resulting loss, inconvenience or injury. We would appreciate it if readers would call our attention to any errors or outdated information. We also welcome your suggestions; please contact us at:
hello@insightguides.com

www.insightguides.com

Editor: Sarah Clark
Author: Linda Hoffman
Head of DTP and Pre-Press: Rebeka Davies
Update Production: Apa Digital
Managing Editor: Carine Tracanelli
Picture Editor: Tom Smyth
Cartography: original cartography Berndtson & Berndtson, updated by Carte
Layout: Aga Bylica

CONTRIBUTORS

This guide has at its foundation the very first edition, published in 1970, which became the ground-breaking prototype that led to the creation of the Insight Guides series. This 21st edition is published 50 years after the original version; it was commissioned by **Tatiana Wilde** and edited by **Sarah Clark**.

The book's updater, American-born **Linda Hoffman**, has lived and worked in Indonesia for thirty years, where her career as a freelance travel writer, tour

leader and guest lecturer has taken her to some of Indonesia's most remote regions on multiple occasions. Having contributed to ten *Insight Guide Indonesia* editions since 2001, she is especially proud to be part of this 50th anniversary *Bali and Lombok* special edition.

Enormous thanks go to Andreas Grosskinsky and his entire team at Destination Asia Bali, Putu Wisnu (Bali), and Lombok Paradise Tours & Travel for their wisdom and support.

ABOUT INSIGHT GUIDES

Insight Guides have more than 45 years' experience of publishing high-quality, visual travel guides. We produce 400 full-colour titles, in both print and digital form, covering more than 200 destinations across the globe, in a variety of formats to meet your different needs.

Insight Guides are written by local authors, whose expertise is evident in the extensive historical and cultural

background features. Each destination is carefully researched by regional experts to ensure our guides provide the very latest information. All the reviews in **Insight Guides** are independent; we strive to maintain an impartial view. Our reviews are carefully selected to guide you to the best places to eat, go out and shop, so you can be confident that when we say a place is special, we really mean it.

Legend

City maps

Freeway/Highway/Motorway
Divided Highway
Main Roads
Minor Roads
Pedestrian Roads
Steps
Footpath
Railway
Funicular Railway
Cable Car
Tunnel
City Wall
Important Building
Built Up Area
Other Land
Transport Hub
Park
Pedestrian Area
Bus Station
Tourist Information
Main Post Office
Cathedral/Church
Mosque
Synagogue
Statue/Monument
Beach
Airport

Regional maps

Freeway/Highway/Motorway (with junction)
Freeway/Highway/Motorway (under construction)
Divided Highway
Main Road
Secondary Road
Minor Road
Track
Footpath
International Boundary
State/Province Boundary
National Park/Reserve
Marine Park
Ferry Route
Marshland/Swamp
Glacier   Salt Lake
Airport/Airfield
Ancient Site
Border Control
Cable Car
Castle/Castle Ruins
Cave
Chateau/Stately Home
Church/Church Ruins
Crater
Lighthouse
Mountain Peak
Place of Interest
Viewpoint

INDEX

A

Abang 166
  Pura Lempuyang 166
accommodation 195, 215
  at Taman Tirtagangga 169
activities 83. *See also* individual
  activities by name
  on beaches 122
addresses 236
admission charges 236
age restrictions 236
agriculture 29, 101, 171, 238
  irrigation 30
  on Lombok 201
  rice **29**, 101, 144, 191, 197
  traditional farming 197
Aik Berik 220
Air Kalak 220
Airlangga 38
Air Sanih 173
Air Terjun Gitgit 176
air travel 230
  Lombok International Airport
    234
  Ngurah Rai International
    Airport 105
Alassari 172
Alas Sari
  Symon's Art Zoo 172
Ambron, Emilio 157
Amed 65, 84, 166, 167, 232
Amlapura 165
  Puri Agung Karangasem 92, 165
  Taman Tirtagangga 166
Ampenan 206, 217, 35
Anak Agung Gede Mandera 137
Anak Agung Nengah 42
Anak Agung Ngurah Gede
  Karangasem, King 203, 208
Anak Wungsu 38, 146
ancient sites 10
animal parks. *See* zoos and
  animal parks
Antosari 193
Anyar 217, 219
Apuan 197
architecture 47, 89
  contemporary 92
  Dutch colonial 206
  temples 90
  traditional 89
art and crafts 27, 46, **75**, 158, 223.
  See also museums and galleries
  basket weaving 137, 164, 207,
    224
  jewellery and metalwork 77,
    127
  Lontar manuscripts 76, 164, 175
  masks 75, 130
  musical instruments 158
  painting 78, 128, 158, 194
  Pitamaha school 79
  Pitamaha School 78, 130
  pottery 194, 201, 208, 223, 224

  puppets 128
  religious art **80**
  silverwork 75
  textiles 76, 77, 128, 156, 159,
    164, 223, 224
  Threads of Life (Ubud) 132
  wood and stone carving 75, 125,
    127, 130, 171
  Young Artists 79, 133, **134**, 135
art galleries. *See* museums and
  galleries
arts, performing 67. *See
  also* music and dance
  shadow plays 71
Asahduren 187
Ayung River 87, 135, 136

B

Badung 42, 101, **105**
  Bukit Pandawa Golf and
    Country Club 85
Balangan 84, 232
Balangan Beach 115
Bali Barat National Park 29, 86,
  87, **185**
Balina 163
Bali Strait 28
Bangko Bangko 227
Bangli 101, 147, 146
  Pura Dalem Penunggekan 147
  Pura Kehen 90, 147
Bangsal Harbour 210, 214, 217
Banjar 176
  Air Panas Banjar 176
  Brahma Arama Vihara 176
Banyumulek 207
Banyupoh 182
Banyuwedang 183
  Mimpi Resort 183
Batavia 41
Bat Rock 87
Batuan 79, **128**
  Pura Puseh 128
Batubelig 65, 120
Batubulan 75, **125**
  Bali Bird Park 127
Batu Layar 209
Batu Mejan 120
Bayan 219
beaches 9, 101
  East Bali 153, 161, 162, 163,
    165, 166, 167
  Gili Islands 214
  Lombok 201, 206, 210, 218, 221,
    223, 226
  North Bali 175
  South Bali 105, 111, 113, 114,
    115, 116, 118, 119, 120, **232**
  West Bali 181, 182, 187
Bedugul 177, 232
  Handara Golf and Resort 84
Bedulu 78, 139
  Gedong Archaeology Museum
    140

  Goa Gajah 139
  Pura Kebo Edan 140
  Pura Penataran Sasih 141
  Pura Pusering Jagat 141
  Pura Samuan Tiga 90, 140
  Yeh Pulu 142
Bedulu, King 38
Belayu 195
  Pura Alas Kedaton 195
Belega 129
Belimbing 193
Belimbingsari 185
Berawa 120
Bertais 207
Besakih 86
Bias Tugal Beach 162
bicycle hire 233
Bingin 232
Bingin Beach 115
bird-life 8
  Bali Bird Park 127
  Bali Starling 87, 184
  Javan pond herons 143
  plumed egrets 143
  sea birds 87
birdwatching 87
black magic 111
Blahbatuh 78, 129
  Pura Gaduh 129
  Sidha Karya Gamelan Foundry
    129
Blahkiuh 195
Blanco, Antonio 134
Blue Lagoon 87
boat trips and cruises 87
  Danau Batur 150, 151
  Danau Tamblingan 174
  dolphin-watching tours 176
  to the Gili Islands 214, 217
Bona 129
Bonjeruk 223
Bonnet, Rudolf 79, 130
Bugbug 165
Buitan 163
Bukit Badung 29, 84, **113**
  Pura Luhur Uluwatu 115
Bukit Demulih 147
Bukit Gumang 165
Buleleng 41, 101
bull races. *See* water-buffalo
  races
business hours. *See* opening
  hours
business travellers 236
bus travel
  Bali 230
  Lombok 235
  tourist shuttles 232

C

Cakranegara 207, 235
  Pura Mayura 207
  Pura Meru 207
  Taman Mayura 207

calendar systems 58
Campuhan 131, 133
  Blanco Renaissance Museum
    134
  Pura Gunung Lebah 134
Campuhan River 133
Candidasa 165, 232
Candikuning 177
  Bali Botanical Gardens 28, 177
  Bali Treetop Adventure Park
    178
Canggu 120, 231
car hire
  Bali 233
  car with driver 233
  Lombok 235
Cekik 185
Celuk 78, **127**
Celukan Bawang 181
children 237
  activities 83
  attractions 149, 117, 178, 237.
    See also zoos and animal
    parks
  Bali for Families 8
climate 28, 237
  monsoons 28
climbing 85, 220
clothing 237
  temple etiquette 237
cockfights 27, 53
consulates 238
crafts. See art and crafts
credit cards 242
crime 27
  in Kuta 118
cruises. See boat trips and
  cruises
cuisine 61
Culik 167
customs regulations 238
cycling 83. See also mountain
  biking; See also bicycle hire

D

Danau Batur 148, 150, 232
Danau Bratan 177, 232
Danau Buyan 87, 178
Danau Segara Anak 220
Danau Tamblingan 87, 178
Danghyang Nirartha 39, 115, 120,
  121, 172, 182, 186, 187
Danghyang Nirartha Nirartha
  130
Dauhwaru 186
Denpasar 77, **105**, 232
  airport 230
  Bali Orchid Garden **111**
  Catur Mukha 107
  Grand Inna Bali Beach Hotel
    109
  Indonesia Australia Language
    Foundation 111
  Lata Mahosadhi Art Museum
    109
  Museum Negeri Propinsi Bali
    107
  nightlife 109
  Pasar Badung 108
  Pasar Burung 109

Pasar Burung Satria 109
Pasar Kereneng 109
Pasar Kumbasari 108
Pura Agung Petilan 110
Pura Jagatnatha 108
Pura Masopahit 109
Puri Agung Kesiman 110
Sekolah Tinggi Seni Indonesia
  (Indonesia Institute of the
  Arts) 109
Taman Puputan 105
Taman Werdhi Budaya Art
  Centre 110
Taman Werdi Budaya Art Centre
  79
diving and snorkelling 83, 162,
  167, 176
  Gili Islands **213**, 214, 215
  Lombok 210
  Nusa Lembongan 161
  West Bali 182, 183
Dreamland 232
Dreamland Beach 115
drinking, legal age 236
driving
  Bali 231, **233**
  Lombok 235
drugs 238

E

East Bali 153
eating out 61. See also food and
  drink
economy 46, 238
education 171
electricity 238
emergency numbers 238
Empu Kuturan 183
environmental issues 21
  coral, destruction of 153
  tourism, effects of 31, 86
etiquette 238. See also temples,
  etiquette
  sunbathing 214

F

ferries 162, **231**. See also boat
  trips and cruises
  to and from Java 185
  to Lombok 231
festivals and events 10
  Alip festival (Bayan) 219
  Bali Arts Festival (Denpasar)
    110
  Bau Nyale festival (Kuta) 225
  fertility rite (Muncan) 155
  Galungan 58
  Kuningan 58
  Nyepi 59
  perang dewa (Bukit Gumang)
    165
  Segara Anak pilgrimage
    (Narmada) 208
  temple festivals 53, 108, 155,
    207, 209, 210
  Usaba Sambah (Tenganan) 162,
    164
food and drink 61. See also eating
  out

babi guling 143
  rice 61
four-wheel-drive expeditions 83
further reading 248

G

Gajah Mada 38, 129
gardens. See parks and gardens
gay and lesbian travellers 241
Gelgel 39, 77, **158**
  Pura Dasar 159
geography and geology 21, 185
Gerupuk 226
getting around
  Bali 231
  Lombok 234
Gianyar 75, 77, 101, 129, **143**
  Puri Agung Gianyar 143
Gili Air 214
Gili Gede 227
Gili Islands 210
  boats to 217
Gilimanuk 185, 231
  Museum Situs Purbakala 185
Gili Meno 215
Gili Nanggu 227
Gili Sudat 227
Gili Tangkong 227
Gili Trawangan 215
golf 84, 121
Gondang 218
  Tiu Pupus Waterfall 218
government and politics 45
Grokgak 181
Gung Kak. See Anak Agung Gede
  Mandera
Gunung Abang 148
Gunung Agung 28, 86, 89, 101,
  153, 155
  eruptions 45, 155, 167
  Pura Besakih 90
  Pura Pasar Agung 156
Gunung Baru Jari 220
Gunung Batukau 197
Gunung Batur 85, 147, 232
  eruptions 149
Gunung Catur 177
Gunung Kawi 145
Gunung Pengsong 208
Gunung Penulisan 150
  Pura Puncak Penulisan 150
Gunung Prapat Agung 83, 184
Gunung Rinjani 201, 217, 219, **220**
Gunungsari 217
Gunung Seraya 166
Gunung Tambora 41
GWK Cultural Park 116

H

handicrafts. See art and crafts
Hatta, Mohammad 44
Hatten Wines 181
health and medical care 239
  dengue fever 239
  HIV-AIDS 27
  methanol poisoning 213
  traditional remedies 54
hiking. See trekking
history 34

Chinese influence 47
Dutch conquest 21, 205
Dutch influence 40, 41, **42**
Indian influence 37
Indonesia, creation of 45
Javanese influence 38
of Lombok 203
prehistoric 37, 185
World War II 44, 205
hitchhiking 233
horse riding 85
horticulture 93
hot springs 151
Air Kalak (Lombok) 220
Air Panas Banjar (Banjar) 176
Banyuwedang 183
Gunung Rinjani 220
Mimpi Resort (Banyuwedang) 183
Toya Bungkah 85
Yeh Panes 196
Houtman, Cornelis de 39

I

Ida Bagus Anom 130
I Gusti Ngurah Rai 45, 196
I Gusti Nyoman Lempad 131, 132
I Ketut Marya 193
Impossibles Beach 115, 232
Indonesia Australia Language Foundation 111
I Nyoman Gunarsa 158
I Nyoman Mandra 158

J

Jagaraga 174
Pura Dalem 174
Jagaraja 41
Jatiluwih 197
Jayaprana 184
Jembrana 28, 101, 181
Jerowaru 226
Jeruk Manis waterfall 224
jet-skiing 112
Jimbaran 46, 105, 113, **116**, 231, 232
eating out 116
Pura Ulun Siwi 116

K

Kamasan 78, 158
Kang, Princess 47
Kapal 194
Pura Sada 194
Karangasem 42, 101
Kayangan. See Labuhan Lombok
Kebo Iwo 129, 142
Kedewatan 135
Kedisan 150
Keliki 79
Kemenuh 75
Kerambitan 78
Kerandangan 210
Kerobokan 65, 117, 120, 231
Kerurak
Kerta Gangga Waterfalls 218
Kintamani 149
Kintamani mountain dogs 47

Klungkung 101
Bale Kambang 157
Bale Kerta Gosa 157
former palace 157
Pasar Klungkung 157
Puputan Klungkung Monument 157
Semarajaya Museum 157
Koke, Robert and Louise 118
Krambitan 194
Puri Agung 194
Puri Anyar 194
Krijgsman, J.C. 139
Kublai Khan 38
Kubu 167
Kubutambahan 173
Pura Meduwe Karang 173
Kusamba 159
Pura Goa Lawah 161
Kuta 40, 41, 84, 101, 105, 117, **225**, 231, 232, 235
Cinema XXI 119
Jalan Legian 119
Jalan Melasti 119
Jalan Pantai Kuta 119
Matahari Kuta Square 119
Museum Kain 119
nightclub bombings 46
safety 238
shopping 119
Kutri 142
Pura Bukit Dharma 142

L

Labuhan Lalang 183
Makam Jayaprana 184
Labuhan Lombok 221
Lange, Mads 40, 117
language 23, 39, **245**
Bahasa Indonesia 24, **245**
Balinese 23
glossary 246
Kawi (Old Javanese) 23, 38
lessons 111
Sasak 205
useful phrases 245
left luggage 241
Legian 101, 105, 117, **119**, 231, 232
Le Mayeur de Merpres, Adrien-Jean 92, 112
Lembar 227, 234
Lenek 223
Les 171
Borboran Yeh Mampeh 171
literature 39, 40, 70, 171. See also further reading
Loloan Timur 186
Lombok 39, 40, 42, **201**. See also individual place names
Central and South 223
ferries 231
North and East 217
safety 238
West 203
Lombok International Airport 234
Lombok Strait 28, 31, 206
lost property 241
Lovina 65, 84, 175, 231, 232
Jalan Raya Lovina 176
Loyok 224

M

Mahabharata 71, 157
Mahendradatta 38
Malimbu 210
Manggis 163
Manggissari 187
Bunut Bolong 187
Mangsit 210
maps 241
Marga 196
Margarana Memorial 196
Puri Taman Sari 195
marine life 8, **83**, 163, 183
coral 114, 153, 163, 182, **183**, 214, 215
dolphins 84, 176
of Nusa Penida 161
Tulamben Marine Reserve 167
turtles 215
Mario. See I Ketut Marya
Markandeya, Resi 134
markets
Ampenan 206
Bertais 207
Kintamani 150
Pasar Badung (Denpasar) 108
Pasar Burung (Denpasar) 109
Pasar Kereneng (Denpasar) 109
Pasar Klungkung (Klungkung) 157
Pasar Kumbasari (Denpasar) 108
Pasar Ubud (Ubud) 131
Tanjung 218
Mas 75, 130
Ida Bagus Anom workshop 130
Njana Tilem Museum 130
Pura Taman Pule 130
Masbagik 223
Mataram 42, 206, 235
Nusa Tenggara Barat Museum 206
Taman Budaya 207
Mawun 226
McPhee, Colin 136
Medewi 187
Melaya 185
Menanga 153
Pura Besakih 153, 155
Mengwi 195
Pura Taman Ayun 195
minivans 230
public minivan routes 235
with driver 233
money matters
budgeting for your trip 236
credit cards 242
currency 241
currency exchange 241
Moon of Pejeng 141
motorcycle hire
Bali 233
Lombok 235
mountain biking 87
Muller, Peter 93
Muncan 155
Munduk 178
Munduk Tamblingan 174
museums and galleries 11
ARMA Museum & Resort (Pengosekan) 137

Batur Geopark Museum (Penelokan) 149
Blanco Renaissance Museum (Campuhan) 134
Gedong Archaeology Museum (Bedulu) 140
Lata Mahosadhi Art Museum (Denpasar) 109
Museum Bali. *See* Museum Negeri Propinsi Bali
Museum Kain (Kuta) 119
Museum Le Mayeur (Sanur) 112
Museum Negeri Propinsi Bali (Denpasar) 107
Museum Puri Lukisan (Ubud) 78, 79, 132
Museum Situs Purbakala (Gilimanuk) 185
Museum Subak (Tabanan) 193
Neka Art Gallery (Ubud) 133
Neka Art Museum (Penestanan) 79, 134
Njana Tilem Museum (Mas) 130
Nusa Tenggara Barat Museum (Mataram) 206
Rudana Museum (Peliatan) 139
Semarajaya Museum (Klungkung) 157
Symon's Art Zoo (Alas Sari) 172
Taman Werdhi Budaya Art Centre (Denpasar) 110
Taman Werdi Budaya Art Centre (Denpasar) 79
music and dance 11, 39, 46, **67**, 127, 186. *See also* I Ketut Marya
Barong and Rangda 38, 47, 67, **68**, 76, 116
Frog Dance 128
gambuh 129
gamelan 27, 72, **73**, 129, 164, 186
Indonesia Institute of the Arts (Denpasar) 109
legong 137
of Lombok 201
of the Haji 220
Sasak 223
tektekan 194
topeng 128
mythology 21, 28, 38, 151
Calonarang 38
keris 42
wong gamang 182

N

Narmada 208
Pura Kalasa 208
Pura Lingsar 208
Taman Narmada 208
national parks and reserves
Bali Barat 29, 86, 87, **185**
Monkey Forest (Sangeh) 195
Rinjani National Park (Lombok) 219
Tulamben Marine Reserve 167
Negara 77, 186
Ngurah Rai International Airport 105, **230**
Nieuwenkamp, W.O.J. 173
Nipah 210

Ni Polok 112
North Bali 171
NTB (Nusa Tenggara Barat) 206
Nusa Ceningan 87, **161**
Nusa Dua 46, 65, 84, 105, **113**, 231, 232, 238
Bali National Golf Club 85
eating out 114
Nusa Lembongan 87, **160**
Dream Beach 161
Jungutbatu 161
Mushroom Bay 161
Nusa Penida 56, 84, 87, 111, **159**
boats to 159, 162
Goa Giri Putri 160
Nyoman Rudana 139

O

opening hours 242
opium 40, 43
orientation
Bali 231
Lombok 234

P

Pacung 197
Padang Bai 162, 231, 232
Padang Padang 84, 232
beach 115
Padangtegal 137
Pakerisan River 145
Palasari 186
Pan Pacific Nirwana Bali Resort 121
Pantai Sire 218
Sire Beach Golf Club 218
paragliding 84
parks and gardens 93
Bali Botanical Gardens (Candikunung) 28, 177
Bali Orchid Garden (Denpasar) **111**
Hutan Wisata Suranadi (Suranadi) 209
Taman Mayura (Cakranegara) 207
Taman Tirtagangga (Amlapura) 166, 168
Taman Ugung 168
Taman Ujung (Ujung) 166
Water Parks of East Bali 168
Pasir Putih 165
passports. *See* visas and passports
Payangan 135
pearls 206
Pecatu
New Kuta Golf Course 85
Pejaten 194
Tanteri Ceramics 194
Pejeng 139
Pekutatan 187
Pelangan 227
Peliatan 75, 131, 137
Puri Agung Peliatan 137
Rudana Museum 139
Pemenang 217
Pemuteran 182, 232
Penatahan 196

Penelokan 148
Batur Geopark Museum 149
Pura Ulun Danu Batur 149
Penestanan 79, 134
Neka Art Museum 79, 134
Pengosekan 78, 79, 131, 137
ARMA Museum & Resort 137
Penujak 224
people 21, **23**
Bali Aga 23, **24**
Christian communities 185, 186
Muslim communities 186
Sasak 201, **203**
Perancak River 186
Pererenan 120
Peteluan 146
Petitenget 65
Petulu 143
pharmacies 240
photography 239
plant-life 28
bamboo 148
biodiversity 197
cacti 113
palahlar trees 195
police spot-checks 233
politics. *See* government and politics
population 27
postal services **242**
courier services 242
packing and shipping 242
Praya 224, 235
Pringgasela 223
public holidays 242
public toilets 243
Pujungan 193
Pulaki **182**
Pura Melanting 182
Pura Pulaki 182
Pulau Burung 87
Pulau Menjangan 83, **183**
Pulau Serangan
Pura Sakenan 113
puppets 67, 71, 128
Pupuan 187, 193
Pura Batu Bolong 121
Pura Gede Perancak 187
Pura Tanah Lot 121
Pusuk Pass 217

R

Raden Saleh 137
Raffles, Sir Thomas Stamford 41
rafting 83, **87**, 136
Ramayana 71, 195
religion 21, 26, 38
Agama Hindu Dharma or Agama Tirtha 51
ancestral graves (makam) 209
animism 163, 205
banten (offerings) 80
Buddhism 51, 205
cosmology 89
cremation ceremonies 57
Hinduism 23, 39, 51, 203, 205
holy eels 209
in Lombok 205
Islam 51, 203, 205
religious art 75

rice, role of 29
rituals 52
sacred dances 68, 128
Wektu Telu 219
religious services 243
Rembitan 225
Rendang 155
Rimba Reptile Park 127
Rinjani National Park 219
Tiu Kelep Waterfall 220
road travel 114

S

Sade 225
Mesjid Kuno 225
sailing 112
Sakah 129
salt 159, 167, 215
Sanda 193
Sangeh 195
Monkey Forest 195
Pura Bukit Sari 195
Sangsit 174
Pura Beji 174
Sanur 65, 79, 105, **111**, 231, 232, 238
Bali Beach Golf Course 85
Grand Inna Bali Beach Hotel 111
Museum Le Mayeur 112
Pura Belanjong 112
Pura Segara 112
Sapit 221
Satria 77
Sawan 78
Sayan 131, 135
seaweed cultivation 87, 159
Sebatu 144
Pura Gunung Kawi Sebatu 144
Sebudi 156
Segenter 219
Sekotong 227
Selakarang 75
Selasih 120
Selat 156
Selat-Duda 156
Selong Belanak 227
Semabaung 142
Sembalun Bumbung 221
Sembalun Lawang 221
Seminyak 65, 101, 105, 117, **119**, 231, 232, 238
eating out 120
Jalan Abimanyu 120
Jalan Kayu Aya 120
Jalan Raya Seminyak 120
nightlife 120
Pura Dalem Petitenget 120
shopping 120
Senaru 219
Sendang Gile Waterfall 219
Senggigi 206, **210**, 235
Senggigi beach 210
Senggigi Point 210
Sengkidu 163
Pura Puseh 163
Seraya 166
Seririt 178, 181
Shark Point 215
Sidan 146

Pura Dalem 146
Sidemen 77, 156
Singapadu 75, 127
Bali Zoo 127
Singaraja 40, 77, 174
Ling Gwan Kiong Chinese Buddhist Temple 175
Museum Gedong Kirtya 175
Singa Ambara Raja 175
Yudha Mandala Tama Independence Monument 175
Smit, Arie 79, 133, 134, 135
snorkelling. *See* diving and snorkelling
society
burials and cremations 150, 162, 163
caste system 24, 39, 43
ritual suicide (puputan) 41, 107, 205
women's role 27
Songan 149, 151
Pura Ulun Danu 151
South Bali 105
Spies, Walter 79, 92, 130, 137
sport. *See* activities
Suharto, General 46
Sukadana 218
Sukarara 224
Sukarno, President 44, 45
Sukawati 77, 128
Banjar Babakan **128**
Pasar Seni 128
Sukawati, Cokorde Gede Agung 130
Suluban 232
beach 115
Sumbawa 41
Sunset Road 231
Suranadi 209
Hutan Wisata Suranadi 209
Pura Suranadi 209
surfing 84, 232
East Bali 161
Lombok 201, 210, 225, 226, 227
South Bali 113, 115, 118, 120
West Bali 187
Suteja Neka 134
Sweta. *See* Bertais
Symon 172

T

Tabanan 42
Pura Luhur Batukau 90
Tabanan (region) 191
Tabanan (town) 191
Gedong Mario Theatre 191
Museum Subak 193
Taman Nasional Bali Barat 29, 86, 87, **183**, **185**
Taman Tirtagangga 168
Taman Ujung 168
Tampaksiring 75, 77, 145
Pura Mengening 145
Pura Tirtha Empul 145
Tanjong Benoa 113
Tanjung 218
Tanjung Aan 226
Tanjung Benoa 105, **114**, 231, 232
Tanjung Luar 226

Tanjung Medana 218
Pura Medana 218
Taro 144
Mason Elephant Park 144
Taun 227
taxes 243
airport taxes 230
exports 238
in bars 236
taxis 236
Bali 231, 232
Bali airport services 231
Bali motorcycle taxis 233
Lombok 234, **235**
teeth, filing 52, **53**
Tegalalang 144
Tejakula 78, 172
Telaga Waja River 83, 87
telephones
area codes 243
Teluk Amuk 163
Teluk Jepun 162
Teluk Lumpur 87
Teluk Nara 210
temples 10, 139
architecture 90
at Gunung Kawi 146
Brahma Arama Vihara (Banjar) 176
dress code 53
etiquette 237, 239
Ling Gwan Kiong Chinese Buddhist Temple (Singaraja) 175
Pura Agung Petilan (Denpasar) 110
Pura Alas Kedaton (Belayu) 195
Pura Batu Bolong (Lombok) 210
Pura Batu Bolong (South Bali) 121
Pura Beji (Sangsit) 174
Pura Belanjong (Sanur) 112
Pura Besakih (Gunung Agung) 90
Pura Besakih (Menanga) 153, 155
Pura Bukit Dharma (Kutri) 142
Pura Bukit Sari (Sangeh) 195
Pura Candi Dasa (Candidasa) 165
Pura Dalem Agung (Ubud) 137
Pura Dalem (Jagaraga) 174
Pura Dalem Penunggekan (Bangli) 147
Pura Dalem Petitenget (Seminyak) 120
Pura Dalem (Sidan) 146
Pura Dasar (Gelgel) 159
Pura Desa (Ubud) 131
Pura Gaduh (Blahbatuh) 129
Pura Gede Perancak 187
Pura Goa Lawah (Kusamba) 161
Pura Gubug (Danau Tamblingan) 174
Pura Gunung Kawi Sebatu (Sebatu) 144
Pura Gunung Lebah (Campuhan) 134
Pura Jagatnatha (Denpasar) 108
Pura Kalasa (Narmada) 208
Pura Kebo Edan (Bedulu) 140
Pura Kehen (Bangli) 90, 147
Pura Lempuyang (Abang) 166
Pura Lingsar (Narmada) 208

Pura Luhur Batukaru
(Wongayagede) 191
Pura Luhur Batikau (Tabanan)
90
Pura Luhur Batukau
(Wongayagede) 197
Pura Luhur Uluwatu (Bukit
Badung) 115
Pura Masopahit (Denpasar) 109
Pura Mayura (Cakranegara) 207
Pura Medana (Tanjung Medana)
218
Pura Meduwe Karang
(Kubutambahan) 173
Pura Melanting (Pulaki) 182
Pura Mengening (Tampaksiring)
145
Pura Meru (Cakranegara) 207
Pura Pasar Agung (Gunung
Agung) 86, 156
Pura Penataran Sasih (Bedulu)
141
Pura Ponjok Batu (near
Tejakula) 172
Pura Pulaki (Pulaki) 182
Pura Puncak Penulisan
(Gunung Penulisan) 150
Pura Puseh (Batuan) 128
Pura Puseh (Sengkidu) 163
Pura Pusering Jagat (Bedulu)
141
Pura Rambut Siwi (Yeh Embang)
187
Pura Sada (Kapal) 194
Pura Sakenan (Pulau Serangan)
113
Pura Samuan Tiga (Bedulu) 90,
140
Pura Segara (Lombok) 209
Pura Segara (Sanur) 112
Pura Silayukti (Padangbai) 162
Pura Suranadi (Suranadi) 209
Pura Tahun (Danau Buyan) 174
Pura Taman Ayun (Mengwi) 195
Pura Taman Pule (Mas) 130
Pura Taman Saraswati (Ubud)
131
Pura Tanah Lot (South Bali) 121
Pura Tegeh Koripan. See Pura
Puncak Penulisan (Gunung
Penulisan)
Pura Tirtha Empul
(Tampaksiring) 145
Pura Ulun Danu Batur
(Penelokan) 149
Pura Ulun Danu Bratan 177
Pura Ulun Danu (Songan) 151
Pura Ulun Siwi (Jimbaran) 116
Yeh Pulu (Bedulu) 142
Tenganan 77, 163
terrorist attacks 46, 118
Tetebatu 224
Tianyar 167
Tihingan 78, 158
Timbanuh 220

Timbis 84
time zone 244
tipping 243
tourism 21, 27, **46**, 105, 118, 238
Lombok 203
tourist offices 244
Toya Bungkah 85, 151
transport
Bali 230
Lombok 234
travellers with disabilities 244
trekking 83, 85, 167
Bali Barat 185
Gunung Agung 156
Gunung Batukau 197
Gunung Rinjani 220
Lombok 224
Rinjani National Park 220
Trunyan 150
Tuban 65, 117, 231, 238
Discovery Mall 117
Waterbom Park 117
Tulamben 83
Tulamben Marine Reserve 167
Tunjuk 196

U

Ubud 65, 46, 65, 79, **130**, 101, 231,
232
Ganesha Bookshop 133
Jalan Kajeng 132
Jalan Raya Ubud 131
Monkey Forest 136
Monkey Forest Road 131, 136
Museum Puri Lukisan 78, 79,
132
Neka Art Gallery 133
Pasar Ubud 131
Pondok Pekak Library and
Learning Centre 136
Pura Dalem Agung 137
Pura Desa 131
Pura Taman Saraswati 131
Puri Saren Agung 131
Threads of Life 132
tourist office 132
Yayasan Bina Wisata 132
Udayana, King 38, 51, 146
Ujung 166
Taman Ujung 166
Uluwatu 84, 232
beach 115
Unda River 87
Unesco World Heritage Site 197

V

vineyards 181
Hatten Wines 181
visas and passports 244
volcanoes 28, 171, 219. See
also volcanoes by name
Batur Geopark Museum
(Penelokan) 149

W

walking 233. See also trekking
Ubud Walks 138
Wallacea 31
Wallace Line 31
Wallace, Sir Alfred Russel 31
Wanasari 196
Bali Butterfly Park 196
water-buffalo races **184**, 186
waterfalls
Air Terjun Gitgit 176
Borboran Yeh Mampeh 171
Gunung Rinjani 220
Jeruk Manis (Lombok) 224
Kerta Gangga (Kerurak) 218
Pujungan 193
Sendang Gile (Senaru) 219
Tiu Kelep (Rinjani National
Park) 220
Tiu Pupus (Gondang) 218
Waturenggong, King 39
weather. See climate
websites 244
weights and measures 244
West Bali 31
West Bali National Park. See Bali
Barat National Park
white water rafting. See rafting
wildlife 29. See also bird-life,
marine life
bats 87, 161, 195
Java deer 183
monkeys 115, 165, 182, 195,
196, 208, 217, 224
snakes 161
windsurfing 112, 226
women travellers 244
Wongayagede 197
Pura Luhur Batukaru 191
Pura Luhur Batukau 197

Y

Yeh Embang 187
Pura Rambut Siwi 187
Yeh Kuning 186
Yeh Panes
Yeh Panes Hot Springs Resort
197
Yeh Panes 196
Yeh Sanih. See Air Sanih

Z

zoos and animal parks
Bali Bird Park (Batubulan)
127
Bali Butterfly Park (Wanasari)
196
Bali Zoo (Singapadu) 127
Mason Elephant Park (Taro)
144
Monkey Forest (Ubud) 136
Rimba Reptile Park 127

B a l i S e a

Kayangan

Gondang

Karanganyar

Gill Islands

Trawangan   Meno   Tanjung
                         Air   Sira   **Tanjung**   Jenggala   **Tiu Pupus Wate**

                                          Pura   Sokong   Bentek
                         Bangsal   **Medana**

                         Teluk   **Pemenang**   *Segara*
                         Nara   Terangan

Nipah

Tanjung Rumbeh   Malimbu

Lendang Luar   *Pusuk*
                                      Pass   Gunung
Mangsit   Meninting
                         Pura   ▲ **1418**
Kerandangan   **Batu**
                         Bolong
Senggigi

                         Batu Layar   Gunungsari   Jangkok   Sesao
                                          Mambalan   **Pura**
                         Pura Segara ★   **Lingsar**   **Pura**
                                                                          ★ **Suranadi**   Pen
                                          Mataram   Bertais   Lingsar   Batukumbung
                         Ampenan ◉   (Sweta)   **Narmada**
                                          Cakranegara   **Taman**   **Pringg**
                                                                          Narmada   Pag
                                          Telagawaru   Bagu   Bonjeruk
                         Nyamarai   Ail
                         Gunung Pengsong ★   Rumak   **Kediri**   Jelantik   Geru
                         Banyumuluk   Jagaraga   **Ubung**
                                          Kuripan   Batutulis   Sukarara
                         Kebonayu   **Pray**
                                          Gerung   *Dodokan*   Ranggagata   Ungga   *Bendung*
                         Dodokan   Darek   *Batujai*
                         Jembatankembar
                         Lembar   Plambik   Setanggor   **Penu**
Tanjung   *Bendungan*   Kabol   Tanakawu
Bangkobangko   **Nanggu**   *Pengga*
Bangko-   **Asahan**   *Gede*   Taun   Sekotong
Bangko   (Sekotong   Timur   Mangkung   Kateng
Labuan   Barat)   Penge
Poh   Pelangan   **Sekotong**
           Barat   **Tengah**
                         Mecanggah   Timbal   Montongsapah   **Man**
                                                                          Resort Develop
Mekaki
Bay   Slodong   Pengatap   **Selong**   **Selong**   Mawun   Ku
                                          Belanak   **Blanak**
           Tanjung   **Beach**
           Belenanggung   Tanjung
                         Ujunglangit

N

Lombok

0 ————————— 10 km

0 ————————— 10 miles